Writing Faith and Telling Tales

ReFormations

MEDIEVAL AND EARLY MODERN

Series Editors:
David Aers, Sarah Beckwith, and James Simpson

WRITING FAITH AND TELLING TALES

*Literature, Politics, and Religion in the Work of
Thomas More*

THOMAS BETTERIDGE

*University of Notre Dame Press
Notre Dame, Indiana*

Manufactured in the United States of America

Library of Congress Cataloging-in-Publication Data

Betteridge, Thomas.
Writing faith and telling tales : literature, politics, and religion in
the work of Thomas More / Thomas Betteridge.
pages   cm. — (Writing faith and telling tales: medieval and early modern)
Includes bibliographical references and index.
ISBN 978-0-268-02239-6 (pbk. : alk. paper) —
ISBN 0-268-02239-9 (pbk. : alk. paper)
1. More, Thomas, Saint, 1478–1535—Political and social views.
2. Reformation—England—Historiography.   3. Christian literature, Latin
(Medieval and modern)—England—History and criticism.   4. Great Britain—
History—Henry VIII, 1509–1547.   5. Religious thought—16th century.
6. Philosophy, Medieval.   7. Humanism—England—History—16th century.
8. England—Intellectual life—16th century.   I. Title.
DA334.M8B48   2013
942.052092—dc23
[B]

2013032614

This book is dedicated to
Janet Betteridge and Priscilla Tolkein.

CONTENTS

ACKNOWLEDGMENTS

Many friends and colleagues have helped me during the course of writing this book. Greg Walker and Eleanor Rycroft have been a joy to work with on all our various and varied productions. Thomas S. Freeman read a draft of this volume and provided me with useful comments. Peter Marshall also gave me invaluable feedback on an earlier version of this book. I have immensely benefited from being a member of a collegiate and collaborative academic community, and I would like to thank the following for their support over the years—Victoria Bancroft, Kim Coles, Katherine Craik, Brian Cummings, Eamon Duffy, Elisabeth Dutton, Vincent Gillespie, Andrew Hadfield, Elizabeth Hurren, Julia Ipgrave, Steven King, Susannah Lipscombe, Eleanor Lowe, Nicole Pohl, Kent Rawlinson, and David Scott Kastan. There are many other colleagues and students who have attended lectures and seminars that I have given over the years and whose insightful comments have helped me in numerous ways to write this book. I would like to thank David Aers, Sarah Beckwith, and James Simpson for their thoughtful and helpful responses to drafts of this volume. I would also like to thank all the staff at the University of Notre Dame Press for the support they have given me.

NOTE ON CITATIONS

I would like this work to be as accessible as possible. I have therefore
modernized the spelling and punctuation of the texts that I refer to
where necessary to elucidate the meaning for readers unfamiliar with
fourteenth-, fifteenth-, and sixteenth-century writing, except when quoting from *The Yale Edition of the Complete Works of Saint Thomas More*, when
quoting poetry, or where I am making a specific philological point. I have
also silently expanded contractions. When quoting from translations of
works originally written in other languages, I have included the original
text as a footnote only where this is necessary for the point I wish to make.

INTRODUCTION

On September 1, 1523, Thomas More wrote to Cardinal Wolsey from Woking, updating him on the correspondence that Henry VIII had recently received.

> It may like your good Grace [Wolsey] to be advertised that I have received your Grace's letters directed to myself dated the last day of August with the letters of my Lord Admiral to your Grace sent in post and copies of letters sent between the Queen of Scots and his Lordship concerning the matters and affairs of Scotland with the prudent answers of your Grace as well to my said Lord in your own name as in the name of the King's Highness to the said Queen of Scots. All which letters and copies I have distinctly read unto his Grace.[1]

More went on to tell Wolsey that Henry, and his queen, Catherine of Aragon, were extremely pleased with the letter that Wolsey had written in Henry's name to Queen Margaret of Scotland, Henry's sister. More told Wolsey, "I never saw him [Henry] like thing better, and as help me God in my poor fantasy not causeless, for it is for the quantity one of the best made letters for words, matter, sentence and couching that ever I read in my life."[2]

In 1523 More was one of Henry's key public servants, a member of the king's council and under treasurer of the exchequer. He was used by Henry and Wolsey as a diplomat, orator, and secretary.[3] More was also a celebrated letter writer and engaged in correspondence with many leading European humanists, most famously Desiderius Erasmus. His praise of Wolsey's letter is therefore extremely generous. Unfortunately it is impossible to know if it was justified, since the original letter Wolsey wrote on Henry's behalf has not survived. The appreciation that More showed for Wolsey's skills as a ghostwriter reflects perhaps a shared sense of the creative requirements but also the compromises involved in being a royal servant: the need to write as someone else, to author another man's words. More, as Henry's secretary, was the king's textual eyes and hands— reading and writing for the king.

Throughout the 1520s More was an important conduit between Henry and his realm, the kind of dependable, discreet civil servant that all regimes require to carry out their business. The letter of September 1523 provides a snapshot of More in his role as royal councilor and secretary, as a trusted servant of the king and Wolsey's confidant. The courtly political milieu of More's letter to Wolsey seems on the surface to be many miles from the world of the author of *Utopia*, *Richard III*, or the *Dialogue concerning Heresies*. This disjuncture is, however, more apparent than real. More, perhaps to a greater degree than any other figure in Tudor history, has suffered from being viewed through inappropriate or partial perspectives. In particular, More's opposition to Henry's religious policies of the early 1530s and his martyrdom profoundly colored the first Tudor accounts of his life, and this has fed into the modern historical record.[4]

Thomas More was born in 1478 into a relatively wealthy, well-connected London family. His father, John More, was a leading member of the legal profession, rising to become judge of the King's Bench in 1520. More's early education was at St. Anthony's School, a leading London grammar school. Sometime around the year 1489 More entered the household of Archbishop John Morton at Lambeth Palace. Also in Morton's household at this time was the playwright Henry Medwall. William Roper, More's son-in-law and early biographer, records More spontaneously leaving his place in the audience and taking part in dramas being performed before Morton's household. Roper writes that "though he [More] was young of years, yet would he at Christmas-tide suddenly sometimes step in among the players, and never studying for the matter, make a part of his own there presently among them, which made the lookers-on more sport than all the players beside."[5] It is difficult to imagine that More's interventions were met with unalloyed pleasure by the players performing the Christmas revels, but they clearly amused those watching the drama.

In 1492 More went to Oxford University, and two years later he returned to London to train as a lawyer. It was while studying law that he lodged in or near the Charterhouse, the home of the Carthusian Order in London. Roper writes that More "gave himself to devotion and prayer in the Charterhouse of London, religiously living there without vow about four years, until he resorted to the house of one Master Colt, a gentleman of Essex, that had oft invited him thither, having three daughters, whose honest conversation and virtuous education provoked him there specially to set his affection."[6]

It is unclear if More lived as a monk during his association with the Carthusian Order.[7] The passage from Roper's life describing More's time "in the Charterhouse" suggests that in this period More lived as a devout Christian as well as a gentleman, taking up offers of hospitality from the likes of Master Colt. In 1505 More married Colt's daughter Jane. The marriage to Jane produced four children between 1505 and 1509, the oldest being his favorite daughter, Margaret. During the period 1505–18 More steadily built up his career as a lawyer. This led to his becoming a member of the important Mercers' guild in 1509 and representing Westminster in Henry VIII's first parliament. At the same time More and his family played host to Erasmus, who appears to have enjoyed staying with More. In 1511 More's wife, Jane, died, and within a short time he married Alice Middleton. In 1518, when More entered the royal service, he was a highly successful London lawyer, a humanist scholar with a European reputation, and a happy family man. Seymour Baker House comments that "when More joined the king's council in 1518, he did so because his training and inclinations had prepared him for exactly that."[8] The story of More's life from his birth until he entered royal service is, based on contemporary historical records, relatively straightforward. This is not, however, how it appears when looked at from the perspective of the various modern accounts of More's early life, which present a bewildering array of different, often incompatible, Mores for the reader to praise or condemn.

The first significant modern study of More was R. W. Chambers's biography, *Thomas More*, published in 1935. Chambers thought it important to address a number of agendas. Above all he wanted to critique the assumption that More the writer of *Utopia* and More the martyr were in conflict. Chambers thought the idea that these two aspects of More clashed was produced by a false assumption that More's "modern" humanism and his "medieval" religion were in conflict. Throughout *Thomas More* Chambers argues that what distinguishes More is his ability to combine the modern with the medieval. Chambers writes that

> More . . . connects Medieval England with Modern England. . . .
> Think of him first in connection with the continuity of the English
> speech, English prose, English literature. To the student of the En-
> glish language he is a vital link between Middle and Modern English.
> To the student of English prose his work is the great link which con-
> nects modern prose with the medieval prose of Nicholas Love, Wal-
> ter Hilton, and Richard Rolle. . . . To the student of English thought
> More is equally vital: he points to our own times; but he also points
> back to William Langland, and More and his writings help us to see
> a continuity running through English literature and history.[9]

Chambers insisted in his work that More's life and work exhibit a basic coherence. In making this argument, however, Chambers painted a simplistic picture of the medieval period as a time without major conflicts or areas of dispute; in particular he depicted More's religion as entirely conventional without pausing to consider what this meant in late medieval England.[10] Chambers's More is a reasonable, witty man—a martyr who put his conscience before the demands of a tyrannical king. Chambers spends some time discussing the similarities between More and Socrates. In particular, he argues that as Socrates transcended the particular history of ancient Athens, so More transcended that of Tudor England.[11] More's transcendent nature is for Chambers largely a product of his status as a martyr for the rights of the individual conscience against the demands of government or state.[12] This claim is, however, profoundly problematic, since More was a consistent critic of those who placed their own conscience before the teaching of the church.[13] Chambers's understanding of More's attitude to conscience reflects the most pressing issue in relation to *Thomas More*, which is that it elides history with hagiography, so that the judgments that Chambers makes, which went on to inform Robert Bolt's play *A Man for All Seasons*, are a strange blend of the historically astute and uncritically acclamatory.

It was this combination that above all drove two highly influential critiques of *Thomas More*, the biography by Richard Marius, published in 1984, and the work on More by G. R. Elton, particularly the article "Sir Thomas More and the Opposition to Henry VIII." Marius's More is a man obsessed with sex, a failed monk who could never forgive himself for giving in to his sexual desires and marrying Jane Colt. Marius assumes that More's time at the Charterhouse represents an attempt by More to become a monk and that it was his sexuality, and the demands of his father, that prevented More from achieving this desire. Marius regards this moment of frustration or failure as the key to More and suggests it created a conflict that runs throughout the rest of More's life. The evidence that Marius advances for More's conflicted state is an obsession with sex that Marius suggests is an important feature of the antiheretical writings More produced at the beginning of the 1530s. For example, Marius suggests that "the *Confutation* rings with the clangour of More's own repressed sexuality."[14] The problem is that there is no real evidence that More did "repress" his sexuality. He had two marriages, both of which, as far as can be ascertained, were entirely happy. Marius suggests that More's second marriage, to Alice Middleton, "was probably a quiet and unobtrusive way of living a life of sexual abstinence while he [More] remained in the world" and that it may even have been "a continuing penance."[15] There is no historical evidence to back these claims. The fact that More's second marriage did not produce any children is not evidence that More and Alice did not have sex. Marius's biography is the mirror image of Chambers's *Thomas More* in that it builds castles in the sky on the basis of limited historical records.

G. R. Elton shared Marius's sense that More was a man caught between competing demands, but for Elton those demands were an obsessive hatred of heresy and a recognition of the need for reform.[16] Elton's attitude to More was critical and strangely uncomprehending. It is clear that he found it simply impossible to understand More as, or forgive him for being, a man of reason, a humanist, the writer of *Utopia*, and a principled opponent of the policies pursued by the Henrician regime in pursuit of Henry's divorce of Catherine of Aragon. Both Marius and Elton suggest that More was "happy" when he was imprisoned in the Tower of London at the end of his life, since finally he could live as a monk. This seems an unfortunate and belittling suggestion. More's final letters, discussed in the conclusion of this study, indicated More feared death and was desperate to return to his family. In his highly influential study, *Renaissance Self-Fashioning: From More to Shakespeare*, Stephen Greenblatt produced an interpretation of More that is more nuanced than but essentially similar to that of Elton. Again More is depicted as caught between the playful humanist writer and the obsessive heresy hunter. Greenblatt comments of More's antiheretical work that "the possibility of playful, subversive fantasy . . . is virtually destroyed."[17] Elton and Greenblatt both see as a central element of More's work and life a tension between the medieval, which they implicitly relate to the campaign against heresy, and humanism, which they see as modern or at least modernizing.

Recent studies of More have followed in the paths laid down on one side by Chambers and on the other by Elton, Greenblatt, and Marius. For example, the More of Peter Ackroyd's *The Life of Thomas More* is, like Chambers's, one of the "last great exemplars of the medieval imagination."[18] There are two central problems to all of these approaches to More. The first is a simplistic approach to the "medieval period," invariably treating it as homogeneous and conservative. For example, Marius writes, "A thesis of this biography is that until his imprisonment More suffered the severe inner struggle of a deeply divided soul. Perhaps the fundamental cause was that he struggled to combine medieval piety with the invincible temptations of Renaissance secularism."[19] In this context "medieval piety" implies a dated emphasis on monasticism and in particular asceticism that any normal person would find less attractive than the "temptations" of the Renaissance. Chambers's apparent exception to this rule is simply a product of his approval of what he saw as medieval homogeneity and piety. The second problem, exemplified in the approach that these scholars have taken to More's attitude to religion, is a marked tendency to move beyond the available facts in order to support what are extreme understandings of More—he is either saint or persecutor, a humanist or medievalist, reformer or reactionary. Sophisticated writers like Greenblatt do produce more subtle versions of this dichotomy, but it still exists in their work as an explanatory framework. John Guy's study of Thomas More, published in 2000, and his earlier work, *The Public Career of Sir Thomas More* (1980), provide a clear-sighted correction to many of the myths about More. Guy comments, "Writing about More presents an extraordinary challenge."[20] There are, Guy argues, two reasons for this. First, he suggests, More's sainthood "obscures, rather than illuminates his historical significance."[21] Second, many of the earliest sources and records of More's life have been strongly influenced by people for whom More's martyrdom was by far the most important aspect of his life.[22]

Writing Faith and Telling Tales: Literature, Politics, and Religion in the Work of Thomas More is a study of More's writing that places it within a tradition of late fourteenth- and fifteenth-century vernacular literature. In some ways it therefore represents a return to the agenda pursued by Chambers in *Thomas More*. The texts that I have chosen to discuss are eclectic, designed to represent the traditions within which More wrote; I am not claiming, however, that More had read, for example, the work of Reginald Pecock. What I am suggesting throughout this volume is that many of the concerns that More addressed in his writings are the same as those that interested late fourteenth- and fifteenth-century English writers.[23] At the same time, unlike Chambers, I will argue that late medieval English writing is not monolithic or homogeneous. More's writing engages with the issues and conflicts that interest authors as diverse as William Langland, John Lydgate, and Geoffrey Chaucer. For More, reading and writing, indeed life, were best understood as a pilgrimage, and, as with Chaucer's pilgrims in *The Canterbury Tales*, the important thing was to keep walking, talking, and listening to each other's tales. More, like Chaucer, was prepared to imagine and defend a promiscuous collection of tales and tellers. The figures that More feared and fought were those like the Pardoner in *The Canterbury Tales*, whose counterfeit, sterile tale and beguiling offer to sell the pilgrims a new pardon "at every miles ende" threaten the very existence of Chaucer's merry company of storytellers.[24] More regarded his opponents as latter-day Pardoners, peddlers in falsehood, endangering the souls of those they attempted to seduce with their offers of instant and immediate gratification, religious, political, and personal.

More's commitment to the ideal of a community of storytellers is born out of his engagement with English vernacular writing of the later fourteenth and fifteenth centuries and his civic humanism. The vernacular as it emerged during the fourteenth century developed a particular sense of itself as offering a language that was an alternative to, and at times more inclusive and authoritative than, learned Latin or other foreign languages. This can be illustrated by briefly examining a scene from the C Text of *Piers Plowman* where the narrator, Will, and Patience sit down to a meal, presided over by Reason, with a learned Friar. Scripture offers them "food"—Augustine, Ambrose, and the four evangelists— which the Friar rejects:

> Ac of these mete the maystre myhte nat wel chewe;
> Forthy eet he mete of more cost, mortrewes and potages.
> Of that men myswonne they made hem wel at ese
> Ac here sauce was ouer-sour and vnsauerly ygrounde
> In a morter, *post mortem*, of many bittere peynes
> Bote yf they synge for tho soules and wepe salte teres.[25]

The Friar desires food that is oversour and unsavory and will lead to bitter pains after death. This episode reflects an important motif in Langland's work, which is the importance of simplicity over complexity. The food the Friar desires is a metaphor for complex, corrupt, over-cooked scholarly discourse that will ultimately lead to bitterness and tears. Nicholas Watson comments, "*Piers Plowman* is . . . one of the first works to argue in English against the formalism of authoritative structures developed in Latin. . . . In *Piers Plowman* we have both a demonstration of the moment at which English, notionally the language of the 'lewd,' challenges this definition of its role, and an analysis of the consequences."[26]

The parable of the Friar and Scripture's meal is about different kinds of language and the authority they confer. It suggests a relationship between ancient Christian teaching and plain, simple wisdom while at the same time criticizing linguistic complexity. Implicit in this moment is a critique of clerical language and, by implication, of scholastic learning, and a claim for the authority of a synergy between the classic Christian teaching and simple or lewd wisdom. Vernacular writing of the fourteenth and fifteenth centuries was not homogeneous, but it did consistently contain a strain, perhaps particularly in relation to religious writing, that emphasized the inclusive nature of writing in English.[27] There is a sense in the writing of authors like William Langland and Geoffrey Chaucer that English not only is a proper and appropriate language to write in but also bears a relationship to the lived reality of the lives of ordinary people, the lewd and everyday, a relationship that gives it a particular status and authority. Late fourteenth- and fifteenth-century vernacular writing is experimental or tentative because its writers were testing in their work the limits and possibilities of their language. This led to some writers celebrating the importance of the vernacular while others expressed anxiety and concern about its spread. *Piers Plowman* and, in a very different way, *The Canterbury Tales* push the limits of what it is possible to say and do in English. More's English writing needs to be seen as part of the same tradition of vernacular writing as that of writers like Langland and Chaucer.[28] In particular, it shares their sense of English as, at its best, combining classical Christian learning with popular sayings, fables, and tales to create an authoritative ethical language.

As well as writing in the vernacular, More was also famous as a Latinist and humanist scholar. His Latin writing forms an important part of the history of humanism in England and Europe.[29] Humanism is a difficult concept to define. It claimed to represent a return to the sources of classical learning, *ad fontes*, freed from medieval commentaries and glosses. Humanism emphasized the educational importance of grammar, rhetoric, and dialectic. This was because humanist scholars insisted on the importance of the practical application of learning to society, which required linguistic skills and eloquence. Humanists like More and Erasmus were strongly influenced by Cicero and his insistence that the learned should play an active part in the public sphere. This had important implications for the kinds of intellectual labor that humanists tended to value. James McConica comments that "the culture of humanism, with its emphasis on the issues of the present, was entirely hostile to philosophical system-building and abstract speculation."[30] This focus on the present and practical was particularly important in relation to the political thought of Northern European humanism, which stressed the Ciceronian understand of learning as, in Brendan Bradshaw's words, a "moral process—directed to the fulfilment of . . . human potential."[31]

More and Erasmus shared an understanding of human potential that was grounded in an Augustinian sense of the mutually supportive natures of reason and revelation. For them the idea that human reason was inherently and irredeemably sinful was anathema, and they both consistently attacked fideism, the belief that faith and reason are incompatible. Central to More's humanism was the ideal of friendship as an embodiment of *amicitia*, or love, on the one hand, and reason on the other. In textual terms the key representation of this ideal was the proverb as represented in Erasmus's highly influential work *Adages* (first published 1500). For Erasmus proverbs were pieces or shards of classical wisdom that could, in theory, be shared by all. As Kathy Eden argues, for Erasmus, "proverbs or adages encode over time and space a collective wisdom that belongs equally to all members of a community."[32] Humanism for More and Erasmus was not an abstract philosophy. It was a vital, exciting, and reforming movement whose aim was nothing less than the renewal of Christianity across Europe.

The vernacular and humanism are two key influences on More's writing. In this introduction I will examine in detail two texts that More wrote relatively early during his writing career, *The Last Things* (c. 1522) and the *Life of Pico* (c. 1510), in order to illustrate More's engagement with late medieval English literature. These works have often been viewed as representing the two sides of More — the medieval and the humanist. I will, however, suggest that it is important to understand them as united in emphasizing the devotional importance of the everyday, of the lived reality of human life. In order to illustrate this argument in detail I will refer to a number of late fifteenth- and early sixteenth-century play texts. Although More never wrote a play, it has long been acknowledged that drama was an important part of his life and work.[33] Early Tudor drama exemplifies late medieval English vernacular culture in its heterogeneity and critical engagement with Christianity. In particular, the issues central to the poetics and ethos of the work of Chaucer and his contemporaries were staged in such plays as *Everyman*, the *N Town Play*, and the Digby *Mary Magdalene*.

Vernacular Writing and *The Last Things*

More's engagement with English vernacular writing was more complex than is sometimes acknowledged. One of his earliest works was "A Mery

Gest How a Sergeaunt Wolde Lerne to Be a Frere," possibly written in
1509.[34] This relatively short poem tells the story of a Sergeant of Law's
attempts to arrest a debtor by pretending to be a friar. It opens by suggesting that people should stick to their trades, since they will make fools
of themselves if they do not:

> Whan an hatter
> Wyll go smater,
> In phylosophy,
> Or a pedlar,
> Waxe a medlar,
> In theolegy,
> All that ensewe,
> Suche craftes newe,
> They dryue so fere a cast,
> That euermore,
> They do therfore,
> Beshrewe themselfe at laste.[35]

This passage could be regarded as expressing a conservative medieval
attitude to society—hatters and peddlers should know their place and
keep to it. Certainly the poem ends by advising its listeners to reject in-
novation and not to repeat the Sergeant's mistake:

> I wolde auyse,
> And counseyll euery man,
> His owne crafte vse,
> All newe refuse,
> And vtterly let them gone:
> Playe not the frere,
> Now make good cheere,
> And welcome euery chone.[36]

The narrator of "A Mery Gest" opens and closes his poem with conventional statements of conservative social wisdom. This is despite the
fact, which the narrator fails to notice, that the poem's story does not

endorse the morality encapsulated in the poem's opening and closing remarks. Instead the story depicts a world of linguistic play and physical comedy. At a basic level the sergeant does not pretend to be a friar in order to improve his social standing. His performance is a product of his existing social role. It is to fulfill his duty as a sergeant of law that he dresses as a friar. The plot of "A Mery Gest" subtly but firmly undermines its narrator's didactic morality by suggesting that "playing the friar" may be necessary to maintain social norms and rules.

As soon as the Sergeant, dressed as a friar, attempts to arrest the debtor, a fight breaks out:

> They rente and tere,
> Eche other here,
> And claue togyder fast,
> Tyll with luggynge,
> Halynge and tugynge,
> They fell doune both at last.
> Than on the grounde,
> Togyder rounde,
> With many sadde stroke,
> They roll and rumble,
> They tourne and tumble,
> Lyke pygges in a poke.[37]

The final image of this line is perhaps intended to remind More's reader of Chaucer's description of the fight between the two clerks and the miller in *The Reeve's Tale*, in particular through its use of the phrase "pigs in a poke."[38] For Chaucer's Reeve and More's narrator the violence that erupts at the end of their texts raises questions about the amount of control they have over their own works. In both cases tales told by advocates of a conservative morality based upon order and restraint undermine that morality. The violence that breaks out at the end of *The Reeve's Tale* is excessive, disturbing, and amusing. It generates textual pleasure that clearly exceeds the didactic requirements of the Reeve's message, which is encapsulated in the two moralizing proverbs with which he concludes his tale.[39] There is also no need for the narrator of "A Mery Gest" to provide a detailed account of the fight between the Sergeant and the Debtor in order to argue for the permanence of the existing social order. It is the requirement to entertain that drives More's description of the fight, with its Skeltonic rhymes and jangles.

The tension between the form of "A Mery Gest" and its narrator's morality comes into particular focus in the poem's emphasis upon the Sergeant's success in impersonating a friar:

> So was he dyght,
> That no man myght,
> Hym for a frere deny,
> He dropped and doked,
> He spake and loked,
> So relygyously.
> Yet in a glasse
> Of he wolde passe,
> He toted and he pered:
> His herte for pryde,
> Lepte in his syde
> To se how well he frered.[40]

This passage suggests that being a friar is largely a matter of performance. More invents a new word, "frered," to encapsulate the extent to which the Sergeant's playacting is real. In the process the poem again puts pressure on its narrator's conservative social ethos. In creating a new word is not More meddling, mixing things up that should be kept apart? What right does More, as a lawyer, have to play the part of a word maker? Clearly the Sergeant is, in one sense, a figure for More, and the former's pride in his "friaring" is a self-deprecating joke on More's "poeting."

"A Mery Gest" was one of the first works that More wrote. It is easy to see it as simple, even naïve. In particular, the poem's apparent moralizing on the importance of knowing one's place could be seen as reflecting a conservative medieval mind-set. In recent years, however, scholars such as David Aers, Lee Patterson, and James Simpson have ably critiqued the idea that in the late fourteenth and fifteenth centuries people uncritically accepted the need to maintain the status quo, social, political, or religious.[41]

"A Mery Gest" can be seen as a typically medieval work, but only on the basis that it offers the modern reader the temptation of medievalism: the possibility of reading without proper care within an existing set of historical and critical assumptions. In "A Mery Gest" More is deliberately and self-consciously mocking a conservative social morality that emphasized the permanency of the existing social order, and he is doing so by deploying the resources of late fourteenth- and fifteenth-century English vernacular writing. Indeed it is arguable that it is the conservative morality of the opening and closing passages of "A Mery Gest" that are modern or, more accurately, typical of the sixteenth century, while the critical, witty middle section of the poem evokes the writing of Chaucer and perhaps specifically *The Reeve's Tale*. More is a medieval writer, and it is his critical engagement with the literature of the late fourteenth and fifteenth centuries that provides him with the intellectual resources to critique the emerging political, cultural, and religious norms of the sixteenth century.

More wrote *The Last Things* at a stage of his life similar to that during which he wrote *Richard III* and *Utopia*. It shares with these works a concern with the ethics of language and the nature of a good life. *The Last Things* was first published in 1557 as part of William Rastell's edition of More's *English Works*. In this work Rastell suggests More wrote *The Last Things* in 1522. This does seem likely. In particular, the reference in *The Last Things* to "a great Duke" has been interpreted as an allusion to the duke of Buckingham, who was executed for treason in May 1521. *The Last Things* is often regarded as an unfinished work and was presented as such by Rastell in his edition of More's works. Possibly, however, it is more than simply coincidence that the final chapter, dealing with the sin of sloth, is short and breaks off before it is finished. Does not an unfinished chapter perfectly illustrate the dangers of slothfulness? The two chapters preceding sloth concern gluttony and covetousness. They are the longest chapters in the work, coveting textual space and consuming narrative motivation so that little of either is left for Sloth. *The Last Things* is not a simple work of conventional piety. It raises questions, for example, similar to those Chaucer poses in *The Parson's Tale* in relation to specific forms of Christian writing, and in particular penitential teaching as a key aspect of fourteenth- and fifteenth-century religious practice. *The Last Things* creates an image of a Christian textual community united in the devotional labor of reading. In the process it critiques the emphasis on clerical authority articulated, for example, in the play *Everyman*.

The Last Things opens with an introduction that includes a discussion of Christian speech. More comments that everything has its time and it is preferable not to speak rather than to participate in a conversation that is ungodly. He goes on, however, to argue,

> Yet better were it then holdynge of thy tong, properly to speake, and with some good grace and pleasant fashion, to break into some better matter: by whiche thy speache and talking, thou shalt not onely profite thy selfe as thou sholdest haue done by thy well minded silence, but also amende the whole audience, which is a thyng farre better and of muche more merite.[42]

In this passage More is seeking to justifying the printing of *The Last Things* as an act of Christian devotion. He imagines the emergence of a Christian community through the shared reading of his work. In particular, *The Last Things* consistently deploys witty and comic language alongside devotional discourse to create a diverse text that happily mixes together different forms and genres.[43] More, like Augustine, while fully accepting the doctrine of original sin, retained a sense of the salvific potential of sensuous human labor and in particular language.[44] This placed him against those fideistic traditions of late medieval religious thought that regarded human wit and imagination as irredeemably sinful and corrupt.

Having discussed the virtue of good speaking, More goes on to reject the imposition of authority upon popular or public speech:

> If thou can find no proper meane to breake the tale, than excepte thy bare authoritie sufficient to commaunde silence, it were peraduenture good, rather to keepe a good silence thy self, than blunt forth rudely, and yrryte them to anger, which shal happely therfore not let to talke on, but speake much the more, less thei should seme to leue at thy commaundement. And better were it for the while to let one wanton woorde passe vncontrolled, than geue occasyon of twain.[45]

More would rather the tale continue than impose a violent, disruptive silence on the community of Christian tale-tellers. In particular, *The Last Things*, despite its focus on the seven deadly sins, is not a penitential work. It does not ask its readers to focus obsessively on their personal sinfulness, and its representation of a good Christian life is far more active and engaged than that of some other early Tudor religious works. *The Last Things* focuses on the need for a Christian to be active in this world. This emphasis upon the active over the contemplative or penitential is ultimately based on the christocentric nature of More's religious beliefs and in particular on the importance he placed upon Christ's role as a teacher. Not for More the suffering, relatively passive, "domestic" Christ of works like Nicholas Love's immensely popular *The Mirror of the Blessed Life of Jesus Christ*.

More's emphasis on reason extends to his understanding of the proper approach to Scripture. The phrase "four last things," referring to death, judgment, hell, and heaven, alludes to Ecclesiasticus 7:36: "Remember thy last thinges, and thou shalte neuer sin in this world." More tells the reader in the opening pages of his work that remembering the last things is a "sure medicine." He then develops this metaphor, comparing the true healing powers of Ecclesiasticus 7:36 with those of human doctors:

> The phisicion sendeth his bill to the poticary, and therin writeth sometime a costlye receite of many strange herbes and rootes, fet out of far countreis, long lien drugges, al strength worn out, and some none such to be goten. But thys phisicion sendeth his bil to thy selfe, no strange thing therin, nothing costly to bie, nothing farre to fet, but to be gathered al times of the yere in the gardein of thyne owne soule.[46]

More in this passage seems to be drawing a relatively simple dichotomy between the physical and spiritual. The passage tempts the reader to assume that the biblical doctor works on the soul in much the same way as the secular doctor works on the body. The two doctors, however, are in practice quite different. The secular doctor's cures are largely powerless, with the patient becoming involved in a series of exchanges that ultimately produce nothing and are almost entirely symbolic. Certainly there is no actual physical cure to be found in the secular doctor's treatments. The biblical doctor, who *is* the words "Remember thy last thinges, and thou shalte neuer sin in this world" works internally and constantly. These words produce their own herbs, "deth, dome, pain and ioy," which cure the soul, and in the process the body, of sin.[47]

More repeats the message later in the opening, telling the reader that

> this shorte medicine is of marueylous force able to kepe vs al our life fro sin. The phisicion canne not geue no one medicine to euery man to kepe him from sicknes, but to diuers men diuers, by reson of the diuersity of diuers complexions. This medicine serueth every man. The phisicion dothe but gesse and coniecture that his receipt shal do good: but thys medicine is vndoubtedly sure.[48]

More's emphasis on "diversity" here is important, since it indicates a key element of the medicinal value of the last things, which is their ability to operate like a proverb or adage. All people can take/read this medicine. Christian healing is open to anyone prepared to engage in the devotional labor of reflecting upon the last things. The metaphor of Scripture as medicine that More deploys in the opening of *The Last Things* is relatively simple and at the same time potentially far-reaching. It reminds one of the meal offered by Scripture to Will and Patience in *Piers Plowman*. Clearly More is creating a tension between the medicinal properties of the powders, herbs, and potions offered by learned secular doctors and the medicinal properties of the last things, which are spiritual. For the last things to be effective, however, those "taking them" must work beyond or through the metaphor, to make the spiritual medicine real or potent. The metaphor of the two kinds of medicine is also a metaphor for different kinds of reading and writing. Some texts, perhaps particularly penitential works, list the deadly sins, often in great detail, and command readers to renounce them.[49] *The Last Things* deploys the metaphor of Scripture as medicine to invite readers to exercise their reason; the last things are healing only if internalized, thought about, and acted upon. It is the reader who needs to provide the actual healing, through active engagement with More's text.

The last sin discussed in detail in *The Last Things* is gluttony. More's discussion appears on the surface to focus upon the sin's effects on the body; however, this turns out not to be the case:

> And who douteth that the body delicately fed, maketh as the rumour saith an vnchast bed. Men are wont to write a short rydle on the wal that, D. C. hath no P. Red ye this rydle I cannot: but I haue hard say, that it toucheth the redines [that] women hath to fleshly filth, if she fal in dronkenes. And if ye fynde one that can declare it, thoughe it be no greate authoritie, yet haue I heard saye that it is very true.[50]

The riddle that More refers to here is, "A drunken cunt hath no porter." The narrator of *The Last Things* claims in this passage not to able to read this riddle, but then goes on to show that this is pretense. More's narrator clearly does know the meaning of "a D. C. hath no P." In this passage More is making fun of the ability and desire of his readers to read "a D. C. hath no P." He is inviting his readers to reflect on the ethics of reading by placing them in a position of knowledge in relation to his narrator's claim, "rede this riddle I cannot." The narrator of *The Last Things* plays at being defeated by this riddle to create space for readers to expose their gluttonous desire to consume textual bawdiness. "A D. C. hath no P." may be true, as More asserts, but what this passage pushes the reader to ask is the extent to which she or he is a D. C. who has no P. when it comes to reading and consuming bawdiness. The section on gluttony in *The Last Things* is an object lesson in the truth of "a D. C. hath no P." A reader who indulges the desire to consume earthly, and in particular bodily, images and words loses control over her or his reading.

In *The Last Things* More stresses the need to moderate the body's desires, and he does so in the context of using the body as a metaphor for devotional labor. He argues that what makes gluttony a particularly pernicious sin is its effect in this world and in particular the bodily pain it causes. More contends that living a godly Christian life will be a source of bodily pleasure, and he clearly understood that this placed his work in conflict with those currents of late medieval Christian thought that made the total renunciation of the world, and in particular of the body, central to a pious Christian life:

If thou wene that I teach thee wrong, when I say that in vertue is pleasure and in sin is pain, I might preue it by many plain textes of holy scripture, as by the wordes of the psalmist where he saith, I haue had a gret pleasure in the way of thy testimonies, as in all maner of riches. And Salomon saith of vertue: her ways are al ful of pleasure, and her pathes are pesable. And further he saith, The way of the wicked, is as it were hedged with thornes but the way of the righteous is without stumbling.[51]

It is of course ironic that More refers to the Psalms as examples of the plain truth, given their poetic form, but this reflects again the extent to which *The Last Things* is concerned, like *Utopia*, with the way a text makes meaning and not simply with what it says. The riddle "a D. C. hath no P." is at one level an example of simple language. But what it provokes in the reader is a gluttonous desire to read the body of a woman and the body of the text. Plain language for More is nongluttonous, and he deliberately chooses the Psalms as an example to avoid suggesting that this means simple or dour. The plainness of the Psalms, like that of Christ's proverbs, was for More a product of their truthfulness. That human beings find riddles like "a D. C. hath no P." easier to understand than the Psalms reflects their sinfulness. More creates a tension in *The Last Things* between the false complexity of riddles like "a D. C. hath no P." and the profound plainness of Christ's teaching. In the process he defends human reason as a Christian good, as a legitimate and necessary weapon in the Christian struggle to lead a good life.

More ends his discussion of gluttony by asking why it is treated so differently from other causes of death:

If there be a man slain of a stroke, there is as reson is muche speache made thereof, the coroner sitteth, the queste is charged, the verdit geuen, the felony founden, the doer endited, the proces sued, the felon arrained, and dyeth for the dead. And yet if men wold enserche how many be slain with weapon, and how many eate and drink themself to death, there should be found (as Salomon saith) mo dead of the cup and kechen, than of the dente of sworde: and thereof is no wordes made at all.[52]

More in this passage is imagining a response to sin, and specifically gluttony, that is based on reason, on the ability of words to find, explain, and defeat sinfulness. He is not suggesting that this is simple or easy. More is no Utopus, the fictional founder of Utopia. He does not believe that sin can be ordered, legislated, or explained away. More did, however, believe that human reason had an important role to play in a Christian commonwealth's moral battle against sinfulness.

The emphasis on reason in *The Last Things* reflects its uneasy relationship to the *ars moriendi* (the art of dying) tradition. More's text constructs itself as a textual weapon in the fight against sin. The section on pride opens by emphasizing the traditional hierarchy of sins, placing pride first: "I haue sene many vices ere this, that at the first seemed far from pride, and yet wel considered to the vttermost, it wold wel appere, that of that rote thei sprang."[53] He then carefully distinguishes different types or forms of pride, reserving his real ire for spiritual pride: "The lechor knoweth he doth nought, and hath remorse therof. The gloten perceiueth his own faut and somtyme thynketh it bestly. The slothful body misliketh his dulnes, and thereby is moued to mend. But this kind of pride, that in his own opinion taketh himself for holy, is farthest from al recouery."[54] More argues that the behavior of these holy sinners is more foolish than that of those "that plainly folow the wayes of the worlde [and] pleasures of theyr body."[55] More's representation of pride, and his singling out of holy pride as particularly dangerous, stresses pride's danger to the commonwealth. Pride affects all classes and all people. It is the universal sin and can be addressed only through collective moral action. More, however, does not imagine the church or the clergy as leading figures in this struggle. Indeed his emphases on the particular dangers of holy pride imply that clerical exceptionalism is itself the worst and most dangerous form of pride.

The Last Things looks like a penitential text, and it does indeed ask its readers to reflect on their lives through the framework provided by the last things. At the same time, the work deploys fictions, stories, and metaphors as part of its teaching to a remarkable extent. For example, in discussing envy More refers to what he tells the reader is one of Aesop's fables—although it is in fact the twenty-second fable of Avianus—to illustrate envy's sterility. In the fable a pagan goddess comes down to earth and offers a covetousness man and an envious man a bargain. She will grant the request of whoever asks first but will give the other man twice what the requester asks for:

> When this condicion was offered, than began there some courtesye betwene the enuyous and the couetyse, whether of them shoulde aske: for that wold not the couetous be brought vnto for nothing, because hymself wold haue his felowes request doubled. And whan the enuious man saw that, he wolde prouide that his felowe should haue lytle good of the doubling of his peticion. And forthwith he required for his part, that he might haue one of his eyen putte out. By reson of which requeste, the enuious man lost one eye, and the couetous man lost both.[56]

More's use of this fable is typical of his vernacular writing. At a simple level it is designed to illustrate the lesson of the book, which is the need to fight against sin. Yet one need not use a fable to make this point. *The Last Things* is a manual designed to guide devotional practice through a focus on the last things. It uses fictions and fables to further its argument, suggesting that these too have a part to play in helping a person lead a good Christian life. Some people in late medieval England, however, would have regarded More's use of fables and fictions as wasteful and inherently sinful.

Chaucer's Parson is just such a person, or rather he is a fictional representation of one. At the end of *The Canterbury Tales* the Host turns to the Parson and demands a tale:

> Unbokele and shewe us what is in thy male;
> For trewely, me thynketh by thy cheere
> Thou sholdest knytte up wel a greet mateere.
> Telle us a fable anon, for cokkes bones![57]

The Parson, however, rejects out of hand the Host's demand, telling him, and the rest of the pilgrims:

> Thou getest fable noon ytoold for me,
> For Paul, that writeth unto Thymothee,
> Repreveth hem that weyven soothfastnesse

And tellen fables and swich wrecchednesse.
Why sholde I sowen draf out of my fest,
Whan I may sowen whete, if that me lest?[58]

The tale that the Parson finally tells is far from being a fable. Indeed it is not a tale at all. Instead what the Parson gives the pilgrims is a treatise on penance. *The Parson's Tale* is one of only two prose tales in the entire *Canterbury Tales*. It is not an easy text to read, let alone listen to while riding on horseback to Canterbury. The Parson is quite open about his lack of poetic skill, telling the pilgrims in the prologue to his tale, "I kan nat geeste 'rum, ram, ruf' by lettre," and later commenting, "I take but the sentence, trusteth weel."[59]

The Parson's Tale is a detailed manual on sin, how it can be known and the ways in which it can be conquered through true penitence.[60] The Parson's rejection of poetry, the deliberately challenging, even turgid, nature of his tale, reflects his fideistic skepticism as regards human reason. The Parson ultimately regards fables and tales as at best a waste of time and at worst inherently sinful. He is a fictional representation of a fideistic current in late medieval religion, orthodox and heterodox, that saw reason and imagination as barriers between humanity and God.[61] The Parson is the last speaker in *The Canterbury Tales*; he ends the pilgrimage, because at one level, once the "parsons" of this world speak, the collective communal voices of the rest of Chaucer's pilgrims are silenced. Their tales simply cannot exist in the reformed, penitential world of the Parson.

The extended discussion of sin by *The Parson's Tale*'s expresses a particular horror of the body. For example, during his discussion of the sin of lechery the Parson tells his listeners that

moore fooles been they that kissen in vilenye, for that mouth is the mouth of helle, and namely thise olde dotards holours, yet wol they kisse, though they may not do, and smarte hem. Certes, they been lyke to houndes; for an hound, whan he cometh by the roser or by othere [bushes], though he may nat pisse, yet wole he heve up his leg and make a contenaunce to pisse.[62]

In this passage the Parson argues that old people kissing is equivalent to dogs cocking their legs and then not urinating. The implication of this passage for the rest of *The Canterbury Tales* is devastating, since the hound's "making a countenance to piss" is a metonym for the desires and pleasures incited by many of the tales told by the Parson's fellow pilgrims. Alison in *The Miller's Tale* is a rose bush designed to incite, and mock, the reader's desires. Although the Parson's treatment of the sin of lechery is orthodox, it exhibits, as David Aers argues, "a hatred of the body and revulsion from all sexual delight which . . . would have seemed 'rigorist' even among orthodox moralists."[63] The Parson expresses a disdain for the body, imagination, and wit. In his world what is the point of *The Miller's Tale* except to encourage sin? There is, however, something excessive, even pointless, about the Parson's cataloguing of sin. It is so extreme that it becomes self-defeating. Katherine C. Little points out that the Parson never connects his discussion of sin with confession and therefore grace. Little asks, "To what use is the [Parson's] list going to be put?"[64] The Parson's rejection of fables, of human wit and imagination, leads him to create a text that, despite its emphasis on penitence, is sterile; there is no confession or forgiveness.[65] Ultimately the Parson's ethos and that of *The Canterbury Tales* are incompatible.[66]

The Last Things rejects the Parson's pessimism through its emphasis on reading as a form of devotion. The medicinal powers of the last things require the reader to use reason to give them potency. More's text locates sin within the real world in order to connect the abstract idea with the reality of people's everyday behavior and to make it something that can be addressed and reformed through human endeavor. More finishes his discussion of the sin of wrath by referring to the anger displayed by some men in church:

> First shame were it for men to bee worth like women, for fantasties and thinges of nought, if ther wer no worse ther in. And now shal ye se men fall at variance for kissyng of the pax, or goyng before in procession, or setting of their wiues pewes in the church. Doubt ye whether this wrath is pride? I dout not but wise men wil agree, that it is eyther follyshe pride or proud foly.[67]

More goes on to ask his readers: "How much is it now the more foly, if we consider that we be but going in pilgrimage, and haue here no dwelling place, than to chide and fight for folyes by the way."[68] The image of

life as a pilgrimage was a very important one for More. He returns to it
throughout his written work. Here it is a metaphor for life but also for
the process of walking and reading that makes the reader think on the
last things. However, thinking, More argues, is not enough: one also needs
to pull up sin from the bottom of one's heart.[69]

At the center of More's Christian thought is a vision of the church as
a community of equals. In his *Letter to a Monk*, around 1519, More writes:
"God showed great foresight when he instituted all things in common;
Christ showed as much when he tried to recall mortals again to what is
common from what is private. For he perceived that corrupt mortal nature cannot cherish what is private without detriment to what is common, as experience shows in all aspects of life."[70] More links the corrupting desire to value the private and individual over the communal and
collective to the vocation of the monk he is writing to:

> For this reason many prize their own ceremonies more than those
> of their religious house, their own house's ceremonies more than
> those of their order, and whatever is exclusive to their order more
> than everything that is common to all religious orders, while they
> prize all that pertains to the religious somewhat more than they do
> those lowly and humble concerns that are not only not private to
> them but are common to the whole Christian people, such as those
> plebeian virtues of faith, hope, charity, fear of God, humility, and
> others of similar character.[71]

In this passage More stresses the religious importance of the communality of Christian people, *populo Christiano communia*. This is where, for
More, one can find the "plebeian" values of faith, hope, charity, and fear
of God. This emphasis upon the virtue of Christian communality is reflected in the devotional teaching of *The Last Things*, which consistently
argues for a communal, collective response to the problem of sinfulness. In these terms *The Last Things* can usefully be seen as part of a tradition of English works of popular theology within which, as Nicholas
Watson has argued in relation to the late fourteenth-century text the *Pore
Caitif*, the vernacular is an emblem for the universality of Christ's teaching and in particular his offer of salvation.[72] *The Last Things* is far from

being an anticlerical work. It does, however, create very little space for the clergy in its imagined community of Christian readers. Or perhaps it would be more accurate to argue that *The Last Things* treats all its readers as equal and therefore does not advance the claims of any specific social or religious group. That this is potentially significant can be illustrated by examining briefly the play *Everyman*, which, like More's text, is centrally concerned with the preparation of the human soul for death.

Everyman was first printed during the 1510s and is a close translation of the Dutch play *Elckerlijc*.[73] It is unclear if *Everyman* was intended for performance. The play stages a number of key early Tudor clerical concerns; in particular it advances a clericalist agenda that emphasizes lay dependency on the clergy, the importance of penitence, and the twin dangers of reason and heresy. In the process it articulates a poetics of which Chaucer's Parson would have approved. *Everyman* is a sophisticated drama that embodies a suspicion of its own form and enacts a desire to separate clerical authority from the world of the play. *Everyman* opens with its eponymous hero surprised by the entrance of Dethe, who informs him that he is about to die. Everyman pleads to be spared until the morning in order to give him time to seek amends. Dethe, however, replies:

> Naye, thereto I wyll not consent,
> Nor no man wyll I respyte,
> But to the herte sodeynly I shall smyte
> Without ony advysement.
> And now out of thy syght I wyll me hy.
> So thou make thee redy shortely,
> For thou mayst saye this is the daye
> That no man lyvynge may scape a-waye.[74]

Dethe's refusal of Everyman's desperate plea for more time forces Everyman to put his affairs into order. In the process, however, Everyman is surprised to be deserted by the world, friends, family, and material wealth, and to discover the importance of good deeds, knowledge, and confession. It is Fyve Wyttes who explains to Everyman that he must turn to the priesthood for salvation:

Fyve Wyttes: God wyll you to salvacyon brynge
For preesthode exceedeth all other thynge.
To us Holy Scrypture they do teche,
And converteth man fro synne, Heven to reche.
God hath to them more power gyven
Than to ony aungell that is in Heven.[75]

At the end of this speech Everyman leaves the stage to be confessed and receive the sacrament from Priesthood. Remarkably the latter, while participating in the drama, does not speak or appear in the playing space. Priesthood is present in *Everyman*, but only as a silent source of authority. Without him Everyman cannot be saved; even his good deeds are useless. *Everyman*'s emphasis on the role of the priest is incompatible with More's argument in *The Last Things* that the spiritual medicine provided by the last things is open to all who read with proper care and devotion. Everyman is saved not by his own efforts but by the off-stage ministrations of a priest. *Everyman*'s didactic or pastoral message is relatively simple—death comes to all, and when it comes it is the state of one's soul that matters, not friends, family, or worldly wealth—but its representation of priesthood is complex and contradictory. *Everyman* lauds the authority of the clergy, arguing that the least priest is greater in the sight of God than any emperor or king, while at the same time depicting priesthood as semidetached from the world of the play. It is as though *Everyman*'s writer is concerned that to give Priesthood words, to explicitly make him a part of the play, would be to endanger his status by suggesting that there is something performative about being a priest.

Everyman spatially divorces the world of the play from that of formal, organized religion. Priesthood and the sacraments occupy a different space, off stage and silent, from that of Everyman's drama. In particular, *Everyman*, as William Munson has argued, is skeptical toward its own form, toward the religious status of the theater. Munson goes on to suggest that "words for Everyman always present the danger of superficiality."[76] *Everyman* is a drama of interpretation. Its eponymous hero has to learn that human language and reason have no place in understanding God's promises; ultimately those faculties are hindrances. What is required is obedience and acceptance of the church's teaching, enacted through penitence. The allegorical figures of the world—Felawship, Kinrede,

Cosyn, and Goodes—are not what they seem. They require interpretation. Good Dedes, Knowledge, Confession, and Fyve Wyttes, Everyman's spiritual qualities, do not ask to be understood. Like the allegorical virtues in other morality plays, for example Henry Medwall's *Nature*, they simply need to be obeyed.

Life of Pico and the Mixed Life

The Last Things creates an image of its readers working together to defeat sin. This is not, however, simply because it is a traditional vernacular or "medieval text." This ideal is also a key element of More's humanism as articulated in his translation the *Life of Pico* (c. 1510). More's work remains largely close to the original Latin text, the life of Pico della Mirandola written by Pico's nephew Gianfrancesco, which prefaced a posthumous *Opera omnia* of Pico's writings first published in 1496. It is unclear how or when More encountered this work. It may have been via John Colet, who had studied in Italy from 1492 to 1495. Other possible sources include Thomas Linacre or Cuthbert Tunstall. It is of course possible that More was introduced to Pico's work by a visiting Italian. Whatever the route Pico's writings took to More, their popularity among European humanists is testified by the publication record of the *Opera* that was reprinted in Lyons before 1498, in Venice in 1498, in Strasburg in 1504, and in Reggio in 1506. More's decision to translate Pico's life into English has in the past been viewed through a biographical framework. Certainly there appear to be interesting similarities between More and Pico. Both established a reputation for precocious learning and may have struggled to reconcile a desire for worldly success with living a religious life.[77] It is, however, dangerous to read More's *Life of Pico* biographically. This is partly because the date when the work was completed by More is uncertain, but more importantly, More's translation remains very close to the original. It is at least possible that what attracted More to Pico was the latter's status within European humanist circles, in which case translating the *Life of Pico* could be seen as a statement of intellectual prowess. Certainly, by translating the *Life of Pico* More was making available in the vernacular an important work of Italian Renaissance learning.

This aspect of More's *Life of Pico* appears in the work's preface, which was not a translation. In this text More dedicates his translation to Joyeuce

Leigh, whose identity has remained a matter of conjecture.[78] More opens his preface by referring to the custom of sending gifts to friends at the beginning of a new year. He then commends his *Life of Pico* as a better gift than those usually given, since it is spiritual rather than carnal:

> But for asmoch as the loue and amyte of christen folke shuld rather be gostly frendsshyp than bodily: sith that all feithful peple are rather spirituall then carnall . . . I therfore myne hartely beloued sister in good lukk of this new yere haue sent you such a present as may bere witness of my tendre loue and zele to the happy continuannce and graciouse encreace of vertue in your soule: and where as the giftis of other folk declare that thei wissh their friends to be worldeli fortunate myne testifieth that I desire to haue you godly prosperous.[79]

More goes on to make some relatively typical claims for the importance of the work he is presenting to Joyeuce: "The warkes are such that trewly goode sister I suppose of the quatitie ther commeth none in your hande more profitable: neither of thachyuyng of temperaunce in prosperitie, nor in the purchasing of patience in aduersite, not to the dispising of worldly vanite, nor to the desiring of heuinly felicite."[80]

The "warkes" that More refers to are the various texts, poems, and letters that compose the *Life of Pico*. The use of the word "warkes" to describe written texts reflects the ironic nature of More's preface, which lauds spiritual gifts over material ones while referring to a physical book. Clearly the "achievement of temperance in prosperity" cannot be accomplished simply by the spiritual quality of More's *Life of Pico*; Joyeuce would need to make the material text "warke." There is also a sense in which More, by rendering the *Life of Pico* into English, has created the possibility for this work to take place. Certainly giving an untranslated *Life of Pico* to someone who could not read Latin would be pointless. It is the fact of translation, of placing Pico's example within the vernacular, that renders it practical, that makes it "warke." More's *Life of Pico*, like *The Last Things*, consistently insists on the need for the spiritual to be combined with the practical or everyday. It is perhaps this emphasis that accounts for the fact that, as the Yale editors point out, many of the excisions More made in Gianfrancesco's original work have the effect of lessening Pico's scholarly activities, the extent of his library, and his secular dealings. More creates a Pico who is a model of devotional activity.[81]

Apart from the preface, More's translation of the *Life of Pico* remains substantially true to its source. The one area where this is not the case is at the end of the work, where More renders into verse and adds considerable material to what are in the original relatively brief lists of spiritual properties and virtues. For example, Pico's sixth rule of spiritual battle is as follows: "Remember that when you have conquered one temptation you should always expect another, since the devil always prowls after someone to devour; that is why we should always serve with fear and say with the prophet, 'I will stand on my guard.'"[82] More's version of this rule reads:

> One synne vainquissed loke thou not tarye
> But lye in await for an other euery howre
> For as a wood lyon the fende oure aduersarye
> Rynneth a bout seking whom he may deuoure.
> Wherefore continually vppon thy towre
> Lest he the vnpurueid and vnredy catche
> Thou must with the prophite stonde and kepe wache.[83]

The changes More makes to Pico's text are limited but significant. He gives the idea of the devil prowling for prey specific form and emphasizes the social nature of the guard that the Christian warrior needs to keep. Pico's text encourages the reader to stand on his or her guard, while More's advises the reader to stand on his or her tower and with the prophet keep watch; More conjures up an image of the Christian watching over others in place of Pico's emphasis on standing one's ground as a solitary individual.

A similar drift can be seen in More's changes to Pico's "Twelve properties of a lover." Pico opens his twelfth property with the phrase "To serve him with no thought of recompense or reward." He then develops the idea of loving God in Platonic terms, commenting that "to serve him is nothing else than to tend toward him, that is, toward the highest good."[84] More's version of Pico's twelfth rule is far more urgent, corporeal, and erotic:

A very louer will his loue obaye
His Ioy hit is and all his appetight
To payne him self in all the euir he may
That parson in whom he set hath his delight.
Diligently to serue bothe day and nyght
For very loue, with owt any regarde
To any profite gwerdon or rewarde.[85]

The words that More deploys in this verse, "joy," "appetite," and "delight," emphasize the potential sensuality of a Christian's love for God. More's verse plays with the tropes and language of courtly love to mock those whose love is purely worldly, but also to question any who imagine that the proper love of God should be entirely abstract and disembodied. There is nothing abstract about a love whose servant feels delight day and night. The way in which More changes the emphasis of Pico's text can be seen as a specifically northern humanist response to Pico's Platonism; in place of abstraction More stresses the joyful, practical nature of a Christian's love for Christ.[86]

In the *Life of Pico* More depicts Christ as engaged in human sensuous activity. The love Christ inspires is joyful and brings delight. More's image of Christ and his ministry is recognizably humanist but also has its roots in late medieval English vernacular literature. Early Tudor religious writing and drama are replete with images of Christ and the godly life, but these are far from homogeneous. This can be usefully illustrated by examining the representation of Christ and the good Christian life in a number of late medieval plays.

As I have suggested, the importance of drama to More's writing has long been recognized. Works like the *N Town Play* and the Digby *Mary Magdalene* embody the tensions that existed within early Tudor orthodoxy and in the process provide the ideal context for understanding More's engagement with what Eamon Duffy terms "traditional religion."[87] For example, the *N Town Play* constructs Christ, and in particular his ministry, in almost entirely clerical and penitential terms.[88] Only two plays in the *N Town Play* cover the period between Christ's temptation in the wilderness and his entry into Jerusalem, "The Woman Taken in Adultery" and "The Raising of Lazarus." The latter focuses upon Christ's status as redeemer and emphasizes the ways in which Lazarus's resurrection prefigures the events of the passion. "The Woman Taken in Adultery" is effectively the only section of the *N Town Play* that stages Christ in his role as teacher and preacher. The play opens with Christ instructing the audience on the need for repentance. It then moves into a detailed staging of a key passage from John 8. This section opens with a scribe and a Pharisee conspiring to bring Christ down. They decide to trap Christ with a "false quarrel" and, on the advice of another character, Accusator, seek out a "fair young queen" to accuse. The play stresses the violence and the pleasure that the arrest of this woman engenders:

> **Scriba:** Come forth, thou stotte, com forth, thou scowte!
> Com forth, thou bysmare and brothel bolde!
> Com forth, thou hore and stynkynge bych clowte!
> How longe hast thou such harlotry holde?[89]

The woman's accusers bring her before Christ:

> **Scriba:** With this woman what xal be wrought?
> Shall we lete here go qwyte agayn,
> Or to hire deth xal she be brought?[90]

Christ does not immediately respond to this question but instead writes in the dust. The Bible does not say what he writes, but in the *N Town Play* Christ's words bear directly on the conclusion of the story:

> **Jesus:** Loke which of yow that nevyr synne wrought,
> But is of lyff clennere than she,
> Cast at here stonys and spare here nowght,
> Clene out of synne if that ye be.[91]

The woman is finally spared as a result of Christ's inviting those who accused her to stone her to death *if* they are free from sin.

Rowan Williams has recently suggested that an important element of the biblical version of this story is the way Christ's writing in the dust creates a space for thought, that Christ pauses and resists the temptation to rush to judgment.[92] The *N Town Play* closes down this aspect of the Gospel story by telling its audience that what Christ writes in the dust is an account of the sins of the woman's accusers:

> **Scriba:** Als the tyme that this betyd!
> Right byttyr care doth me embrace.
> All my synnys be now unhyd,
> Yon man befor me hem all doth trace.[93]

The *N Town Play* also depicts the woman as repentant before Christ writes in the dust:

> **Mullier:** Now, holy prophete, be mercyable!
> Vpon me, wrecch, take no vengeaunce.
> For my synnys abhomynable
> In hert I haue grett repentaunce.[94]

In the biblical version of this story Christ's mercy is not produced by the woman's prior acceptance of her sinfulness. Indeed the scriptural version of this episode creates the radical possibility that the woman does not repent, only that Christ asks her not to sin again.[95] The story of a woman taken in adultery reflects Christ's consistent refusal to participate in existing social norms and rush to judgment. It is an implicit criticism of all forms of condemnatory power and authority. In particular, it can be read as an enacted parable in which the way meaning is produced is at least as important as what the text means. The *N Town Play*, for entirely legitimate pastoral reasons, turns the story of the woman taken in adultery into a lesson on the need for penitence. It closes down the space for religious reflection that Christ creates by writing in the dust. The *N Town Play* stages a moment of forced public confession. Christ compels the woman's accusers to publicly confess when he writes their sins in the dust. The author of the *N Town Play* uses the story of the woman taken in adultery to participate in a scholastic and pastoral debate over the relationship between penitence and confession and to argue strongly the clerical position that for penitence to be real it has to be accompanied by public confession.[96] The *N Town Play*'s retelling of this narrative exemplifies a tradition of fifteenth-century religious writing that, while interesting and original, is nonetheless conservative in its desire to close down the space for religious thought.

The clericalist ethos of the *N Town Play* is reflected in its focus on the pastoral needs of the laity and its emphasis upon the authority of the clergy, particularly in relation to religious teaching and the sacraments.[97] It would, however, be quite wrong to assume that the positions adopted by the author of the *N Town Play* represent fifteenth-century English religious thought. A key problem with claims that More's piety was "medieval" or based on the religious principles of his childhood is that they invariably deploy a monolithic image of pre-Reformation English religious life. As Duffy has argued, "traditional" religion in early Tudor England "exerted an enormously strong, diverse, and vigorous hold over the imagination and loyalty of the people."[98] The Digby *Mary Magdalene* play reflects the perspicacity of Duffy's argument, since, while it is religiously orthodox, the model of a good Christian life it embodies is quite distinct from those articulated in the *N Town Play* or *Everyman*. The Digby play of *Mary Magdalene* cannot be dated with any certainty but was probably produced during the early sixteenth century.[99] It is a fascinating work that manages to stage the saint's entire life, including her fall, her meeting with Christ, and her subsequent voyage to Marseille, where she acts as regent while Marseille's king makes a pilgrimage to the Holy Land. The play ends by depicting Magdalene as a contemplative who, having left Marseille behind, lives and dies in the desert.

The Digby *Mary Magdalene* represents the saint's life as exemplary because it is so mixed and varied. The play includes scenes based on the New Testament alongside others set in hell and Marseille. An important aspect of the Digby *Mary Magdalene* is the comparison it stages between the effectiveness of one kind of knowledge or power and that of another: Mary's knowledge and that of a heathen priest in Marseille. The latter is depicted as a charlatan who deputizes his duties to a boy in his employment:

Rex: Now, prystys and clerkys, of this tempyll cler,
Yower servyse to sey, lett me se.
Prysbytyr: A, soveryn lord, we shall don ower devyr.
Boy, a boke anon thou bryng me!

Now, boy, to my awter I wyll me dresse—
On xall my westment and myn aray.
Boy: Now than, the lesson I woll expresse,
Lyke as longytt for the servyse of this day.[100]

The service that follows is a strange mixture of dog-Latin and nonsense. It concludes with the Boy instructing the audience:

Howndys and hoggys, in heggys and hellys,
Snakys and toddys mott be yower bellys!
Ragnell and Roffyn, and other in the wavys,
Gravntt yow grace to dye on the galows.[101]

These lines combine references to folk wisdom, "hell-hounds and hedge-hogs," with the names of demons, Ragnell and Roffyn. The Boy's "sermon" is parodic and mocking. Its direct target is "heathen" religion, but implicitly this scene asks the audience to question the relationship between religious authority, language, and performance. In this context it is no coincidence that the Prysbytyr behaves like a priest, albeit a bad one.

When Mary arrives in Marseille, the king immediately threatens her and questions her faith:

Rex: Jhesu? Jhesu? Qwat deylle is hym that?
I defye thee and thyn apenyon! [opinion]
Thow false lordeyn, I xal fell thee flatt!
Who made thee so hardy to make swych rebon?
Mary: Syr, I com natt to thee for no decepcion
But that good Lord Crist hether me compassyd.
To receyce hys name, itt is yower refeccyon,
And thy forme of mysbelef by hym may be losyd![102]

Mary goes on to explain Christ's teaching so successfully that not only does the king of Marseille go on a pilgrimage to the Holy Land, but he also leaves her behind as regent. The Digby *Mary Magdalene* stages a confrontation between false, empty knowledge of the heathen prince that is based on linguistic skill and professional status and the simple, empowered wisdom of Mary. In the process it draws on a biblical construction of wisdom as feminine and implicitly contrasts this with the masculine bombast of the heathen priest.[103] This scene also reminds one of the contrast set up in *Piers Plowman* between the simplicity of the meal served by Scripture and the overcooked, complex stew demanded by the learned Friar.[104] The Digby *Mary Magdalene* celebrates the saint's life as an image of a good and pious Christian life that is devotional in its combination of the active and contemplative. Mary lives in the real world, she rules as regent of Marseille, and at the same time she remains true to Christ's teaching.

The Digby *Mary Magdalene* creates an image of the godly Christian life as an epic struggle between embodied biblical wisdom and the wiles of the devil, which are at once comic, seductive, and dangerous. In contrast to works like *Everyman*, or indeed the *N Town Play*, the Digby *Mary Magdalene* articulates a positive attitude toward lay activity and the potential for mixed works—texts that combine a whole range of generic forms and tropes—to be edifying. In particular, like Julian of Norwich's *Showings*, the Digby *Mary Magdalene* has confidence in its audience's ability to understand the way it weaves together fact and fiction, Scripture and hagiography, romance and saint's life. To watch the Digby *Mary Magdalene* is to participate in the saint's life, following her on her journeys and making sense of them as Christian fellow travelers. The Digby *Mary Magdalene* is unconcerned with textual and spatial decorum. It expresses a confidence in the ability of human reason to contribute to God's work on earth. In these terms it is incompatible with the pessimistic view of human wit articulated in works like *Everyman*. More's English writing, indeed his sense of the shape and sound of a good Christian life and commonwealth, are part of the same vernacular tradition as the Digby *Mary Magdalene*, *Piers Plowman*, and *The Canterbury Tales*.

———

In one of his early epigrams More told the story of some sailors on board a boat that was struck by a violent storm. Fearing that the storm was caused by their sinful lives, the sailors decide to confess to a monk who happens to be aboard. Unfortunately this does not have the desired effect; the storm does not abate. One of the sailors then cries out: "No wonder our ship is barely afloat! All this time it has been weighed down by our cargo of sin. Why not throw overboard this monk who now carries the guilt of all of us, and let him take our sins away with him?"[105] Hearing this, the sailors heaved the monk into the sea, and the "ship sailed lighter than before."[106] More concludes this story, which appears on the surface to be of dubious moral value and to mock popular superstition while simultaneously endorsing its effectiveness, by commenting: "From this story—yes, this story—learn how heavy is a load of sin, since a ship cannot sustain its weight."[107] Throwing the monk overboard works. But it does so because sins *are* heavy and the act of confession *does* work; it relieves sinners of the weight of their sins. The basic message of More's epigram endorses the emphasis on clerical confession articulated in *Everyman*, but its ethos is that of the Digby *Mary Magdalene*.

The Last Things opens with a clear statement of the primacy of Scripture:

> If there were anye questyon amonge menne, whyther the woordes of holy scripture, or the doctryne of anye secular authour, were of greater force and effecte to the weale and profyte of mannes soule . . . yet this onely text writen by the wise man in the seuenth chapter of Ecclesiasticus is suche, that it conteineth more fruitfull aduise and counsayle, to the formyng and framing of mannes maners in vertue, and auoyding of sinne, then many whole and great volumes of the best of old philosophers, or anye other that euer wrote in secular literature.[108]

This passage on the face of it seems to negate the rest of the work. Why produce another great volume of secular learning, as More's work would have been if he had completed it according to his plan, when it could add nothing to the wisdom of Ecclesiasticus 7:36? More goes on to expand upon the primacy of Scripture:

> Long would it be to take the beste of theyr woordes [secular writers] and compare it with these wordes of holy writ: Let vs consider the frute and profit of this in it selfe: which thyng wel aduised and pondered, shal wel declare, that of none whole volume of seculare litterature, shall aryse so very fruitful doctrine.[109]

The opening of *The Last Things* is self-parodic. It starts by rejecting the utility of secular learning. It then, however, produces a learned secular frame for the verse from Ecclesiasticus that it is based upon. This is not to suggest that More did not take *The Last Things* seriously. Rather he took the idea of sinfulness, repentance, and forgiveness so seriously that, like the author of the Digby *Mary Magdalene*, he was not prepared to restrict the scope of his writing to the factual or scriptural. *The Last Things* deploys a whole range of comic and gothic moments, and an impressive array of secular learning, philosophical, medical, and political as well as proverbial and popular, to support its didactic aim. At the same time More's work, unlike *Everyman*, embodies a basic confidence in the ability of human wit to grow and water the herbs of Christ's teaching. It is this devotional confidence, an affirmation of the religious potential of human labor, physical and mental, that links More's religious sensibility to popular pre-Reformation forms of Christian devotion and places it within a tradition of vernacular English writing stretching back to Chaucer.

Chapter 1

POLITICS

Thomas More first met Desiderius Erasmus, who was in the company of Lord Mountjoy, in the summer of 1499. Mountjoy was a pupil of Erasmus, and it was probably due to this relationship that the meeting with More took place. It was to result in a friendship that would last for the rest of More's life. Mountjoy was also a companion of Prince Henry, at the time the younger son of Henry VII. At some point during the summer of 1499 More, Erasmus, Mountjoy, and Edward Arnold, a friend of More's, visited the royal palace of Eltham and met Henry. There is very little evidence concerning what happened at this meeting, but twenty years later More entered royal service. Henry was eight in 1499 and destined for a life playing second fiddle to his older brother, Arthur. It was Arthur's death in 1503 that changed everything for Henry. In 1509 Henry succeeded his father. More greeted this event with a number of celebratory Latin poems, which he presented to Henry. It is impossible to know what Henry thought of More's poems, but throughout the 1510s More became increasingly involved in the government of the country, until he entered royal service in 1518.[1] It was during these years that More wrote two of his most famous texts, *Richard III* and *Utopia*. Both works are centrally concerned with power and its relationship to language. In the following chapter I will discuss *Utopia*; here I want to examine *Richard III* as a work of history and as a piece of political theory.

More wrote *Richard III* between 1513 and 1519. William Rastell's suggestion in his 1557 edition of More's English work that More wrote *Richard III* "about" the year 1513 is clearly wrong, since More was definitely still working on the manuscript after 1514, when Henry Howard was made earl of Surrey. The work exists in two related versions, English and Latin. The relationship between the two is problematic, but it is clear that neither should be regarded as inherently more authoritative than the other. Indeed in many ways, as Richard S. Sylvester has suggested, it is more appropriate to talk about the texts rather than text of *Richard III*.[2] The work has been viewed as a work of political skepticism, as a study of tyranny heavily influenced by the depiction of Herod in English *Corpus Christi* plays, and as a piece of prose drama.[3] In particular, *Richard III* has been discussed as a work of humanist history.[4] Antonia Gransden has suggested that it is "the first and last humanist history written by an Englishman."[5] More was clearly influenced by a number of classical historical texts when writing *Richard III*, including Sallust and Tacitus.[6] *Richard III* is a self-consciously historical text. It asks its reader to witness the creation of history from the textual scraps of the past. This creative process is, for More, not simply historiographical but also political. *Richard III* is a meditation upon historical politics and the politics of history. It reflects upon the political dangers of rampant boundless monarchical power and the dissolution of meaning by endlessly circulating texts, lies, documents, smears, ballads, and rumors.

In this chapter I focus upon the English version of *Richard III*.[7] First I will examine a small selection of More's Latin epigrams as well as discussing several early Tudor works written in the same decade as *Richard III*. I then move back into the late fourteenth and early fifteenth centuries to discuss how writers like William Langland and Geoffrey Chaucer reflected upon the politics of the Peasants' Revolt of 1381. The chapter concludes by returning to *Richard III*. This rather circuitous route illustrates *Richard III*'s place within a tradition of fourteenth- and fifteenth-century Aristotelian English political writing that, in James Simpson's words, assumed that "the ideal form of a given entity is an *embodied* form; that the political order is a natural and desirable phenomenon, produced, intelligible, and controlled by human powers; and that the political order is either self-sufficient or at the very least a desirable good in and for itself."[8]

In *Richard III* More creates a text that is Aristotelian not simply because of what it says but also because of the way it says it. For More, Richard's real crime is not legal, although he clearly is a criminal; it is communal. Richard broke the bounds of community that, within the tradition of political thought inspired by Aristotle's thought, are the basis of ethical government. Herbert McCabe comments: "The Aristotelian tradition does not reject the ideas of right, rights, or law, but puts them in a secondary place. They have validity and necessity within, and only within, the quest for human excellence or satisfaction. . . . Community is not founded upon law: rather, law is founded upon community."[9] Richard's lack of community, his alienated uniqueness, reflects and embodies his criminality. At times More suggests that Richard does manage to give his actions a veneer of legality. In the process, however, the author shows that legal forms of government are susceptible to providing legitimation, even if only partial and flawed, to evil rulers.[10] Within More's Aristotelian approach to politics, moreover, such legitimacy is fundamentally undermined by Richard's violent assault on the community. In *Richard III* More places himself within the same political tradition as Langland and Chaucer. The good that all these writers seek to protect is the space of the political that *Richard III* depicts as beset by tyranny—monarchical, historical, and linguistic.

More's *Epigrams, Richard III*, and the Politics of Henrician Kingship

The shape of Tudor political history and, in particular, the importance given to the developments surrounding Henry's divorce have occluded the growing criticism of Henry's kingship that marked the period following the celebration of the new king's succession. There persists within modern literary and historical scholarship an assumption that until the 1530s political debate in early Tudor England was nonideological and moralistic as opposed to theoretical or principled. This is wrong. More wrote his Latin epigrams sporadically between 1497 and 1517 and published them in 1518. Several are intensely political and ask the reader to reflect upon the political relationship between form and language, rhetoric and ethics.[11] More's epigrams were praised by contemporaries for their style and subject matter. The political ones embody a Ciceronian concern with the proper or best order of the commonwealth.

One of More's most striking epigrams is the one he presented to Henry VIII, along with a number of others, to commemorate Henry's coronation. Not surprisingly, it celebrates the new reign: "If ever there was a day, England, if ever there was a time for you to give thanks to those above, this is that happy day. . . . This day is the limit of our slavery, the beginning of our freedom, the end of sadness, the source of joy."[12] It is difficult to believe that More would have meant this passage to be read ironically; however, there is clearly something extreme about the claims being made here. Did Henry's succession really bring an "end to sadness"? Was England enslaved by Henry VII? More goes on: "Now the people, freed, run before their king with bright faces. Their joy is almost beyond their own comprehension. They rejoice, they exult, they leap for joy and celebrate such a king. 'The King' is all that any mouth can say."[13] The extremity of the people's joy as imagined in this passage is clearly linked to the extravagant claims that More made earlier in the epigram. Again a slight sense of unease hovers around the celebration of Henry's succession. What is implied by the people's joy being beyond their comprehension? Does this suggest a lack of reason? What kind of public sphere is being imagined in this passage in which all that anyone can say is "the King"?

This sense that this epigram, "On the Coronation Day of Henry VIII," has a slightly ironic tone is confirmed when More turns his attention to king's person: "There is fiery power in his eyes, beauty in his face, and such colour in his cheeks as is typical of roses. In fact, that face, admirable for its animated strength, could belong to either a young girl or a man. Thus Achilles looked when he pretended to be a maiden, thus he looked when he dragged Hector behind his Thessalian steeds."[14] It does not appear entirely positive to use the example of the death of Hector and Achilles' treatment of his body to praise Henry. More presented his epigram celebrating Henry's succession to the king, which makes it highly unlikely that he intended the praise it contains to be anything other than unambiguous. As Alastair Foxe has suggested, More's presentation of his poems to Henry was clearly "an attempt to gain favour and attention."[15] At the same time it is difficult to read "On the Coronation Day of

Henry VIII" and not feel slightly uneasy. More's focus on the king's person and its impact on the shape and sound of the politics became a key element in the criticisms of Henry's kingship that started to appear in the 1510s. It was perhaps appropriate that at his coronation the people were so beyond themselves with joy that the only words they could say were "the King," but what were the implications if this monological focus continued? What kind of politics was implied by a polity in which only "the King" is heard or where the entire focus of the political gaze is upon the figure of the ruler? Where is its measure or mean? Its point of fixity?

In *Richard III* More describes monarchical politics as stage plays performed before an audience of "poor men": "These matters be kings' games, as it were, stage plays, and for the most part played upon scaffolds, in which poor men be but the lookers-on. And they that wise be will meddle no farther. For they that sometime step up and play with them, when they cannot play their parts, they disorder the play and do themselves no good."[16] In describing Richard's succession, More used a theatrical image for several reasons. *Richard III* consistently suggests that a thin line separates fiction and truth. By placing Richard's succession within a dramatic framework More implies that it had no more value than a stage play, with the various participants simply acting out fictional roles. At the same time, More's use of this image places his work alongside a number of political plays produced during the 1510s, which often reflected in highly critical ways on Henry's kingship. Monarchy was literally the stuff of drama during the decade in which More wrote *Richard III*. The play *Youth* was almost certainly written in 1513 or 1514.[17] Peter C. Herman has suggested that in this play Henry is satirized as frequenter of brothels and associate of Lady Lechery.[18] John Skelton probably wrote his drama *Magnyfycence* to comment upon the expulsion of the "minions" from Henry VIII's court in 1519.[19] In both plays, and in the rabidly anti-Yorkist *Hick Scorner*, politics takes place around a central figure whose flawed morality is shown to have direct and dire political consequences. Depicting Richard III as a player king invited More's readers to see him alongside such theatrical rulers as Magnyfycence and Youth. In the process it created the disturbing possibility that Richard was, like these theatrical kings, a version or image of Henry—albeit one mediated through the prism of history.[20]

The anonymous play *Youth* and John Skelton's *Magnyfycence* both reflect upon the dangers of a polity in which there appear to be no bounds to the desires of a monarchical ruler. *Youth* depicts the eponymous hero's fall from grace under the tutelage of a number of vices: Riot, Pride, and Lechery. The play opens with Charity on stage explaining to the audience that "of all virtues it is the king."[21] Youth then enters, praising himself and in particular his body:

> Who may be likened unto me
> In my youth and jollity?
> My hair is royal and bushed thick,
> My body pliant as a hazel stick:
> Mine arms be both big and strong;
> My fingers be both fair and long.[22]

After a brief, rather heated exchange, Youth drives Charity off stage. Almost at once Riot, having just escaped being hanged at Newgate (the rope broke) enters, joins Youth, and, with Pride and Lechery, indulges in a round of drinking, gambling, and whoring. The vices and Youth proceed to fetter Charity, who has to be released by Humility. Only at the end of the play is Youth brought to see the error of his ways:

> **Charity:** Youth, leave that counsel, for it is nought,
> And amend that thou hast miswrought,
> That thou mayst save that God hath bought.
> **Youth:** What say ye, Master Charity?
> What hath God bought for me?
> By my troth, I know nat
> Wether that he goeth in white or black.
> He came never at the stews,
> Nor in no place where I do use.
> Iwis, he brought not my cap,
> Nor yet my jolly hat.
> I wot not what he hath brought for me.
> And he brought anything of mine,
> I will give him a quart of wine
> The next time I him meet.

Charity: Sir, this he did for thee:
When thou wast bond he made thee free
And bought thee with his blood.
Youth: Sir, I pray you, tell me
How may this be.
That I know, I was never bond
Unto none in England.[23]

Youth is naïve but also arrogant. He cannot conceive of a world beyond that provided for him by his vice companions, that of new caps and jolly hats, of brothels, and wine. Youth's statement that he "was never bond / Unto none in England" reflects his arrogance but also the particularly problematic nature of Youth's understanding of his role as monarch. Youth cannot imagine being bound by anything, since the vices have encouraged him to indulge all his desires. He is a parodic version of an absolutist king existing in a state of boundless power—a youthful Utopus. The existing order, the one Youth lived within and tolerated before being seduced by the vices, has no purchase on his imagination. Indeed the playwright stresses Youth's genuine perplexity in the face of Charity's teaching.

After Charity has explained to Youth the nature of the bond—original sin—that Christ has freed him from, Youth immediately renounces the vices:

Youth: Here all sin I forsake
And to God I me betake.
Good Lord, I pray thee have no indignation
That I, a sinner, should ask salvation.
Charity: Now thou must forsake Pride
And all Riot set aside.[24]

The story of Youth's fall and redemption appears on the surface to be entirely conventional. All morality dramas are based on similar redemptive narratives. Youth's journey, however, shows a number of unusual aspects. For instance, Youth starts his downward journey by driving Charity off stage before any of the vices enter; temptation comes first from his own excessive self-regard and arrogance. In other morality plays, like *Wisdom*, the central character's fall happens, at least on the surface, as a result of temptation by vice figures. Youth's conversion is also significantly more simplistic and sudden than similar conversions in other morality plays. It is as though the playwright wishes to stress the potentially provisional or temporary nature of Youth's reformation. He has heeded Charity's words and turned his back on Riot, Pride, and Lechery, but there is something tentative, even slightly mocking, in the speed with which Youth renounces his erstwhile friends. The audience is left wondering whether Youth's reformation is genuine or whether it is simply driven by his riotous, prideful desire for personal salvation.

In his authoritative modern edition of *Youth*, Ian Lancashire has argued that Youth is an allegorical figure for Henry VIII.[25] He points out that in his songs Henry called himself "Youth" and that in 1513, when the play was probably written, Henry's prodigality and self-conceit were already a political issue.[26] In particular, Lancashire argues that Youth's toleration of Riot is a pointed allusion to Henry's failure as a monarch to control civil disorder or "riot." Lancashire suggests: "In cheerfully tolerating Riot, the highway robber of a 'courtier lad,' Youth is allegorically young Henry VIII in his policy of weakening all justice not strictly tied to the court. The snapping of Riot's Tyburn rope is, in this light, the most serious political allusion in the play."[27] *Youth* is critical of the emerging norms of Henrician kingship. It demands that the king respect the teaching of Charity and rule as a Christian bound by ties of sociability and fraternity. At the same time the dramatic center of the play is provided by the pleasurable spectacle of the vices' seduction of Youth. The audience's gaze is gripped by Youth's fall from grace, which is depicted in excessive comic detail. *Youth* confronts its audience with the social cost of a political gaze focused exclusively on the person of the king. Its solution, the moral reformation of Youth, is also an attack on the audience's voyeuristic pleasures in consuming Youth's seduction, fall, and redemption. Charity's message equates a covetous desire to consume with a form of politics that has no place for Charity. Youth's reform satisfies the audience's desire for political closure, but its simplistic focus on the monarch's personal redemption is an implicit critique of the forms of early Tudor political discourse.

More's epigram "What Is the Best Form of Government" echoes, in its Latin title "*Quis Opitmus Reipublicae Status*," a key aspect of *Utopia*. It opens with a bald statement that republican government is better than monarchical: "You ask which governs better, a king or a senate. Neither, if (as is frequently the case) both are bad. But if both are good, then I think that the senate, because of its numbers, is better and that the greater good lies in numerous good men."[28] The epigram then distinguishes between republican and monarchical government on the basis that in the former people are elected through reasonable argument while in the latter a person becomes king through blind chance. The epigram ends by asking its reader why he or she is even considering the question of which form of government is best: "What started you on this inquiry anyway? Is there anywhere a people upon whom you yourself, by your own decision, can impose either a king or senate? If this does lie within your power, you are king. Stop considering to whom you may give power. The prior question is whether to give it at all."[29] The epigram "What Is the Best Form of Government" is not evidence that More was a republican. It is a Latin poem designed to give pleasure to other learned humanists. What is significant, however, is the extent to which it opens up the idea of debate over the best form of government. It is precisely this kind of debate, and the language that it required, that More imagined being silenced in his epigram "On the Coronation Day of Henry VIII" and that has no place in the world created by Youth's arrogance and folly.

When More produced the epigram "On the King and the Peasant," it appears he was reflecting again on the moment of Henry's succession. The epigram tells the story of a peasant who comes to town when a royal procession is imminent. The peasant is concerned to see the king and asks a passerby where the king is: "And one of the bystanders replied, 'There he is, the one mounted high on that horse over there.' The peasant said, 'Is that the king? I think you are fooling me. He seems to me to be a man in an embroidered garment.'"[30] More contrasts the plain wisdom of the peasant with the foolish display of monarchical power. The peasant's disquiet clearly implies that kingship is only a matter of playing the part or acting the role, that there is nothing to being a king beyond wearing a magnificent gown.[31] The apparent contradiction between the emphasis on political skepticism and reason in some of More's Latin epigrams, on the one hand, and the celebration of Henry's succession in "On the Coronation Day of Henry VIII," on the other, partly reflects the different intended audiences of the texts. It may also relate to the different dates of composition, although this is hard to be certain about since the precise date of composition for many of More's epigrams is unclear. The contradiction between specific epigrams, however, is less important than the basic political thrust of More's work, which is crucial. The Latin epigrams all display an understanding of the political sphere as a space sustained by skeptical, applied reason. They are not populist or indeed inherently republican, but what does concern them is the relationship between power and language. The peasant's wisdom is an antidote to the uncritical cheers of the crowd. The epigram's aim is not to argue for the abolition of monarchy as a form of government but to question its status and scope. If monarchical power is simply an act, what keeps it within its proper bounds? Who controls Youth? What makes a king a king? Is it more than blind chance and a fancy robe?

John Skelton's play *Magnyfycence* also reflects upon monarchical power. It tells the story of its eponymous hero's fall and redemption. Unlike in *Youth*, in Skelton's play the vices, principally Fansy, cause the collapse of political order by tempting the protagonist, in this case Magnyfycence, to indulge his desires. The play opens with a debate between Magnyfycence, Measure, Felycyte, and Lyberte. The crux of this debate is the need for measure in all things, and in particular in relation to Lyberte, whose role in *Magnyfycence* can be equated with that of Lady Mede in *Piers Plowman*, since in both cases what causes corruption and disorder is less that liberty or mede is inherently wrong than the way they circulate within society.[32] Measure is for Skelton an overarching principle that ensures order even in a society in which the distribution of wealth and power is unequal. At the end of the debate Fansy enters, demanding to be heard and claiming to be Largesse. At this stage Magnyfycence resists Fansy's "charms," telling him, "Though Largesse ye hyght, your language is too large; / For which end goth forwarde ye take lytell charge."[33] To be accepted at court by Magnyfycence, however, Fansy has only to resort to some simple trickery and produce a forged letter of recommendation from Sad Cyrcumspeccyon. From this moment Magnyfycence's fate is sealed. Fansy gives Liberty his freedom and introduces a range of vices into the court, including Counterfeit Countenaunce and Crafty Conveyance. Having reduced Magnyfycence to poverty and then despair, the vices depart, leaving the stage to Sad Cyrcumspeccyon, Redresse, and Perseveraunce. These three virtues instruct Magnyfycence in the way of the world, advising him in particular that "in this worlde there is no erthly truste."[34] *Magnyfycence* concludes with an image of the world as a savage sea that absorbs people into a chaos of treachery:

> **Sad Cyrcumspeccyon:** Of the tereste [t]rechery we fall in the flode,
> Beten with stormys of many a forwarde blast,
> Ensordyd with the wawys savage and wode.
> Without our shyppe be sure it is likely to brast.
> Yet of magnyfycence oft made is the mast;
> Thus none estate lyvynge of hym[selfe] can be sure,
> For the welthe of this worlde can not indure.[35]

The play is no longer simply about Magnyfycence's fall and redemption; instead it takes on a more general moral message in which "our ship" represents a Christian commonwealth whose mast ought to be Christ but is often magnificence.

What causes corruption in *Magnyfycence* is the eponymous hero's weakness in the face of Fansy's lies. The play opens with a rational, measured debate about the limits of liberty, but with the entry of Fansy a very different language is introduced. Fansy is able to subvert all order. This is reflected in his speech, which is invariably comic and often borders on the ridiculous:

> **Fansy:** Lo, this is
> My Fansy, iwys.
> Now Cryst it blysse!
> It is, by Jesse,
> A byrde full swete,
> For me full mete.
> She is furred for the hete
> All to the fete;
>
> Her browys bent,
> Her eyen glent.
> From Tyne to Trent
> From Stroude to Kent.[36]

The disorder of Fansy's speech does not prevent him from turning to writing and using a forged letter to achieve his ends. Jane Griffiths has suggested that Fansy locates authority "in the act of speaking and writing."[37] It is precisely Fansy's ability to subvert language that gives him the power to corrupt Magnyfycence. Skelton's play suggests a profound weakness within the Henrician polity. Depicting a world in which one simple forged letter can allow all measure to be driven from the commonwealth, *Magnyfycence* implies that monarchical power is dangerous because it relies too heavily on the judgment of an individual person. Skelton's play, like *Youth*, expresses anxiety over the direction of Henrician kingship, which is also a key element of More's *Richard III*.

The 1510s, when both *Youth* and *Magnyfycence* were probably written, saw a number of potentially disturbing developments in the English political scheme. The occupation of Tournai from 1513 to 1519 created new stresses within the polity. Although it now seems unlikely that in this period Tournai became the testing grounds for a Henrician model of imperial kingship, the expulsion of the "minions" in 1519 may well reflect a concern among senior councilors about the drift of royal policy.[38] The "minions" were a collection of young courtiers who, having been appointed to the new position of gentleman of the privy chamber in 1518, were being exiled from court in apparent disgrace within nine months. It has been assumed that this expulsion was political and related to the minions' advocacy of a pro-French foreign policy. Greg Walker, however, has persuasively argued that in 1519, "the minions were proving themselves to be conceited and obnoxious young men whose contempt for anything which was not in the latest, French, fashion, coupled with their unseemly overfamiliarity with Henry, were antagonizing the more conservative elements at court. It was in their 'French vices and bragges' that their objectionable Frenchness expressed itself, not in any advocacy of a pro-French foreign policy."[39] The genesis of More's *Richard III* can be located in the early Henrician political crisis that reached a peak with the events of 1519. T. F. Mayer has argued in this context that *Richard III* "considers what happens when English conciliar institutions break down and ambition of 'sovereignty' and faction combined led to tyranny."[40] Henry VIII in 1519, and before this, appeared to men like More to be in danger of becoming a tyrant, ignoring the proper bonds that bound the polity together, giving riot and fancy a place at the court, and coveting political power.

Richard III opens with an account of the final year of the reign of Edward IV. More then describes Richard, duke of Gloucester. This description, however, is strangely aslant. More's Richard is a figure of evil. At the same time, Richard's almost physical presence in *Richard III* is itself problematic since it raises the question of the relation between meaning and form which More's history echoes in its self-reflective staging of the production of history. More describes Richard as "malicious, wrathful, envious, and from afore his birth, ever forward."[41] He continues: "It is for truth reported that the duchess his mother had so much ado in her travail, that she could not be delivered of him uncut, and that he came into the world feet forward, as men be borne outward, and (as the fame runneth) also not untoothed—whether men of hatred report above the truth, or else that nature changed her course in his beginning, which in course of his life many things unnaturally committed."[42] Richard in this passage is depicted as something outside nature. His birth was unnatural or reflected nature's rejection of such an evil person. At the same time, More opens up the possibility that the claims about Richard's birth are "above the truth." More then acknowledges that Richard was a "none evil captain in war" before commenting: "Free was he called of dispense, and somewhat above his power liberal; with large gifts he get him unsteadfast friendship, for which he was fain to pill and spoil in other places and get him steadfast hatred. He was close and secret, a deep dissimuler, lowly of countenance, arrogant of heart, outwardly coumpinable where he inwardly hated, not letting to kiss whom he thought to kill. . . . Friend and foe was much what indifferent: where his advantage grew, he spared no man's death whose life withstood his purpose."[43]

More's Richard is a man without measure. Not only is he too liberal to his "friends"; more importantly, he recognizes no limits to his desire for power; he will allow no bonds to stand in the way of his ambition. He is also unbounded by nature, turning the natural order of birthing on its head. More portrays Richard as a tyrant. This portrayal is entirely conventional, inverting the image of a good or virtuous ruler as articulated in numerous works of Aristotelian political theory, which placed measure or mean at the heart of good governance.[44] It also mirrors the image of Henry VIII that More produces in his poem "On the Coronation Day of Henry VIII," in which the person of Henry dominates the

political sphere. Richard is an inverted Henry, filling up the space of
More's history with his boundless, fascinating presence.

Richard III creates readerly expectations that it then subverts and
mocks. The opening description of Richard incites the reader to see him
as a traditional tyrant. More, however, in the following paragraph opens
up a number of provocative historiographical questions:

> But of all this point is there no certainty, and whoso divineth upon
> conjectures may as well shoot too far as too short. Howbeit, this I
> have by credible information learned, that the self night in which
> King Edward died, one Mistlebrook, long ere morning, came in haste
> to the house of one Potter dwelling in Redcross Street without Crip-
> plegate; and when he was with hasty rapping quickly letten in, he
> showed unto Potter that King Edward was departed. "By my troth,
> man," quod Potter, "then will my master, the Duke of Gloucester,
> be king." What cause he had so to think, hard it is to say—whether
> he being toward him anything knew that he such thing purposed, or
> otherwise had any inkling thereof, for he was not likely to speak it
> of nought.[45]

More's opening comment can be read as simply relating to the immediately preceding suggestion that Richard was involved in the death of his
brother, Clarence. But the phrase "of all this point" raises the disturbing
possibility that the entire description of Richard is based on nothing more
than conjectures. More then uses a proverbial expression to sustain the
authority of his text, but again places the reader in the position of having to judge the mean between shooting too short and shooting too far.
In particular, given the extreme nature of More's description of Richard, it is hard to imagine that anyone could "shoot too far." Indeed one
could suggest that More is deliberately mocking his own history at this
point. Has the reader not just read a description of Richard that, built
largely on conjecture, could be seen as an object lesson in shooting too
far? The story of Mistlebrook and Potter, which is based on "credible
information" but whose ultimate significance is "hard to say," confirms
the skeptical tone of this section. The reader is left at the end of these
two passages unclear how to read More's text, poised between shooting

too far and too short in a world in which meaning is constantly asserted and then undermined.

More's history then recounts the events immediately following Edward's death. The key moment in this narrative is the decision of Edward's queen, Elizabeth Woodville, to seek the sanctuary of Westminster Abbey with her younger son when she hears that Richard has arrested her family and supporters and has taken her elder son, Edward V, into "protective" custody. More writes that when the Archbishop of York went to the queen, "he found much heaviness, rumble, haste and business, carriage and conveyance of her stuff into sanctuary—chests, coffers, packs, fardelles, trusses, all on men's backs, no man unoccupied, some lading, some going, some discharging, some coming for more, some breaking down walls to bring in the next way, and some yet drew to them holp to carry a wrong way. The queen herself sat alone alowe on the rushes, all desolate and dismayed."[46] One reading of this passage is that Richard's behavior has already created a state of confusion, which is reflected in the behavior of the queen. This would, however, be to preempt the historical record, since at this stage it was not clear that Richard would usurp the throne. More's description of the queen's entry into sanctuary is excessive. It creates an image of confusion and enacts on the page, through the piling up of words and phrases, the rumble and haste that it is describing. At the center of all this activity More places the queen in an image that evokes a classical or biblical image of a lamenting women— Andromache or Mary. At the same time there is also a comic aspect to More's description of the queen's entry to sanctuary. She seems to be bringing with her an awful lot of "stuff."

The description illustrates a measureless world. Yet significantly, the piling up of words, echoing of phrases, and repetition in this passage create a text that asks to be read not as an exercise in history or reason but rather at a poetic or simply phonic level. As a reader, one need not carefully distinguish between the various items and actions described. Indeed to do so would undermine the integrity of the passage and one's enjoyment of More's language. Reason has no place in More's description of the queen's entry into sanctuary.[47] It is as though Richard's actions, his ambitions, have already so corroded the English polity that language has become irrational. In this passage, and more generally in *Richard III*, More collapses the failure of rationality caused by Richard's usurpation into readerly pleasure. He equates the desire of readers to consume a text without limits, without measure, with Richard's tyrannical desire to rule beyond social and political bonds.

Richard III's concern with the relation between politics and language reflects the work's place in an emerging critique of Henrician kingship. It is also, however, an aspect of More's engagement with issues central to vernacular English political writing of the late fourteenth and fifteenth centuries. In particular, *Richard III* can be read as part of an English tradition of Aristotelian political writing reflected in Passus III of the C Text of *Piers Plowman* and Fragment VII of *The Canterbury Tales*.

Late Fourteenth-Century Political Writing

The late fourteenth and fifteenth centuries have in the past been seen as a period of relatively limited political thought. This view has, however, recently been questioned by a number of scholars. In particular, David Lawton has argued that the public poetry of the fifteenth century, building on the work of Chaucer and his contemporaries, creates an image of a public sphere, "parallel to and connected with the structures of power."[48] Lawton's article emphasizes that the political writing of the fifteenth century is "to a great extent the literature of public servants."[49] More's political writing, like that of his fifteenth-century predecessors, reflects upon the reality of early modern politics and at the same time deploys tropes and ideas first fully articulated in English during the late fourteenth century. In particular, while we must note that influence of humanist thought on More, it is equally vital to acknowledge the extent to which writers like Chaucer also engaged in a debate with classical writers like Cicero. The emphasis in *The Tale of Melibee*, told by Chaucer in *The Canterbury Tales*, on prudence is profoundly Ciceronian.[50] *The Tale of Melibee* articulates and implicitly critiques a form of instrumental political reason that, like that which governs Utopia, has no place for Christian grace.[51] In this section I will discuss a number of late fourteenth-century texts in order to illustrate the importance of this vernacular tradition of political writing in More's work.

In 1381 the Peasants' Revolt rocked English society. Thomas Walsingham, in his *Historia Anglicana*, reflects the trauma caused by the rebellion in his descriptions of the peasants as inhuman animals:[52]

> When the Archbishop arrived at the place of execution a most hor-
> rible shouting broke out, not like the clamour normally produced
> by men, but of a sort which enormously exceeded all human noise
> and which could only be compared to the wailings of the inhabi-
> tants of hell. Such shouts used to be heard whenever the rebels be-
> headed anyone or destroyed houses, for as long as God permitted
> their inquiry to be unpunished. Words could not be heard among
> their horrible shrieks but rather their throats sounded with the bleat-
> ing of sheep, or, to be more accurate, with the devilish voices of
> peacocks.[53]

In Walsingham's account of the Peasants' Revolt the peasants are simultaneously monstrous beasts, the agents of God's vengeance, limbs of Satan,
stupid rustics, *and* clever, resourceful criminals capable of persuading the
Londoners that their aim is only to "discover the traitors of the kingdom."[54] Later, in a telling phrase, Walsingham describes the rebels' activities in the city as a "solemn game."[55] A visceral hatred of the peasants runs
through the account of the Peasants' Revolt in *Historia Anglicana*. The histories of the revolt written by the victors are replete with gothic images
of animalistic rioters indulging in a carnival of carnage and express a desire to see similar violence inflicted upon the defeated peasants, albeit in
the name of order and justice.[56]

Despite the impression created by writers like Walsingham, there
was not a mass slaughter of lawyers and aristocrats in 1381, although the
rebels did massacre London's Flemish population on the night of June 14;
and while the restoration of order following the revolt's collapse was
arbitrary and oppressive, it did not amount to a reign of terror. These
events in 1381, however, rent asunder for a moment the norms of late
fourteenth-century English life, the polite fiction that went by the name
of the commonwealth, and threw into sharp relief the deep antagonisms
and conflicts of English society.[57] Late fourteenth- and early fifteenth-
century writers like William Langland and Geoffrey Chaucer responded

to the events of 1381 by reflecting upon the costs and dangers to the society of the fantasies of retributive, carnivalesque violence shared by Walsingham and his peasant opponents.

Langland wrote the C Text of *Piers Plowman* during the years following 1381.[58] It contains several significant revisions, including a new passage in Passus III, in which Langland equates the breaking of grammatical boundaries with the corrupting effects of Mede on the commonwealth:

> "Relacioun rect," quod Consience, "is a record of treuthe,
> *Quia antelate rei recordatiuum est,*
> Folowynge and fyndynge out the fundement of a strenghe,
> And styfliche stande forth to strenghe the fundament
> In kynde and in case and in the cours of nombre.
> As a leel laborer byleueth in his maister
> In his pay and in his pitie and in his puyr treuthe —
> To pay hym yf he parforme and haue pite yf he faileth
> And take hym for his trauailed al that treuthe wolde."[59]

This passage creates an analogy between the truth of grammar, or the proper ordering of relations between words, and the web of relationships that is society. In a potentially provocative move, however, Langland chooses the bond between laborer and master to illustrate his argument. In particular, he plays with the word "pay" to emphasize the extent to which a laborer's wages are more than simply cash and instead represent a wider web of rules, a social grammar, that creates a set of mutual and implicitly equal relations between members of the social body.[60]

In *Magnyfycence* the political world falls apart when Fansy releases Liberty from Measure's control. Mede is Langland's Liberty.[61] She is not inherently sinful, but at the same time her effects on the commonwealth seem to be almost entirely baleful.[62] In the C Text of *Piers Plowman* Langland carefully distinguishes between good and bad "mede," through the distinction between "mede" and mercede." The former is simply reward or payment; the latter, however, adds a moral element, since it refers to due or earned reward.[63] In particular, Langland stresses the importance of payment being made at a proper time. Mercede is payment for something done; mede, however, is often paid in advance:

Harlotes and hoores and also fals leches
They asken here huyre ar thei hit haue deserued,
And gylours gyuen byfore and good men at the ende
When the dede is ydo and the day endit;
And that is no mede but a mercede, a manere dewe dette,
And but hit prestly be ypayed the payere is to blame,
As by the book that byt nobody with-holde
The huyre of his hewe ouer eue til amorwe:
Non morabitur opus mersenarii, etc
And ther is resoun as a reue rewardynge truethe
That bothe the lord and the laborer be leely yserued.[64]

In this passage Langland contrasts the behavior of harlots and whores, who ask for payment in advance, with a laborer's properly waiting to be paid by the lord at the end of a day's work. He is not, however, drawing a merely economic distinction. Langland's use of the loaded words "reason" and "truth" reflects the ethical importance of mercede. He equates due reward with the rules of grammar, "relacioun rect." The passage is a lesson in careful reading. It equates reading without care, the desire to consume the text in advance of understanding, with the behavior of those who demand mede before they have earned it.[65] For plowing the field, reading the poem, one does deserve reward, but only after completing it, doing the work. *Piers Plowman* asks to be read with care. It demands that the reader, like Will, explore the poem and find meaning in an accumulative, sometimes even meandering, fashion.[66]

Langland's discussion of the distinction between mede and mercede is particularly pointed in relation to the clergy: "The mede that many preste taken for masses thei syngen / *Amen, Amen*, Matheu seyth, *mercedem suam recipient.*"[67] These lines draw a parallel between the laborer in the field being paid at the end of the day and the priest being paid for saying mass. Both should wait to be paid until they have completed the work. But what is the priest's work? When can it be called complete? There is a potentially apocalyptic feel to these lines, since for a priest, "to wait until the end of the day" could be read as "to wait until the end of time." Mass has to be said, the field needs to be plowed, until Christ returns. At the same time these lines stress the extent to which priests are part of the

social order, not a separate, privileged group existing above or beyond
its bounds. They, like the lord and laborer, deserve to be rewarded for
their work, once it is done.

In the C Text of *Piers Plowman* Langland explicitly equates the grammatical and social order:

Ac relacoun rect is a ryhtful custume
As a kyng to clayme the comune at his wille
To follow and to fynde hym and fecche at hem his consayl
That here loue to his lawe thorw al the lond acorde.
So comune claymeth of a kyng thre kyne thynges,
Lawe, loue and lewte, and hym lond antecedent,
Bothe heued and here kyng, haldyng with no parteyye
Bote standynge as a stake that stikede in a mere
Bytwene two lordes for a trewe marke.[68]

This passage appears to be a simple assertion of a conservative model of
society, with the commons required by nature to accept their subservient
position. In *Piers Plowman*, however, conservative formulations often articulate potentially radical implications. This passage suggests that society is balanced and true through the proper relation between terms, between "two lords," the king and the commune. Passus III of the C Text
of *Piers Plowman* deploys the language of stability and order based upon
an analogy between the rules of grammar and the ties that bind society
together. Langland's "trewe mark" is analogous to Skelton's measure; in
both cases what is important is to maintain the boundaries of the social
bond. Fansy and Mede subvert the social order by encouraging people to
indulge their desires and fancies. The "trewe mark," like mercede, embodies an Aristotelian sense of the political order as located in the real
world of sensuous human activity and based upon mutually beneficial,
self-sustaining rules. It is this world that More depicts Richard as tearing
up in his remorseless pursuit of power. There is no "trewe mark" for
Richard beyond his desire, which is all-encompassing and all-corrupting.

Fragment VII of *The Canterbury Tales* is centrally concerned with the
role of the reader in the production of meaning and the politics of reading.[69] The fragment opens with the disturbing *Shipman's Tale*, with its re-

ductive and banal sexual puns. In particular, in this tale the idea of wifely debt becomes an excuse for adultery and adulterous words. *The Shipman's Tale* incites the reader to accept uncritically a collapse of the sexual and the monetary. Helen Cooper suggests, "Of all the fabliaux in the *Canterbury Tales*, [*The Shipman's Tale*] is the only one to be totally amoral."[70] The tale concludes with the merchant's wife explicitly engaging in an act of self-commodification:

> For I wol paye yow wel and redily
> Fro day to day, and if so be I faille
> I am youre wyf; score it upon my taille,
> And I shall paye as soone as ever I may.
>
> . . . .
>
> Ye shal my joly body have to wedde;
> By God, I wol nat paye yow but abedde![71]

The wife constructs herself in this passage as a book or ledger in which her husband can read what she owes him. This is a "parodic," reductive version of fourteenth-century charters of Christ that, as Emily Steiner has recently discussed, depicted the body of Christ as a book containing Christ's promises to humanity.[72] The wife's offer of her "joly body" to her husband as always available in payment of her debts mocks Christ's similar offer of salvation based upon the universal availability of his bodily death to all Christians.[73] The wife implicitly offers her body to all the readers of *The Shipman's Tale*. She will always be available, like the body of Chaucer's text, for our pleasure. Cathy Hume has pointed out that "there is no final exposure of the wife in *The Shipman's Tale*, no poetic justice or moral censure."[74] This is undoubtedly the case. But it leaves the purpose of the tale open. If the wife can escape punishment for her adultery simply by making a pun literal, then the reader is back in the corrupt world of Langland's Mede, where the right relations between words are turned upside down. *The Shipman's Tale* depicts a world in which honest men are tricked and humiliated by those for whom the collective meaning of words, the bonds of society and grammar, have no intrinsic worth or value.[75] They are there simply to be played with, mocked and ignored in the pursuit of one's desires and pleasures.

Fragment VII asks questions of its readers. It is Chaucer's response to the public poetry of the late fourteenth century that Anne Middleton, in an important article, suggested was fundamentally concerned with "worldly felicity" and "peaceful, harmonious communal existence."[76] In 1381 the desire for a "harmonious communal existence" provided the ideological motivation for apocalyptic violence and fantasies of retributive justice. The opening tales of Fragment VII confront readers with the extent of their desire to read and consume bodily images. *The Prioress's Tale* is a miracle story focused on the Virgin Mary. It tells the story of a young boy murdered by Jews. The tale emphasizes the violence of the Jews, in particular in relation to the child's body, to justify the emergence of fantasies of retributive justice directed against the enemies of the church. It chillingly evokes the discourse of persecution. Indeed it can be read as Chaucer's poetic response to those calling for the followers of John Wycliffe to be persecuted.[77] *The Prioress's Tale* asserts an absolute, closed orthodoxy that sustains itself through persecution. There is no room in this tale for religious reflection or even thought. Indeed the images of domesticity and innocent ignorance that cluster around the young boy suggest that orthodoxy does not require readers' active reasoned involvement, beyond their imaginative and emotional engagement with the tale's narrative. In these terms *The Prioress's Tale* looks forward to such persecutionary texts as Nicholas Love's *The Mirror of the Blessed Life of Jesus Christ*.[78]

The Tale of Melibee is Chaucer the pilgrim's second attempt to tell a tale. In his first, *Sir Thopas*, the host stopped him for "drasty rymyng."[79] *The Tale of Melibee* is one of only two tales Chaucer describes as a "tretys." Paul Strohm has suggested that the word "tretys" is "the perfect designation for a narrative which is a 'tale' only with respect to its oral nature, and which is neither 'storie' nor 'fable' in its rejection of plot."[80] *Melibee* is a translation of *Le Livre de Melibee*.[81] It tells how Prudence, the wife of a "yong man," Melibee, persuades him to forgo vengeance after their daughter, Sophia, is attacked and wounded. The tale opens with a brief but nonetheless disturbing account of the attack:

> Upon a day bifel that he for his desport is went into the feeldes hym to pleye. His wyf and eek his doghter hath he left inwith his hous, of

which the dores were fast yshette. Thre of his olde foes hath it es-
pyed, and setten laddres to the walles of his hous, and by wyndowes
been entred, and betten his wyf, and wounded his doghter with fyve
mortal woundes in fyve sondry places.—This is to seyn, in her feet,
in hire handes, in hir erys, in hir nose, and in hir mouth—and leften
hire for deed, and wenten awey.[82]

One way of reading this passage is to see it as setting up *The Tale of Melibee* as an allegory. Indeed, later on Prudence confirms the potential allegorical meanings of the assault on Sophia when she tells Melibee that it
is his sin that has let the three enemies of mankind—the flesh, fiend,
and world—into his soul/house and that they have wounded his five
senses.[83] Alongside the allegorical aspects of the tale are several features
that resonated politically with readers at the end of the fourteenth century.[84] Kathleen E. Kennedy has argued, "In the *Tale of Melibee* Chaucer
narrates a chain of events including offense, counsel taking, and reprisal
that were all too typical of the fourteenth- and fifteenth-century English
legal landscape."[85] *The Tale of Melibee* is an allegory, but it is also an attempt
by Chaucer to create a work in which relations are always right in the
context of 1381. To achieve this, however, he must renounce the pleasures of reading and produce a text so pure in its pursuit of reason or
prudence that it closes down any space for political thought.

The Tale of Melibee is composed almost entirely of Prudence's attempts
to counsel Melibee and persuade him to seek reconciliation with his enemies rather than vengeance. She succeeds so well that Melibee agrees to
be guided by Prudence and apparently to forgo his desire for revenge.
However, when Melibee's enemies present themselves before him to be
judged as part of the reconciliation process proposed by Prudence, Melibee immediately forgets all of his wife's earlier advice. He tells her he intends to "desherite hem of all that evere they han and for to putte hem in
exil for evere."[86] Prudence counters:

Certes, . . . this were a crueel sentence and muchel agayn resoun.
For ye been riche ynough and han no nede of oother mennes good,
and ye mighte lightly in this wise gete yow a coveitous name, which
is a vicious thyng, and oghte been eschued of every good man.[87]

Having listened to Prudence's reasons, Melibee's "harte gan enclyne to the wil of his wif, considerynge hir trewe entente, and conformed hym anon and assented fully to werken after hir conseil."[88] The tale ends with Melibee forgiving his enemies their sins. His final words, and the conclusion of the tale, relate the need for forgiveness to God's mercy: "If we be sory and repentant of the synnes and giltes which we han trespassed in the sighte of oure Lord God, he is so free and so merciable that he wole foryeven us our giltes and bryngen us to blisse that nevere hath ende. Amen."[89] *The Tale of Melibee* is a lesson in reason that ultimately undermines its own argument by illustrating reason's limitations. It depicts its central character, Melibee, as incapable of being reasonable for more than the time it takes his wife to persuade him of reason's worth. Certainly the tale ends with an apparently uncontroversial invocation of God's mercy and its applicableness as a model for relationships between humans on earth. The conclusion, however, does raise, or rather elides, the need for justice. Indeed the tale's ending leaves behind the initial allegorical interpretation of Sophia's wounds, since if Melibee's enemies are the flesh, fiend, and world, then he cannot really reconcile with them. Thus Chaucer illustrates that different reading strategies, specifically the desire to allegorize, have costs. Sophia, not Melibee, pays the price for Prudence's reason. Indeed Melibee's plan to take the goods of her attackers commutes their violent attack on her body, their indebtedness, into monetary terms. In the process, however, Melibee is simply acting within the logic of the text, in which Sophia's wounded body, like the "joly body" of the wife in *The Shipman's Tale* or the body of the young boy in *The Prioress's Tale*, becomes an object to be consumed by Chaucer's readers. To read *The Tale of Melibee* prudently is to learn a deliberative logic that ultimately reduces Sophia's body to an illustrative example within a generalized and generalizing moralistic discourse.[90]

The Tale of Melibee is a cruel sentence, punishment for the reader's enjoyment of the shipman's and prioress's tales. On the surface its political message is positive. During the course of the tale Melibee denies himself the pleasure of violent revenge, the pleasure that flows through the texts of 1381, and he does so as a result of the efficacy of his wife's reason. At another level, however, *The Tale of Melibee* is a deeply pessimistic work. It suggests that reason can be successful in a tightly controlled, "utopian" world. Above all it implies that a political world in which reason is dominant will emerge only at the cost of the disappearance of the body. David Wallace suggests that "Prudence . . . embodies her own discourse: she is prudence, the matter of which she speaks."[91] *The Tale of Melibee* formally embodies prudence. In rejecting the poetic norm of *The Canterbury Tales*, it also rejects a particular gendered understanding of poetry as inherently feminine. Lee Patterson has discussed in detail the ways in which writers in the fourteenth century equated the body of the poetic text with female copiousness and suggests that for male readers, "feminine speaking is never wholly divested of the titillating ambivalences of eroticism."[92] Prudence's speech, the body of *The Tale of Melibee*, is, however, entirely and deliberately non-erotic. Indeed Chaucer goes out of his way to close down any possibility of the reader "enjoying" reading Prudence's body. Amanda Walling points out that "if the Wife of Bath's discourse is directly fuelled by her carnality, her sexuality, and her experience as a wife, Prudence's is made possible only as her own body, wifehood, and motherhood are sublimated into language."[93] *The Tale of Melibee* celebrates reason and at the same time does not trust the reader's ability to be a reasonable reader, to renounce the pleasures of a text's "joly body." In this work Chaucer creates a text whose body is entirely prudent. The reader of *The Tale of Melibee* does learn prudence, does participate in the creation of a reasoned space of politics, but it is a forced participation, a forced lesson. Chaucer leaves no room for a nonprudent, an irrational reading of the tale.[94] In *The Tale of Melibee* relations will always be right because Chaucer has removed any grounds for them not to be. In particular, the disappearance of Sophia's wounded body and of the demand for justice that is marked in its wounds reflects the disembodied nature of the reason at the heart of Prudence's discourse. *The Tale of Melibee*, like Sir John Fortescue's *On the Laws and Governance of England*, and in a very different way More's *Utopia*, celebrates a reason that is absolute, disembodied, and ultimately sterile. The tale's reasonableness also, however, again like *Utopia*'s, seems to have no place for the church or the sacraments.[95] As a response to the political issues confronting England at the end of the fourteenth century, it is simply inadequate. In particular, it totally fails to address the desire for carnivalesque violence and retributive justice that fueled the crisis of 1381. *The Tale of Melibee* articulates a political ethos so general that it is equally applicable everywhere and nowhere.

After *The Tale of Melibee* in Fragment VII comes *The Monk's Tale*. This is another failure, but like *Sir Thopas*, it fails because of its content, which the knight regards as too depressing. The host agrees, telling the monk, "Youre tale anoyeth al this compaignye. / Swich talkyng is nat worth a boterflye, / For therinne is ther no desport ne game."[96] The host then turns to the Nun's Priest for a tale that will satisfy his desire for "game." *The Nun's Priest's Tale*, a beast fable set in a poor widow's croft, tells the story of the cock Chauntecleer and the hen Pertelote. Though following *The Monk's Tale* and therefore concluding Fragment VII, it is more specifically an answer to *The Tale of Melibee*'s politics of disembodied reason. *The Nun's Priest's Tale* offers its "joly body" to be consumed by the readers and at the same ultimately resists simplistic forms of consumption or reading. It is a story that celebrates the copiousness of the poetic text as a potential answer to the political crisis of 1381.

It is difficult to describe *The Nun's Priest's Tale*, as the narrative often digresses and defers. After much discussion the tale concludes when a fox catches Chantecleer and is then chased around the yard by the cock's owner, an old widow, and her daughters, who make a great noise:

> So hydous was the noyse — a bendicitee!—
> Certes, he Jakke Straw and his meynee
> Ne made nevere shoutes half so shrille
> Whan that they wolden any Flemyng kille,
> As thilke day was maad upon the fox.
> Of bras they brogthen bemes, and of box,
> Of horn, of boon, in whiche they blewe and powped,
> And therwithal they shriked and they howped.
> It seemed as that hevene sholde falle.[97]

This passage can be read, like the whole of *The Nun's Priest's Tale*, as a rejection of reasoned reading as modeled in *The Tale of Melibee*. There is nothing prudent, decorous, or safe about these lines, or indeed the entire tale. In this passage a simple example drawn from the recent past to illustrate the noise made by the widow and her daughters plunges the reader into the world of 1381, where carnivalesque whooping was driven by an apocalyptic desire for the heavens to fall and justice to be rendered on earth. But perhaps this passage is simply descriptive? Perhaps the reference to Jack Straw is nothing more than a rather risky joke? The problem is that, unlike *The Tale of Melibee*, *The Nun's Priest's Tale* provides no real guidance to how it should be read. Or rather the guidance that it does provide is not the sort that allows readers to indulge their desire for the kind of pleasures, albeit very different, offered by the shipman's and prioress's tales. Nor is it the kind of forced guidance offered by Prudence.[98] *The Nun's Priest's Tale* celebrates the ability of literary texts to create a space for reason that, while shot through with ideological pressures, still manages to escape their totalizing grasp.[99] As Lee Patterson argues, "Chaucer quite self-consciously writes what we call 'literature': a discourse that insists upon its autonomy from both ideological programs and social appropriations."[100] In *The Nun's Priest's Tale*, as Lynn Staley has recently suggested, Chaucer consistently connects the widow's croft and the commonwealth.[101] The literary space of the tale is at once autonomous and a model for the proper ordering of the commonwealth. *The Nun's Priest's Tale* invites its reader to accept an Aristotelian text/commonwealth in which relations are right not because they adhere to preexisting structures or laws but because they have a communal integrity that can on its own terms sustain the space of the tale.[102]

In the shadow of the traumatic events of the Peasants' Revolt, Langland and Chaucer both try to imagine a politics that prevents a repetition of the violence of 1381 but does not close down the political sphere. Their commitment to keeping the space of politics open contrasts markedly with the response to 1381 by people like Walsingham, who demanded retributive revenge for those responsible for the social legislation of the Cambridge Parliament of 1388, which attempted to create a series of laws that, in nonconsensual versions of Langland's "relacioun rect," would have set in stone what the Parliament regarded as the social order.[103] The social legislation that was put before the Cambridge Parliament embodied a utopian desire for a fully transparent, ordered social sphere. It intended to fix symbolically, and for working-class people literally, the social order and to close down the space for politics. Indeed if all the social legislation placed before the Cambridge Parliament had been enacted and enforced, England would have become a version of Utopia 150 years before More wrote his *Utopia*. When writers like Langland and Chaucer create texts that defend and celebrate an Aristotelian political sphere, they are doing so in the context of the competing and completely incompatible politics of Walsingham and the Cambridge Parliament. In *Richard III*, albeit within a different political context, More was seeking, like Chaucer and Langland, to protect a space for politics against what he saw as the linked dangers of tyranny and chaos.

Richard III and Tyranny

Richard III is bad history. It opens with a factual inaccuracy, Edward VI's age when he died. It consistently breaks the rules of history writing by introducing doubt where there should be certainty. In this work More seems to go out of his way to include a kaleidoscope of different texts, generic forms, and historical models. *Richard III*, like Fragment VII of *The Canterbury Tales*, self-consciously mixes genres.[104] Like Chaucer, in *Richard III* More deploys the possibilities offered by generic mixing to reflect upon the politics of reading and to defend the space for an Aristotelian political sphere.

In *Richard III* texts circulate and are written, rewritten, and unwritten in front of the reader. More forces readers to confront their desire for simple pleasures, for a history that is black and white, by producing simultaneously a parodic moralistic history and one in which the moral is at best unclear, if not completely obscure. It is around Richard's body that the relationship between the body and the text plays out most clearly, since at one level his grotesque body marks him out as uniquely evil, as almost a devil, while at the same time being the thing that locates him within the textual world of history; all the bodies in *Richard III*—Richard's, Jane Shore's, Hastings's—are ultimately made into text through the same process, rendered into the matter of More's historical writing. The "joly body" of *Richard III* is offered to the reader as an object of consumption, and in the process, More poses with particular intensity the dangers of the politics of pleasure in the context of royal tyranny. In particular, More, like Chaucer, theorizes politics through and around the figure of the reader.

Tyranny produces, and is produced by, readers whose gaze is transfixed by the protean "joly body" of an image, figure, or text.

Scholars have long recognized More's portrayal of Jane Shore in *Richard III* as one of the key moments of the text. When Richard Grafton published a version of *Richard III* in his *Chronicle*, he added a few marginal notes, including three indicating where More described leading characters in history: Richard III, Edward IV, and "Shores Wife."[105] The presence of Shore alongside these two kings is, however, difficult to explain on purely historical grounds, since she was involved in the events leading up to Richard's usurpation of the throne only to a very limited extent. Yet Grafton's marginal note recognizes the importance of Shore to More's history, in which she is introduced after the execution of Hastings and immediately following a passage where More mocks Richard's "miraculous production" of a proclamation justifying Hastings's death: "Now was this proclamation made within two hours after that [Hastings] was beheaded, and it was so curiously indited and so fair written in parchment in so well a set hand, and therwith of itself so long a process, that every child might well perceive that it was prepared before."[106] More's mockery of Richard here, however, extends to a more general point about the historical reliability of official documents. We sense that the historical fact that the proclamation justifying Hastings's death was written in advance will ultimately disappear and only Richard's beautiful formal proclamation will remain. Thus More confronts the reader with the provisional nature of history produced by relying upon written records and prompts the recognition that such a history can only ever be a part of the story.

To turn from this moment of metahistorical reflection to the relatively simple story of Shore appears to uncannily reflect the scholarly positioning of More as sitting between the modern and the medieval. He presents Shore's story as an archetypal morality drama of a person's rise and fall, and as such it could be seen as profoundly medieval. More opens his account of Shore by commenting that Richard initially tried to condemn her for trying to bewitch him and for being a partner to Hastings's "plots," but that when he found "no colour could fasten upon these matters, then he laid heinously to her charge the thing that herself could not deny, that all the world wist was true, and that nevertheless every man laughed at to hear it then so suddenly so highly taken—that she was naught of her body."[107] Richard tries to impose two particularly lethal ideological constructs upon Shore: treason and witchcraft. Only when these will not stick does he accuse her of immorality. More stages for the reader's benefit the way in which ideologies seek to create explanations for social and political conflict that are either ridiculously extreme or banal. Richard's attempt to distract the citizens of London by accusing Shore of witchcraft or treason, and his failure, invite the reader to reflect on those moments in the past when these and similar ideological labels—"foreigners," "aliens," "revolting peasants," and "bloodsucking clergy"—have been used to justify violence and oppression.

More then describes how Richard persuaded the bishop of London to condemn Shore to do public penance,

> in which she went in countenance and pace demure so womanly, and albeit she were out of all array save her kirtle only, yet went she so fair and lovely, namely while the wondering of the people cast a comely rud in her cheeks (of which she before had most miss), that her great shame won her much praise among those that were more amorous of her body than curious of her soul. And many good folk also, that hated her living and glad were to see sin corrected, yet pitied they more her penance than rejoiced therein, when they considered that the protector procured it more of a corrupt intent then any virtuous affection.[108]

In this passage the reader is positioned alongside those who originally watched Shore's penance. This, however, creates a potential parallel between More's behavior and that of Richard III. In particular, this passage raises the disturbing possibility that More undertook this detailed description of Shore for corrupt and not virtuous reasons.[109] Does the reader need to know that Shore's shameful blushing made her even more attractive? Why add this detail? It could be argued that this is simply a historical fact and that therefore there is no reason not to add it. More, however, consistently foregrounds the extent to which what history notices and what it ignores are ideological. History sees Richard's formal proclamation. It sees Shore's body. And it sees these things because they are what readers expect and desire to find in a historical text. Shore's body operates as a metonym for the reader's desire to consume the text at a corporeal or sensual level. The "joly body" of More's text incites the unwary reader to indulge in a model of historical reading that is based on a denial of the reader's culpability and responsibility. More consistently shows in *Richard III* that readers get the histories they desire and deserve.

Shore's body, like Richard's, gives More's text at this point a specific corporeal inflection. In the same way that Chaucer creates a parallel between prudence and the body of the text of *The Tale of Melibee*, More stages the emergence of a parallel between the desirable female body and the body of the text of history. In particular, at the end of his description of Shore, More refers explicitly to the question of its appropriateness:

> I doubt not some shall think this woman too slight a thing to be written of and set among the remembrances of great matters, which they shall specially think that haply shall esteem her only by that they now see her. But me seemeth the chance so much more worthy to be remembered, in how much she is now in the more beggarly condition, unfriended and worn out of acquaintance, after good substance, after as great favour with the prince, after as great suit and seeking to all with those that those days had business to speed, as many other men were in their times, which be now famous only by infamy of their ill deeds.[110]

This passage argues that the story of Shore's rise and fall is worthy of telling because it illustrates the fickleness of worldly success. This, however, only partly justifies the early detailed description of Shore's body. Looking at the story of Shore as a whole, we see that More used it to reflect upon the ways in which readers are implicated in the texts they read and, more specifically, upon the political question of responsibility. Shore as a witch or traitor has nothing to teach the reader. As an example of the instability of fortune, however, she can be seen as an excellent illustration. In particular, More's deployment of her body as an object to be consumed by the reader emphasizes how the lesson of Shore's life applies to everyone. Ideology singles out, as Richard tried to, specific people and groups to blame for social and political conflict. The story of Shore, however, as told by More, enacts the truth that no one is perfect, no one fully or completely virtuous. This emphasis on a commonplace universality links this section of *Richard III*, and indeed the entire work, to Chaucer's *Nun's Priest's Tale*. More effectively uses the story of Shore as a parable in which the readers are parties. To try to understand this section of *Richard III* in judgmental terms, to treat it as simply a morality tale, would be to fail to acknowledge the extent to which the reader's desire is implicated in Shore's story as More tells it.[111]

Richard III constantly emphasizes the dangers of adultery and lust, of sacrilegious, untrammeled desire. John Bossy has argued: "The critical moments in More's story were not acts of usurpation, not even perhaps acts of murder, but acts in violation of the holy: of the sanctity of holy places in Richard's removal of his brother's son from sanctuary, and of the sanctity of his brother's marriage. The clergy, whose duty was to be a living embodiment of the sacred, had through worldliness connived at these violations. At the centre of the community there had opened an abysmal void."[112] The void that Bossy sees at the center of the community in *Richard III* resembles that imagined in the C Text of *Piers Plowman*. For Langland and More the collapse of social norms and that of linguistic norms are bound together, and both writers deploy images of corrupt, unlicensed perverse sexual desire to imagine a world in which right relations have been abandoned. There is no transparency in *Richard III*. Richard's tyranny undermines all bonds and "trewe markes." Despite its reputation as a piece of simplistic Tudor propaganda, there is nothing certain about More's work. It is a profoundly opaque text.[113]

Indeed, given *Richard III*'s constant reference to other texts and given its own unfinished status, it might be more accurate, as Richard S. Sylvester suggests, to refer to it as a collection of texts that consistently incite the reader to produce simple meanings, while at the same time mocking this desire and holding it up as at best politically naïve and at worst a recipe for tyranny. There is something incestuous about the relationship between Richard's body and the text of More's history. Both seem incapable of remaining within existing boundaries, corporeal and generic. Bossy's void is a product of Richard's tyranny but also of the way More's work seems to excavate any place or moment from which to understand the text, to deny the possibility of right relations in its undermining of history's lessons.

Hanan Yoran has argued that a basic tension runs through *Richard III*. He suggests that More's work can be read as "an unequivocal condemnation of the sort of 'external evil' that overturns the natural order of things," or it can be seen to imply that "human politics is irredeemably corrupt." Yoran points out, however, that these two readings cannot be "harmonized."[114] The equivocation is particularly pronounced in the Latin version of More's work. For example, having described Edward IV as England's most popular king, More comments, "Even so, from early youth throughout his life, whenever business did not call him away, he was particularly given to dissipation and wantonness, like virtually everyone else; for you will hardly persuade anyone in good health to restrain himself when his fortune permits great extravagance."[115] The English version makes the same point but reduces its scope: "He was of youth greatly given to fleshly wantonness, from which health of body in great prosperity and fortune, without a special grace, hardly refraineth."[116] The Latin version universalizes the tendency to wantonness where fortune allows it, while the English version makes the same point in a more muted form. When writing for the benefit of fellow learned Latinists, More stresses the extreme difficulty of persuading anyone not to be as wanton as his or her health allows. The Latin version of *Richard III* doubts its own status as an authoritative, persuasive text, and it does so in such a way as to raise serious doubts over the ability of any text to escape the compromises of the world and the corruptions of human sinfulness.

The Latin version of *Richard III* also stresses the distorting, protean quality of Richard. More writes that Richard "could adopt any role, then play it out to perfection, whether cheerful or stern, whether sober or relaxed, just as expediency urged him to sustain or abandon it. There was modesty in his countenance when in his heart there was arrogance, uncontrollable, boundless, and monstrous."[117] The reference to modesty in this passage, not repeated in the English version, is a worrying echo to "On the Coronation Day of Henry VIII," which suggested that Henry's face guaranteed his fitness to rule: "How great his care to honor modesty! How serene the mercy which warms his gentle heart! How far removed from arrogance his mind! Yes, of all these gifts, the very countenance of our prince, extraordinary as it is, wears upon itself sure evidence which cannot be falsified."[118] Richard's face is modest but hides a boundless arrogance. Henry's face wears sure evidence of his lack of arrogance and his "care to honor modesty." The Latin version of *Richard III* stages the danger that monarchical power can be just an act and that behind the actor's mask lurks tyranny. The commonsense insight of the peasant that to be a king is simply to wear an embroidered coat is suggested in the English version of *Richard III*, but, ironically, is only fully articulated in the learned, Latin version of More's text. The Latin version of *Richard III* implicitly poses the question, if Richard's boundless, uncontrolled arrogance was hidden by a cloak or mask of modesty, what horrors might be hidden under other royal countenances?

Richard III gives its readers the same choices as Fragment VII of *The Canterbury Tales*, albeit much more concisely. Caught between the reductive punning of *The Shipman's Tale*, the voyeuristic pleasure of *The Prioress's Tale*, and the chaste sterility of *The Tale of Melibee*, Chaucer offers the reader the space for reasoned ethical reflection created by the open fable that is *The Nun's Priest's Tale*. More's *Richard III* fails as history because it does not successfully obscure the tension between writing and history; it does not deliver simple or clear messages. As a piece of political writing, however, it is a profound critique of tyranny and an implicit critique of emerging Henrician political tropes.[119] *Richard III* is a sustained argument for the need to maintain a space for political thought that is not entirely centered on the monarch, and perhaps in particular on his body. It is a lesson in critical historiography as the key to resisting royal tyranny and protecting an Aristotelian political sphere of reasoned argument.[120]

The Spoiled King

In 1510 there was a pageant at court. It was a typical Henrician affair, and Edward Hall recorded what happened in detail. At the end of the pageant there was, however, what appears to be a very un-Henrician moment:

> After the king and his companions had danced, he appointed the ladies, gentlemen and the Ambassadors to take the letters of their garments, in token of liberalitie, which thing the common people perceiving, ran to the king and stripped him into his hosen and doublet,

and all his companions in likewise. Sir Thomas Knevet stood on the stage, and for all his defence he lost his apparel. The ladies likewise were spoiled, wherefore the king's guard came suddenly, and put the people back, or else it was supposed more inconvenience had ensued.[121]

It is very difficult to imagine what could be more inconvenient then being stripped of one's clothes. Throughout his account of the 1510s Hall constantly notes moments when the surface of Henry's court—its pageants, jousts, and disguisings—breaks down. Henry VIII as portrayed in *Hall's Chronicle* is a medieval monarch, not because he was interested in the reality of fifteenth-century kingship but because, unlike his father, he was committed to a fantasy chivalric image of the past in which noble knights jousted over fair ladies. In conducting himself in this manner, as in 1510, Henry placed himself, and in particular his body, within the public sphere in a way that demanded attention but was also dangerous:

> The king being lusty, young and courageous, greatly delighted in feats of chivalry, in so much that he made a challenge of jousts, against all comers . . . which noble courage, all young people highly praised, but the ancient fathers much doubted, considering the tender youth of the king, and divers chances of horse and armour: in so much that it was openly spoken, that steel was not so strong, but it might be broken, nor no horse could be so sure of foot, but he may fall: Yet for all these doubts, the lusty prince proceeded to his challenge.[122]

There is something disturbing about the phrase "lusty prince." It evokes the excesses of Youth and Magnyfycence. It also implies a cavalier disregard for responsibility. If the monarch was a "trewe marke," a central component of the social bond, what were the implications of Henry's insistence on placing himself in danger?

Jeanne H. McCarthy has commented on the "medieval" ethos of the early Henrician court. In particular, she has suggested, in relation to Henry's participation in pageants, jousts, and disguisings, that "it is hard to escape the conclusion that in such entertainments Henry occasionally lost control over his monarchic role. His almost compulsive violations of decorum, his habit of levelling rather than elevating his authority, could actually result in the diminishment of his 'honour.'"[123] Hall portrays Henry as the youthful new monarch bringing glamour, honor, and good governance to the realm. But at the same time Hall's account of the 1510s is haunted by a very different Henry, an excessive, out-of-control monarch, disordered and disordering; a monarch not prepared to live within proper bounds and respect social bonds; someone who is no longer a "trewe marke" but instead is prepared to completely ignore "relacioun rect" in order to satisfy his personal desires.

In *Richard III* More confronts issues similar to those Langland addressed in Passus III of the C Text of *Piers Plowman*. For both writers a key theme was the way in which a particular covetous use of language reflected a more pervasive corruption of society by those not prepared to accept any boundaries or limits upon their desires. The peasants and their opponents in 1381 are, in Langland's eyes, incestuous in their refusal to live within the bounds of mutual grammatical and social dependence. Richard III was for More a symbol of those in power whose covetous desires corrupt all human bonds: familial, political, and corporeal. Late fourteenth-century writers like Chaucer faced a political world riven with violence and class conflict. The shadows of 1381 consistently fall across their work. In this context the kind of fixity that Langland seeks through his use of the grammatical metaphor is completely understandable. Chaucer, however, responded differently, trying to imagine in texts like *The Nun's Priest's Tale* a space for political debate and reason that was not corrupted by either popular violence or princely tyranny. Maura Nolan has recently argued that "Chaucerian verse demands close reading; close reading disrupts abstraction."[124] More's *Richard III* also demands close reading as a key element in its Aristotelian defense of the bonds of community against the dangers of princely tyranny.[125] In *Utopia*, the subject of the next chapter, More reflected upon the dangers of abstract reason and its costs — social, political, and religious.

Chapter 2

REASON

In May 1515 Thomas More went to Flanders as part of a royal trade commission. The negotiations were protracted, and More did not return to England until the end of October. It was during his time in Flanders that More probably wrote book 2 of *Utopia*, adding book 1 after he returned to London.[1] In this chapter I start by discussing *Utopia* and the ways in which its treatment of reason reflects More's Christian humanism. Next, I examine the representation of reason in a number of late fourteenth- and fifteenth-century texts, including Fragment 1 of *The Canterbury Tales*, the work of Reginald Pecock, and *The Tale of Beryn*. *Utopia*'s vision of a fully public world based on reason appears to epitomize its originality and modernity. These aspects of *Utopia* are, however, prefigured in the work of writers like Chaucer and Pecock.[2] *Utopia* is modern, but as with much of More's written work, its modernity is an aspect of its engagement with the "reformist" norms of late fourteenth- and fifteenth-century literature.[3] Finally, I examine the *Dialogue concerning Heresies* and illustrate the extent to which the concerns and issues that More discussed in *Utopia* remained an important aspect of his thought throughout his life. There is not a "good," humanist More and a "bad," persecuting one; the man who wrote *Utopia* also produced works like the *Dialogue concerning Heresies*. Indeed, as this chapter will demonstrate, many of the themes that More addresses in the *Dialogue concerning Heresies* echo those that he discussed in very different circumstances over ten years before in *Utopia*.

Utopia and Absurd Reason

In a seminal article, "Thomas More: On the Margins of Modernity," the historian J. H. Hexter discussed the "problem" of *Utopia*—is it a medieval or modern work?[4] The position that scholars have adopted toward this question, however, as Hexter demonstrated, relates at least as much to their approach to More the man as to *Utopia* the text. Scholars sympathetic to More's opposition to Henry VIII's religious polices on the whole view *Utopia* as a medieval work in order to stress the consistency of More's views throughout his lifetime. On the other side historians and critics who have emphasized the modernity of *Utopia* have tended to regard More's rejection of Henrician religious and political change as an act of betrayal. Unfortunately, as Hexter demonstrates, neither position is very useful in terms of understanding *Utopia*: "To describe *Utopia* as merely medieval or merely Renaissance both unduly restricts its significance, and poses the difficult question of why so many people still read it, since they could find the medieval and the Renaissance points of view far more clearly, precisely, and fully expressed in other writings."[5] What makes *Utopia* a medieval and modern work is its central concern with the possibilities and boundaries of reason. It is a critique of a particular kind of reason, diachronic and absolute, anticorporeal and antiperformative. In this work More imagined a fully functioning rational, non-Christian society; one, moreover, whose rationality is so total and all-encompassing that it appears to drive the irrational to the very margins of society.

More, however, was aware of the paradoxes implicit in his utopian vision. His fantasy of a totally rational world is contradictory and disturbingly irrational. Utopia is based on a royal fiat. Hythloday, the narrator of book 2 of *Utopia*, describes utopian society in detail but does not discuss how it came to be, how the rules that structure every aspect of Utopia were devised and enacted. It appears that they were conceived and set down by Utopus, Utopia's founder. Utopian society is therefore based upon an arbitrary imposition of one man's will; it is a fully public society that validates debate and discussion but is founded upon a private act of monarchical power; and it is a virtuous land whose rules are so exacting as to make the pursuit of virtue largely meaningless. Hythloday praises Utopia as a fully reasonable society but seems strangely unaware of its irrational origins.[6]

Reason in Utopia the place is quite different from reason in *Utopia*. In the former there does indeed seem to be no limit to the rational, not even the absurd. *Utopia* the book, however, invites its readers to engage in reasoned debate. More's target in *Utopia*, as it would be in his later polemical works like the *Dialogue concerning Heresies*, is modes of thought that oscillate between a complete rejection of reality, such as Utopus's fantasy world, and an overwhelming pessimism in the face of human sinfulness, such as Hythloday's sweeping rejection of even the possibility of meaningful social reform. The Aristotelian ideal that More celebrates in *Utopia* is a form of analogical rationality that is incompatible with the kind of dialectic reasoning that More's work ironically and quite deliberately offers the reader as a tempting but ultimately sterile solution to the "problem" of *Utopia*'s meaning.[7]

Utopian reason has a number of sources. The most obvious one is perhaps Epicurean. Hythloday tells his listeners that the Utopians put the pursuit of pleasure as the highest good. Stephen Greenblatt has recently commented, "As More imagines it . . . an entire society—not simply a philosophical viewpoint but a complex set of laws and institutional arrangements—could be founded on explicitly Epicurean principles."[8] Utopian society views itself as inherently superior to those surrounding it because of its rationality.[9] Its Epicureanism is rigorous and stoic, focusing on what the Utopians regard as true pleasure, which is intellectual and spiritual as opposed to physical or material. Several other important classical sources influenced Utopia, perhaps most obviously Plato's *Republic* and Saint Augustine's *City of God*.[10] Significantly, however, *Utopia*, though written in Latin, also has roots in late medieval English vernacular writing. Henry Medwall's play *Nature* was probably composed and performed between 1490 and 1500, while Medwall was employed by Archbishop John Morton. At the same time More was a member of Morton's household. *Nature* is a psychomachia. Its action takes place within the mind of its central character, Man, and it is an allegorical battle for his soul between various virtues and sins. The two most important allegorical figures are Reason and Sensualyte. Medwall's play is in many ways a typical morality play. What distinguishes it, however, is its interest in reason as a concept. Daniel Wakelin has recently suggested that in *Nature* Medwall theorized the practice of reason as it appeared in Medwall's other play, *Fulgens and Lucres*.[11] Certainly the depiction of the relationship between Reason and Sensualyte in *Nature* is stark, pushing to the limits similar representations of this relationship in other late medieval texts. The most obvious example of these works is perhaps John Lydgate's poem *Reson and Sensuallyte*, which opens by stressing the geographical nature of the choice between Reson and Sensuallyte; reason is located in the east, while sensuality lies in the west.[12]

Nature is effectively in three parts. The first is a debate between Nature, Reason, and Sensualyte within Man. This part of the play is formal, with each of the figures indulging in relatively long set-piece speeches. The middle part depicts the effects of Man's decision to trust in Sensualyte at the expense of Reason. *Nature*'s final section shows Man returning to Reason and repenting of his indulgence of Sensualyte. As is clear from this structure, there is nothing particularly original about Medwall's play in terms of genre or form. What is significant is the way it depicts Man's move from Reason to Sensualyte and his subsequent penitent return. Unlike movements in such plays as *Magnyfycence*, in *Nature* the moves from virtue to vice and back again are sudden and unmotivated. Man simply decides to embrace Sensualyte and later to return to Reason. This creates a situation in which *Nature* produces an absolute dialectic division between the world of reason and sensuality. This has important implications in terms of the play's drama. It is the middle section of the play, over which Sensualyte presides, that is playful, comic, and witty. Pryde spells out the reasons for this, telling Man:

Yt ys ryght syttyng
That a man of your behaving
Shuld have alway suffycyent conyng
Of worldly wyt and policy.[13]

Man is reassured by Pryde's words, even though they directly contradict what Reason told him earlier:

Man: Now certayne, thank be heven Kyng,
I have a ryght quyk understanding:
If ye shew me any thyng
I can sone perceive yt.
But I was forbid by Reason
On myne own fantasye to ron
Or to take any presumpcyon
Of myne own wyt.[14]

Man's claims for his "quick understanding" and ability to "perceive any-thing" are designed to illustrate his fallen state. He does not realize that human wit and cunning are sinful and incompatible with Reason, which *Nature* depicts as abstract and absolute in its demands.

Nature ends with Man renouncing Sensualyte and returning to Reason:

Reason: Syr, have ye done as I wylled you to do?
Man: Ye, that have I don, and what trow ye more?
I have ben wyth Repentaunce also,
Whyche fro my hart shall never go,
For he brought me unto Confessyon,
And anon I was acquainted with Hartys Contrycyon.[15]

Man's return to Reason is a return to the penitential world of Chaucer's Parson, in which there is no room with human cunning or wit. *Nature* stages a confrontation between two worlds. The argument of the play is that Reason should be preferred to Sensualyte, but as a piece of theater, *Nature* demonstrates that it is Sensualyte's world that is dramatic, comic, and full of memorable characters. An audience member watching this drama, as perhaps More did in Morton's household, would see played out a stark choice between the abstract, dramatically sterile world of Reason and the sinful, comic, corrupt, and exciting play of Sensualyte.

Utopia rejects the dichotomy insisted upon by *Nature*. It is a witty, cunning defense of human reason. At its heart is More's commitment to the northern humanist ambition of uniting classical learning with Christ's teaching. This ideal was perhaps most powerfully articulated in Erasmus's collection of proverbs, the *Adages*.[16] In the introduction to the 1508 edition of the *Adages*, as part of a discussion of the importance of proverbs, Erasmus wrote: "There are two things which are peculiar to the character of a proverb, common usage and novelty. This means it must be well known and in popular currency . . . and then it must be shrewd, so as to have some mark, as it were, to distinguish it from ordinary talk."[17] Having discussed what makes proverbs novel, Erasmus illustrates his argument by referring to the proverb "Between friends all is common." Erasmus soon makes his discussion of this proverb explicitly Christian, arguing: "What other purpose had Christ, the prince of religion? One precept and one alone He gave to the world, and that was love; on that alone, He taught, hang all the law and the prophets. Or what else does love teach us, except that all things should be common to all?"[18]

Erasmus goes on to equate human friendship with the mystical unity of the "many grains into one flour" and "one liquid from many clusters of grapes" embodied in the eucharistic bread and wine.[19] His discussion of the proverb "Between friends all is common" ends with him asking the reader to "see what an ocean of philosophy, or rather theology, is opened up to us by this tiny proverb."[20] Erasmus regarded proverbs as exemplary forms of Christian language because they united classical wisdom with the everyday. Daniel Kinney argues that for Erasmus, "Every adage represents a charmed union of *verba* and *res*, and the source of the charm is the God-ordained bonding of social *consensus*."[21] Erasmus's discussion of the proverb "Between friends all is common" pronounces and performs the social and communal production of meaning. Erasmus argues that the grains that come together to create bread and the grapes that mix to produce wine in the sacrament of the altar are metaphors for the letters and words that come together in Christ's teaching. The reader of the *Adages*, in bringing together the diverse aspects of Erasmus's work, participates in a textual friendship whose ultimate goal, always deferred but also always desired, is to fully understand Christ's message of love. It is this that prevents Erasmus's emphasis on the communal production of meaning, on consensus, from becoming a weak, quietist position. Erasmus and More shared a similar understanding of Christian wisdom. In particular, as Brendan Bradshaw has persuasively argued, both men emphasized the Christian importance of human reason against a fideistic emphasis on the inherent irredeemable sinfulness of the human intellect.

Proverbs, like Christ's teaching, were for Erasmus and More simple and commonplace, but at the same time the wisdom they contained was potentially transformative.[22] They do not exist apart from the world, nor do they turn their back on the world's sinfulness; rather they emphasize the communal and social as the arena in which meaning is produced. In Christian terms, for More and Erasmus proverbs enacted the truth of Christian wisdom; they embodied faith.[23]

Another crucial influence on *Utopia*, as I suggested, is Saint Augustine.[24] In particular, *Utopia* reflects the importance of Augustine's views on education and language to More's thought.[25] Augustine's *On the Trinity* (*De Trinitate*) ends with a prayer, "Deliver me, O God, from the multitude of words with which I am inwardly afflicted in my soul."[26] The idea of Augustine praying at the end of a long and complex work to be delivered from words is ironic and humbling. It reflects Augustine's consciousness of the necessarily linguistic nature of the human self and the extent to which this is at once humanity's cross and the basis for human salvation. In book 14 of *On the Trinity* Augustine spells out the relationship between God's remission of sins and leading a Christian life by focusing on the requirement that Christians constantly seek to renew themselves as the image of God:

> This renewal, of course, is not brought about in the one moment of the conversion itself, as in Baptism that renewal is brought about in one moment by the remission of all sins, for there does not remain even one sin, however small it may be, that is not forgiven. But just as it is one thing to be free from fevers, and another to recover from the weakness which has resulted from the fevers . . . so the first step in a cure is to remove the cause of the disease, which is done through the remission of all sins; the second is to heal the disease itself, which is done gradually by making progress in the renewal of this image.[27]

In this passage Augustine is emphasizing the importance of renewal not because he thinks it is possible for humans to escape the disease of sin but rather to stress the Christian imperative to work patiently to recover from its effects.

In *Utopia* More creates the image of a world split between two failures. He represents contemporary Europe as hopelessly mired in sin—pride, wrath, and sensuality—and he imagines an "ideal" state, fully and transparently reasonable, in which Augustine's renewal would be entirely redundant. The solution to these failures, More argues in *Utopia*, can be found only in the collective communal Christian wisdom celebrated by Erasmus in his introduction to the *Adages*. The target of *Utopia*'s satire is a reductive pessimism personified in Hythloday's simultaneous and linked rejection of the possibility of meaningful social reform and his championing of Utopia as the perfect commonwealth. By the horrors described in book 1 of *Utopia*, More makes plain to the reader the dire implications of the refusal of people like Hythloday to even attempt to reform early sixteenth-century England. The costs of Utopia's perfection are, however, if anything, even more drastic than these horrors, since ultimately what Utopia loses is Christ's message of hope, the possibility of Augustinian renewal. *Utopia* is a Christian parable. Utopia is a wretched place.[28] And its wretchedness reflects the extent to which it embodies a fideistic pessimism concerning human wit and imagination similar to that which drove Chaucer's Parson to reject fables and tales as empty, pointless chaff.[29]

Utopia opens with a letter from More to Peter Giles that represents itself as a preface to More's work but immediately undermines this claim by refusing to behave like one. Prefaces are meant to introduce a work to its reader. More's letter does this, but in such a way as to generate for readers more confusion, not less, about what they are about to read. "Truth in fact," states the letter, "is the only quality at which I should have aimed, or did aim, in writing this book."[30] Later he repeats the point, telling Giles, "As I've taken particular pains to avoid untruths in the book, so, if anything is in doubt, I'd rather make an honest mistake than say what I don't believe. In short, I'd rather be truthful than correct."[31] At the end of the preface, however, the irony of More's claims to truthfulness appears plainly when he asks Giles, "Get in touch with Hythloday—in person if you can, or by letters if he's gone—and make sure that my work contains nothing false and omits nothing true."[32] Deferring to a fictional character, and one whose name means "expert on nonsense" or "nonsense peddler," is ridiculous. It also constructs the question of *Utopia*'s truthfulness as depending upon a contrast between fact and fiction.

This is also the main issue addressed in another letter to Giles, attached to the 1517 edition of the work. In this text More claims to be responding to a "sharp fellow" who has questioned whether *Utopia* is fact or fiction:

> When he questions whether the book is fact or fiction, I find *his* judgement quite awry. There's no denying that if I had decided to write of a commonwealth, and a tale of this sort had come to my mind, I might not have shrunk from a fiction through which the truth, like a medicine smeared with honey, might enter the mind a little more pleasantly. But I would certainly have softened the fiction a little, so that, while imposing on vulgar ignorance, I gave hints to the more learned which would enable them to see through the pretence. . . . If the veracity of the historian had not actually required me to do so, I am not so stupid as to have preferred those barbarous and meaningless names of Utopia, Anydar, Amaurot and Ademos.[33]

More's claim that it is the demands of history that force him to tell the truth about Utopia should be treated as seriously as Chaucer's similar suggestion in the prologue to *The Miller's Tale*: "I moot [must] reherce / Hir tales alle, be they bettre or werse, / Or elles falsen som of my mateere."[34] *Utopia*, like *The Canterbury Tales*, is false matter, fiction, but as Chaucer and More knew, this was not a bar to a work's being truthful.[35] The truths that *Utopia* contains are both fictional and factual. One of them is that the learned, in More's time and our own, are far happier discussing the differences between fiction and fact in relation to imaginary worlds than addressing the reality of human suffering and sinfulness. More's "sharp fellow" is happy to dispute, question, and deconstruct Utopia while ignoring book 1's critique of Tudor society as oppressive, conflict ridden, and filled with injustice.

Book 1 of *Utopia* opens with a fictional More being introduced by Giles to Hythloday. Very quickly the conversation between the three men turns on the question of counsel, and in particular More and Giles's argument that Hythloday should enter the service of a ruler so that his wisdom can contribute to the common good.[36] Hythloday responds by rejecting the possibility that as a learned man he could make any impact as a counselor. He produces numerous reasons. In the process, however, More places into Hythloday's mouth a critique of the existing social order. For example, Hythloday comments that in England, "there are a great many noblemen who live idly like drones off the labour of others, their tenants whom they bleed white by constantly raising their rents."[37] Hythloday forcibly insists upon the failure of Tudor England to live up to the precepts of Christian teaching, arguing that "if we dismiss as out of the question and absurd everything that the perverse customs of men have made to seem unusual, we shall have to set aside, even in a community of Christians, most of the commandments of Christ."[38] He criticizes the English legal system in detail before concluding by rejecting the possibility that counsel can be anything more than the craven acceptance of terrible decisions: "In a council, there is no way to dissemble or play the innocent. You must openly approve the worst proposals and warmly urge the most vicious policies. A man who went along only half-heartedly would immediately be suspected as a spy, perhaps a traitor."[39] Hythloday's rejection of the value of counsel is absolute and extreme.[40] It is uncounseled, and he refuses to engage properly with the advice offered to him by More and Giles. Book 1 of *Utopia* depicts a society in desperate need of reform but in which those who, because of their wisdom, ought to be doing the most to change the world for the better are locked in an extreme pessimism that at once prides itself on its ability to fully see how desperate the situation is and refuses to exert itself to make things better.

There is a brief moment at the start of the discussion between More, Giles, and Hythloday that encapsulates their different attitudes not only to reform but, more fundamentally, to language itself. Giles expresses surprise that, given Hythloday's learning, he does not enter a king's service. Hythloday, however, states very clearly that he will not, even for the sake of his family and friends, "enslave" himself "to any king whatever."[41] Giles's response is witty but also telling: "'Well said,' Peter replied; 'but I do not mean that you should be in servitude to any king, only in his service.' 'The difference is only a matter of one syllable,' Raphael replied."[42] Syllables, however, matter. They matter in particular in relation to Utopia, since it is created out of combinations of syllables. Indeed Hythloday himself is only three syllables welded together. Hythloday's wisdom, like

Utopian reason, is strangely unaware of its own limitations. Its remorseless desire for order blinds it to the sensuous reality of human life. Hythloday and Utopus are convinced that all can be explained, all can be ordered, humanity can be made perfect—and if a few syllables are lost in the process, that is a price worth paying. The cost of Utopian perfection, however, as More knew, is much higher than Hythloday appears to realize or acknowledge.

In book 2 of his work More, through Hythloday, gives a detailed account of Utopia. As described by Hythloday, it is a strange combination of freedom and constraint. Peter Iver Kaufman points out that the Utopians' freedoms are "hedged about on all sides with rules."[43] For example, Utopians are free to travel within their own districts, provided they have all the necessary permissions. Hythloday strongly approves of the rules governing travel, commenting, "So you see there is no chance to loaf or kill time, no pretext for evading work; there are no wine-bars, or alehouses, or brothels; no chances for corruption; no hiding places; no spots for secret meetings. Because they live in the full view of all, they are bound to be either working at their usual trades or enjoying their leisure in a respectable way.[44] Utopia is not an entirely urban land, but, as Lawrence Manley has suggested, early Tudor London is a constant presence: "While More's *Utopia* surveys a host of problems besetting the contemporary world, it imagines their solution within a conceptual framework whose material counterpart is a perfectly ordered urbanistic space."[45] *Utopia*'s fully public reformed world is a fantasy image as different as possible from the London More knew. It is a space whose rules and regulations ensure that sin is not possible.[46] The Utopians may be virtuous, but they actually have very little choice in the matter. Utopia is London as a large, perfectly functioning monastery. The rules of the Utopians' society, as laid down by Utopus, force them into a regime that is monastic in intent and detail. In these terms Utopia can be seen as More's version of a perfected commonwealth only if one thinks that he desired to create just such a law-bound community.[47]

Many scholars have indeed made this assumption. For example, Richard Marius argues that "the relentless openness of the society, the resolute eagerness of the Utopians to spend time with each other and to check up on what everybody is doing, the loathing of idleness—all are part of More's recognition of sin's terrible power, a power he must have felt continually in himself. If the Utopians let down their guard for an instant, sin will rush in."[48] As Marius suggests, Utopia is based on a deeply pessimistic view of humanity. Arthur F. Kinney points out that "nowhere do the Utopians display a desirable humanist faith in humanity."[49] Utopia embodies a Pelagian fantasy of human perfectibility. A key element of Augustine's rejection of Pelagius's teaching was the way it imposed impossible demands on ordinary Christians—Pelagius wanted all Christians to live perfect, sin-free lives.[50] Utopia is the only place in which Pelagius's desire could be realized.[51] Not, however, because Utopians are naturally more virtuous than other people. Utopia is a Pelagian paradise because it forces people to be virtuous and in the process embodies a deeply pessimistic, wretched attitude to humanity. Only if there are no brothels, no inns, no hiding places, will people resist sin. And significantly, as Gerard Wegemer has pointed out, "universities do not exist in Utopia."[52]

For Augustine the potential richness of human language was a danger, but also a source of strength, a reservoir of God's grace. In *On Christian Teaching* (*De Doctrina Christiana*) Augustine writes, "The human condition would be wretched indeed if God appeared unwilling to minister his word to human beings through human agency."[53] Brian Stock has suggested that in *On Christian Teaching*, "the entire Christian community is envisaged, potentially at least, as a body of readers, either as clergy or as cultured laypersons."[54] It was the labor of renewal, the preparedness to work as a community to restore the image of God, that for Augustine made a person a good Christian, not the achievement of an ideal that was beyond most people. At the end of book 2 Hythloday turns from his description of Utopia to attack the one sin that he regards as, above all others, responsible for the failure of all Christians to live as virtuously as the Utopians—pride. Hythloday's attack on pride is pointedly allegorical:

> Pride measures her advantages not only by what she has but by what other people lack. Pride would not deign even to be made a goddess if there were no wretches for her to sneer at and domineer over. Her good fortune is dazzling only by contrast with the miseries of

others, her riches are valuable only as they torment and tantalise the poverty of others. Pride is a serpent from hell that twines itself around the hearts of men, acting like a suckfish to hold them back from choosing a better way of life.[55]

Hythloday's purpose in describing pride in such metaphoric detail is clearly to make the reader reflect on the lack of pride in Utopia. Indeed a central aim of Utopus's rules and regulations was to create a society without pride, a fully reasonable world similar to that of Reason in the final section of Medwall's *Nature*. Utopia, however, is awash with precisely the sin that its founder sought to banish. It is Utopus's pride made concrete, enacted and embodied in the land that he founded. The reason that fills Utopia, and that Hythloday so admires, is ordered, public, and fundamentally flawed since it excludes the sensuous, lived reality of humanity.[56] Utopia is designed so that there is literally no place for sin; it has no dark corners or hidden nooks, but it also has no place for the Christ, the friend of innkeepers and prostitutes, the lost and the rejected. Certainly Hythloday tells his listeners that the Utopians are very interested in Christianity, but he does not seem to realize that Christ's teaching would transform Utopia as completely as it would Tudor England—if it were to be put into practice.

Utopia was written in Latin and was clearly intended to be read by a relatively small number of learned humanist scholars. But at its heart is an attempt to create through the act of storytelling a community united in a common Christian agenda of social reform and transformation. The parables that Christ constantly tells as part of his ministry are a strange collection of the relatively obvious and the deeply obscure. What they all share, however, is a desire to unsettle the given—the extent to which the existing order, at the level of individual, family, temple, and state, is natural or reasonable. Christ's wisdom is collective. It is produced through the process of parabolic exchange and discussion.[57] The attack in *Utopia* on private property as the corrupting force in Tudor England reflects More's commitment to an ideal of an equalitarian community produced in and through the act of storytelling. At the heart of the *Utopia* is a desire for a textual community conterminous with a reformed, just Christian commonwealth.

Kingship, Falsehood, and Reason in the Late Fourteenth and Fifteenth Centuries

Utopia is steeped in humanist concerns and ideals. Scholars often use it as an exemplary Renaissance text. As I have already suggested, however, Chaucer and other late fourteenth- and fifteenth-century writers had already addressed many of the issues it addresses. In particular, a number of writers in this period produced works that prefigured More's utopian fantasy in their concern with the boundaries and possibilities of reason.

The three major tales that make up Fragment 1 of *The Canterbury Tales*, the Knight's, the Miller's, and the Reeve's, raise a number of important issues. In particular, they stage a confrontation between different versions of reason and irrationality. *The Knight's Tale* is set in pagan Greece. One of its key themes is the confrontation between human reason and fate, which, in a world without grace, can never be resolved beyond a reasoned acceptance of arbitrariness. Lee Patterson comments: "Whatever final meaning the *Knight's Tale* may bear, it is clear that the knight himself intends to celebrate Theseus as a model of rational governance and chivalry as a force of civilisation."[58] *The Knight's Tale* tells the story of two knights, Palamon and Arcite, and their love for Emelye. Although it appears on the surface to be a romance, in practice this tale is an interrogation of the limitations of a particular form of human reason. In particular, Chaucer quickly shows that the surface courtly decorum of the tale is brittle and easily shattered. *The Knight's Tale* is a courtly romance that mocks the central romantic narrative motivation of the genre. The tale ends when Arcite, who has just won the right to Emelye in a tournament, is mortally wounded by an infernal fury. After his death Theseus persuades Palamon to set aside his defeat by Arcite and marry Emelye, telling him,

Thanne is it wysdom, as it thynketh me,
To maken vertu of necessitee,
And to take it weel that we may nat eschue,
And namely that to us alle is due.[59]

The final image that the Knight leaves his reader with is of the harmony produced by the marriage between Palamon and Emelye:

Bitwixen hem was maad anon the bond
That highte matrimoigne or marriage
By al the conseil and the baronage.
And thus with alle blisse and melodye
Hath Palamon ywedded Emelye.[60]

What is left out of this moment of resolution is the violence, and its
causes, that flows throughout the tale, and in particular the model of
knightly or courtly masculinity that fueled the competition between Palamon and Arcite. Also silenced in this moment of harmony is Emelye's
desire to live a chaste life.[61] Theseus's necessity is not symmetrical or
balanced. Rather it works to provide a gloss that finesses the extent to
which humans are victims of fate; it reasons away the inexplicable and
does so in such a way as to endorse existing political and gender relations.
Reason in *The Knight's Tale* is a force for order. But it is entirely practical
and instrumental. The pagan setting of *The Knight's Tale* restricts the scope
of its action and leaves its actors caught in a graceless world. It is this
that ultimately gives *The Knight's Tale* is constricted atmosphere; Theseus's
order, like that created by Utopus in Utopia, is reasoned; it works. But it
ignores the messiness, the failure, and also the joy of sensuous human
life. Theseus creates order (or at least thinks he does); Chaucer leaves it
to the Miller to produce bliss.[62]

The Miller's Tale is a perfectly balanced response to the Knight's. It is
a fabliau and, as such, at one level a celebration of human wit.[63] James
Simpson argues that "the *Knight's Tale* implies a melancholic acceptance
of the fact that the political order can only ever be constructed, arbitrary
as it is to the order of the universe; fabliaux, by contrast, celebrate that
makeshift, provisional order, since it gives scope for the exercise of a
worldly self-interested prudence, and produces new hierarchies founded
on gradations of professional skill."[64] Necessity has no place in *The Miller's
Tale*. Nicholas does not need to seduce Alison, and he certainly does not
need to construct the elaborate scheme he uses to trick John, Alison's
husband. In *The Miller's Tale* Chaucer creates a self-contained human world.
It is witty, clever, and amusing. In particular, the tale's detailed description of Alison, who was "ful moore blissful on to see / Than is the newe
pere-jonette tree," embodies a sense of beauty that, Maura Nolan has

argued, is free from "didacticism and exemplarity."[65] Alison is bliss to see or to read. *The Miller's Tale* ends with laughter. It does not have a moral. Caught between Theseus's reasoned order and the Reeve's pessimistic disorder, *The Miller's Tale*, like *Utopia*, celebrates a textual community produced through the blissful process of storytelling.

The Reeve's Tale opens with a prologue in which the Reeve tells his listeners his philosophy of life:

> Oure olde lemes mowe wel been unweelde
> But wyl ne shal nat fallen, that is sooth.
> And yet ik have alwey a coltes tooth,
> As many a yeer as it is passed henne
> Syn that my tappe of lif bigan to renne.
> For sikerly, what I was bore, anon
> Deeth drough the tappe of lyf and lette it gon,
> And ever sithe hath so the tappe yronne
> Til that almoost al empty is the tonne.[66]

The Reeve imagines life as a barrel that starts to empty the moment a person is born. There appears to be no place in the Reeve's world for purposeful human agency. There is just a remorseless, reductive, dying flow. Despite the Reeve's claims to morality, his prologue and the subsequent tale are amoral in their lack of Christian faith. As V. A. Kolve argues in reference to the Reeve's prologue: "There can be no Christian meditation on death that stops short of Christ's victory over Death, no Christian discourse on sin that can entirely neglect the possibility of virtue and man's freedom to amend."[67] Freedom in *The Reeve's Tale* is simply the possibility to sin; it is freedom to cheat, lie, rape, and fight.

The Reeve tells the story of a miller, Symkyn, and two students from Oxford, John and Aleyn, who try to pay him back for his constant pilfering of their college's grain. Instead Symkyn not only steals their grain but also humiliates them into the bargain. In response John and Aleyn contrive to have sex with Symkyn's wife and daughter. At this point in the tale Symkyn wakes, and in the ensuing chaos he is soundly beaten. There is no disputing the relish with which the Reeve concludes his tale:

Thus is the proude millere wel ybete,
And hath ylost the gryndynge of the whete,
And payed for the soper everideel
Of Aleyn and of John, that bette hym weel.
His wyf is swyved, and his doghter als.
Lo, swich it is a millere to be fals!
And therefore this proverbe is seyd ful sooth,
"Hym thar nat wene wel that yvele dooth."
A gylour shal hymself bigyled be.[68]

The Reeve seems to imagine that by ending his tale with two proverbs he makes it moral, or at least didactic. The details of the story he has just told, however, suggest that everyone is a liar, all do evil. There is closure at the end of *The Reeve's Tale*. But at the same time there is no space in the tale for positive human action; the best one could hope for is self-denial and self-abnegation.

Fragment 1 of *The Canterbury Tales*, like *Utopia*, offers its readers a range of possible meanings and responses. In particular, Chaucer, like More, seems to be tempting the reader with a simple, but false, dialectic choice—either to embrace the world of Theseus/Utopus or to be condemned to live in the world as it is portrayed in *The Reeve's Tale* or book 1 of *Utopia*. It is, however, precisely the simplicity of this choice that More and Chaucer rejected. James Simpson has argued that all hermeneutic traditions are ultimately based on faith and "that the greater the level of faith required, the more likely the level of violence" will be high— interpretative, judicial, and real. Simpson suggests that a way of avoiding this violence is to adopt a "friendly hermeneutics," based on "faith in persons as ethical agents."[69] *Utopia* and Fragment 1 of *The Canterbury Tales* tempt their readers with reductive choices—the Knight or the Reeve, book 1 or book 2, a fantasy world of total reason or brutish reality. But in each case the real violence is in the choice, the failure to become a friend, a pilgrim, a member of Chaucer's or More's good company working through or walking around two equally flawed options.

During the course of the fifteenth century, writers continued to reflect upon the issues that Chaucer addressed in Fragment 1 of *The Canterbury Tales*. For example, writers like Reginald Pecock created works that foreshadowed Utopus's fully transparent rational world. Under the pressures of political failure and religious conflict, Pecock produced vernacular works that proposed a utopian solution to England's problems. At the same time More's concerns over the scope of reason and its relationship to the reality of lived human life are foreshadowed in a number of other fifteenth-century texts. *The Tale of Beryn* shares *Utopia*'s sense of the twin dangers of the kind of reasoned order imagined in *The Knight's Tale* and of the pessimistic realism of the Reeve.

Reginald Pecock, bishop of Chichester, developed in his work a particularly idiosyncratic understanding of the relationship between reason and revelation as part of his attack on Lollard criticisms of the English church.[70] In the wonderfully named *The Repressor of Over Much Blaming of the Clergy* (c. 1455), Pecock stressed repeatedly the primacy of reason over Scripture. Norman Doe points out that, for Pecock, "even if scripture did not exist man could still discover the principles of divine and natural law."[71] Pecock goes out of his way to stress the inadequacy of Scripture as a source of knowledge, for example arguing that while Christ "biddeth a man to be meek . . . he teaches not before what meekness is."[72] Pecock's target in *The Repressor* is principally what he constructed as the reductive scripturalism of his Lollard opponents. Pecock stresses in his work the inadequacy of Scripture across a whole range of registers: "Scripture is not ground to any one such said virtue, governance, deed, or truth . . . but only doom of natural resoun, which is moral law of kind and moral law of God, written in the book of law of kind in men's souls."[73] The virtues, deeds, truths, and governance that Pecock refers to in this passage cover practically all human activity; very little indeed is left not only for the church but, more generally, for religion. The judgment of reason is for Pecock a force of totalizing reform that not only erases existing intellectual traditions and schools but effectively renders them redundant.

In particular, in the place of church, fathers, and Scripture Pecock emphasizes the book of reason, supported by references to his own works and commonsensical observations drawn from daily life. For example, in order to illustrate the extent to which Christ's teaching is grounded in reason, Pecock uses an image of fishermen and their baskets, asking his readers: "What if Christ and his Apostles would fish with boats in the sea, and would afterward carry those fishes in panniers upon horses to London, should men say for reverence or love to Christ and his Apostles that those fishes grew out of the panniers . . . or out of the hands of Christ and of his Apostles, and that the ground and fundament of the fishes' substances and beings were the hands of Christ and of his Apostles while they took those fishes, or while they carried those fishes?"[74] Building on this example, Pecock then argues, "All the truths of law of kind which Christ and his Apostles taught and wrote were before their teaching and writing and were written before in the solemnest inward book or inward writing of reason's doom passing all outward books in profit to men for to serve God, of which inward book or inward writing much thing is said in the book called *The just apprising of Holy Scripture.*"[75]

Pecock's privileging of reason over Scripture, and indeed almost any other source of knowledge or authority, allows him to argue that what distinguishes the clergy from the laity is their rationality and not virtue or sacramental status. Stephen E. Lahey has summed up Pecock's argument by suggesting that for Pecock, "to approach Holy Scripture one needs a facility in the 'doom of resoun'; without it, the result must be misinterpretation, heresy and the inevitable social turmoil that follows. Thus the signal criterion for understanding Scripture is not moral purity, but rational acuity. This means that a learned clergy is necessary for ecclesiastical—and social—health, and is more important than a moral clergy. As a consequence, the 'doom of resoun' is needed even regarding scriptural truths not evident to its purview."[76] *The Repressor* responds to heretical or Lollard anticlericalism by changing the terms of debate. Pecock outflanks his opponents by asserting the primacy of reason over church and Scripture. He accuses Lollardy of not being sufficiently Lollard, of not pushing to its logical conclusion what Pecock saw as Lollardy's reasoned rejection of ecclesiastical authority and extending this critique to Scripture itself.

Pecock's privileging of reason was, however, ultimately self-defeating. This is not only because the Lancastrian church found his arguments completely unacceptable. The real problem is that Pecock's "doom of reason" lacks the consistency that it would require to support his constant insistence that it is the foundation of all knowledge. Certainly Pecock does try to avoid this problem by suggesting that God is the ground of reason, but unlike earlier thinkers, for example Aquinas, he does not mean by this that revelation can be used to test a proposition's rationality. As Everett H. Emerson points out, "Again and again, especially in *The Repressor*, Pecock argued that moral philosophy is more important than Scripture for salvation, more important concerning even such matters as the sacraments (which he of course recognized as being based on revelation)."[77] A key problem in Pecock's thought is that he does not, and probably could not, define reason's boundaries. This leads him to deploy a number of strategies that are ultimately incompatible. For example, Pecock consistently refers to the inward book or inward writing of reason—and one should note that these are subtly different things, although Pecock does not acknowledge this. Pecock's references to the book of reason tend to suggest that this is a complete, albeit metaphorical, text accessible to the learned, particularly the clergy, and largely inaccessible to the laity. At the same time his writings are extremely prolix. They are repetitive and self-regarding, as if the constant repetition of a point makes it more rather than less persuasive. Pecock argues endlessly that only reason and not Scripture can provide a firm basis for knowledge, commenting that if "the lay party would attend and trust to their own wits, and would learn from texts of the Bible only, I dare well say so many diverse opinions should rise in lay men's wits by occasion of texts in Holy Scripture . . . that all the world should be cumbered therewith, and men should accord together in keeping the service to God, as dogs do in a market, when each of them tears the other's coat."[78]

The solution to this breakdown in religious and social order is, of course, for the lay party not to rely on their own interpretations of Scripture but instead to listen to the counsel of "substantial clerks well learned in logic and in moral philosophy."[79] Pecock clearly regards himself as one of these men. But during the course of *The Repressor* it becomes obvious how unsubstantial its argument is. Consistently Pecock concludes his arguments by referring to other works he has written, is writing, or plans to write.[80] He does this also in other works. He wrote *The Folower of the Donet* to support the arguments of the earlier work *The Donet* and to teach the lay party how to reason. Pecock explains in detail the relationship of *The Folower of the Donet* to *The Donet*, and indeed to his other work: "All the said 'donet' and all this present book is made in order and process to

be learned before 'the book of christen religion' and the book 'spread-
ing the IIII tables' and other books in like manner to 'the book of christen religion.'"[81] Pecock endlessly argues that the "doom of reason" is
the foundation or ground for all knowledge, that it is the only stable point
of fixity in terms of interpretation, while at the same time writing works
whose form completely undermines this argument. As the words, sentences, and texts pile up, it becomes apparent how unstable the "doom
of reason" is, how much it depends on being grounded in texts whose
exuberance marks their provisional and partial nature. *The Repressor* is an
impassioned defense of clerical status and legitimates an intellectual rational iconoclasm that flattens everything in its path.[82] Pecock's "doom
of reason," instead of creating a world of transparent rationality, produces
a maze of ever-expanding words, sentences, and texts.[83]

For Pecock, reason had the power to resolve all religious debate and
to fix the meaning of Scripture once and for all. One senses that what
lies behind Pecock's works—and this is true of other fifteenth-century
writers, for example Sir John Fortescue—is a burning desire for order
and a fear of disorder. It was this desire that drove writers like Pecock
to see the world in such starkly diachronic terms, as a choice between
Theseus and the Reeve, order and disorder. During the fifteenth century, however, as James Simpson has shown in his study *Reform and Cultural Reformation*, there existed an alternative tradition of reformist writing that was suspicious of power or authority that claimed to be fixed or
absolute. In particular, this tradition, Simpson argues, was committed to
"an affirmation of the possibility of human initiative, whether in politics
or theology."[84] The fear of disorder and the desire for order that runs
through *The Repressor* leads Pecock to create works that are pessimistic
about the scope and potential of humanity, and in particular human wit
or imagination. Late medieval works like *The Tale of Beryn*, however, not
only question the status of worldly authorities; they also privilege the
world and the wisdom of simple, fallen humanity over authorities that
claim to be absolute and all-powerful.

The Tale of Beryn is a continuation to *The Canterbury Tales*. It is a re-
working of a French text, the *Roman de Bérinus*, and dates from the mid-
fifteenth century. *The Tale of Beryn* is in two parts. The first is a witty prologue describing what Chaucer's pilgrims did after they had reached

Canterbury and visited Thomas Beckett's shrine; for example, the Knight and the Squire visit the town walls to see the new defensive arrangements, while the Wife of Bath and the Prioress retire to the garden of an inn to gossip.[85] The prologue to *The Tale of Beryn* reflects its author's close knowledge of *The Canterbury Tales*. In particular, its account of the Pardoner's attempts to seduce a tapster called Kit, who works at the inn where the pilgrims are staying, echoes the events and imagery of *The Reeve's Tale*. When, after a day and evening of trying to seduce Kit, the Pardoner discovers that he has been tricked, a fight breaks out between him, Kit's lover, and the Innkeeper. In the darkness all the men ended up injured, while "she that cause was of all had therof no sorowe."[86] The Pardoner suffers the worst indignity, since, having been roundly beaten, he ends up sharing the bed of a large, violent dog:

> He coude noon other help, but leyd adwon his hede
> In the dogges litter, and wisshed after brede
> Many a tyme and offt, the dogg for to plese,
> To have i-ley more nere for his own ese.
> But wissh what he wold, his Fortune seyd nay.
> So trewly for the Pardoner, it was a dismol day.[87]

The Pardoner's punishment for his lust is to spend the night trying to please a dog. Clearly this is at one level symbolic. At the same time it reflects the extent to which the prologue to *The Tale of Beryn* critically engages with *The Canterbury Tales* and in particular *The Reeve's Tale*. The tale depicts the Pardoner's sexual desire as animalistic. Despite all the wit and comedy that this desire produces, its end is dismal. This is not to suggest that the author of the prologue of *The Tale of Beryn* endorses the views of the Reeve, or indeed the Parson. The Pardoner's fall results from his inability to contain his desires for Kit despite his status as a clergyman. None of the other pilgrims suffer the same fate as the Pardoner. He is the exception, not the norm.

The Tale of Beryn tells the story of a Roman nobleman, Beryn, and his disastrous visit to Falsetown. It mocks English legal practice and, as Richard Firth Green has argued, in particular the Law Merchant as administered in fifteenth-century England.[88] From the moment the tale's eponymous hero, Beryn, lands in Falsetown, he finds himself facing ridiculous, but nonetheless dangerous, lawsuits. He is saved only when another Roman, Geoffrey, uses his knowledge of Falsetown's legal system to defeat Beryn's accusers. Geoffrey explains to Beryn that Falsetown is ruled by Lord Isope, who, Geoffrey claims, is "so inly wise / That no man alyve can pas his devise."[89] *The Tale of Beryn*, however, implicitly questions Isope's wisdom, since it illustrates the limitations of human reason. Isope has made lying punishable by death in Falsetown, and the effect is to make all of Falsetown's inhabitants liars, since their response to this rule is to never contradict each other:

> For hir lawes been so streyt, and peynous ordinaunce
> Is stalled for hir falshede; for this is hir fynaunce
> To lese hir lyff for lesing, and Isope it may knowne
> That lord is riall of the town and holdeth hem so lowe.
> Wherfor they have a custom, a shrewed for the nones,
> If eny of hem sey a thing, they cry all atones
> And ferm it for a soth, and it bere any charge.
> Thus of the daunger of Isope, they kepe hem ever at large.[90]

The people of Falsetown treat the most outrageous lies as truths as a direct result of Isope's attempt to impose complete truthfulness on his subjects.[91] Isope, like Utopus, seeks to create a fully transparent realm, one of absolute truth. Instead he creates Falsetown, a false place, where truth is a lie and where the imposition of reason by an enlightened ruler produces a world of shifting meanings, irrationality, and violence.[92] Falsetown suffers from rules imposed by a ruler whose presence is all-pervasive but whose person is absent.

The two parts of *The Tale of Beryn* seem on first reading to be largely unconnected, but, as John M. Bowers points out, "Beryn's difficulties with the people of Falsetown . . . complement . . . the Pardoner's bitter experiences as a stranger in Canterbury."[93] Indeed Beryn finds himself in a much more difficult and dangerous situation than the Pardoner. The latter has only himself to blame for the beating he receives. Beryn is in danger of losing everything. Isope's land without falsehood is more false, more dangerous, and ultimately more irrational than the teeming urban world of the prologue. Fifteenth-century Canterbury as depicted in the prologue to *The Tale of Beryn* is self-regulating. It does allow the Pardoner to sin, or at least to attempt to, but it also metes out appropriate punishment. It is a comic, self-contained world, which has a place for religion, pleasure, gossip, and a whole plethora of human activities. It is real in a way that Falsetown palpably is not. Isope's attempt to create a world without falsehood produces a situation far more lethal and corrupt than that which exists in fifteenth-century Canterbury. The Pardoner chooses to sin; Beryn cannot help but break Falsetown's rules.

Hythloday looks at early sixteenth-century Europe and throws his hands up in horror. He is, quite rightly, disgusted by its inequalities, the violence and oppression. In its place, like Pecock, he advances the claims of an alternative world, one ruled by reason and in which the messiness and failings of humanity have been reformed away. In the process, however, he places himself in the absurd position of advocating Utopian society because of its virtue without noticing that in Utopia to be virtuous simply means following the rules laid down by Utopus. Utopia is a mirror image of Falsetown. Isope creates a world in which it is impossible to tell the truth, Utopus one in which virtue has become meaningless. *Utopia* mocks the desire for a fully transparent ordered world of the kind imagined in Pecock's work. Above all it critiques the false choice effectively offered by Hythloday between a world of sin and Utopia's "virtue." More rejected Hythloday's fundamentalism, and in its place celebrated the consensual, compromised, messy web of stories, proverbs, and texts that is *Utopia*.[94] More understood that it is only within the reality of sensuous human life that virtue and truth are meaningful.

Reason in the *Dialogue concerning Heresies*

More's response to Luther was driven by the same, basically optimistic vision of humanity as that which informs *Utopia*. In particular, in the *Dialogue concerning Heresies* More attacks what he sees as heresy's pessimistic rejection of any place or role for human agency in the process of renewal that Augustine placed at the heart of a Christian's life.[95] The *Dialogue* was first published in 1529, with a second edition being produced in 1531 containing some extensive additions. More wrote the work as part of an accelerating campaign by the religious establishment against what it saw as the dangerous infiltration into England of Lutheran ideas and texts.[96] In particular, the *Dialogue* targets the work of William Tyndale. In the process, however, More also attempts to map out the boundaries for proper, legitimate religious debate. The work is framed as a dialogue between two fictional characters, "More" and a young Messenger who is portrayed as sympathetic to the arguments of writers like Tyndale, in particular concerning the importance of Scripture and the status of the church. More also depicts the Messenger as having swallowed uncritically a large dose of anticlericalism and with it an assumption that men like Thomas Bilney and Richard Hunne were victims of clerical oppression.[97]

Often throughout the *Dialogue concerning Heresies* More responds to the Messenger's questions, doubts, and criticisms simply and directly. For example, in response to the Messenger's argument that Scripture should take precedence over the church, More answers, in an entirely orthodox and Augustinian manner, that "the scrypture self maketh vs not byleeue the scrypture, but the chyrch maketh vs to know the scryptur."[98] Statements of this kind are precisely what Pecock sought to avoid in *The Repressor* on the entirely logical grounds that his opponents, like More's, could simply respond with an equally valid assertion of the primacy of Scripture over the church. More's assertion of the church's primacy over Scripture, however, comes at the end of a detailed, and in places witty, engagement with the specifics of the Messenger's counterargument.

It is this detail that makes the *Dialogue concerning Heresies* far more than simply a defense of a number of specific religious positions. In this work More seeks to defend an image of what it means to be a Christian and above all the proper shape and sound of Christian thought. In the *Dialogue concerning Heresies* More deploys a provocatively eclectic and potentially risky range of discourses to attack heresy. For example, after a long discussion of the failings of the clergy, instigated by the Messenger, More accepts many of the Messenger's criticisms and comments:

> The tyme was . . . whan few men durst presume to take vpon theym the hyghe office of a preste, not euen when they were chosen and

called there vnto. Nowe ronneth euery rascall and boldely offreth
hym selfe for able. And where the dygnyte passeth all pryncys, and
they that lewde be, desyreth it for worldely wynnynge, yet cometh
that sorte therto with suche a madde mynde, that they reken almost
god moche bounden to theym that they vouchesaufe to take it. But
were I pope.

By my soule quod he I wolde ye were, and my lady your wyfe
popesse to.

Well quod I than sholde she deuyse for nonnes. And as for
me touchynge the choice of prestys, I coulde not well deuys better
prouysyons than are by the lawes of the chyrche prouyded all redy,
if they were as well kept as they be well made.[99]

The idea of a female pope, a popesse with charge of nuns, is intended to
be risible. But this exchange is not simply a joke, since in it More acknowledges the failings of the clergy and, more importantly, lays the blame for
this failure squarely at the feet of the church. This passage also illustrates a process of debate and discussion concerning the state of the
church that, while it ends with More accepting many of the Messenger's
criticisms, is miles away from the sweeping anticlericalist attacks of writers like Tyndale. The process is as important to More as the detail, if not
more important. In *Burning to Read* James Simpson discusses the difference between the models of reading espoused by More and his opponents. Simpson argues that in works like the *Dialogue concerning Heresies*
More defends a "trustful, nonliteralist, and conversational pragmatism"
against what More sees as the textual absolutism of early Protestants like
Tyndale.[100] The form of *Dialogue concerning Heresies* critiques the Messenger's positions not simply because they are wrong but also because they
are the result of haste and a utopian desire for certainty. More knew that
a conversation requires time, space, and trust. He was happy if after the
debate he had happened to be proved wrong, although of course he did
not expect to be, but what really worried him was forms of thought that
collapsed hermeneutic space and time in pursuit of the fantasy of final,
ahistorical, atextual, disembodied truth.

The *Dialogue concerning Heresies* mixes gossip, popular tales, and
orthodox teaching in such a way that it both mocks heretics and pro-

vides religious guidance to the Messenger. During the discussion of how
Thomas Bilney fell into heresy, More argues that a key element in his fall
was overscrupulous praying. The Messenger mocks this argument, suggesting that it implies that praying leads one to heresy. More's response
to this is to recount the story of the collapse of a church in Beverly:

> thys ys mych lyke as at Beuerlay late when myche of the people
> beynge at a bere baytyng the chyrch fell sodaynly down at euen-
> songe tyme, and ouerwhelmed some that than were in yt, a good
> fellow that after herde the tale tolde, lo quod he now maye you see
> what yt ys to be at euensong whan ye shold be at the bere baytynge.
> How be yt the hurt was not therin beynge at euensong, but in that
> the chyrch was falsely wrought.[101]

In his account of Bilney's fall into heresy, More consistently seeks to
instruct the Messenger on the importance of finding a mean between
"scrupulous superstycyon, and rechelesse neglygence."[102] In particular,
he argues that one cannot achieve this mean on one's own. For More it
is only within a faithful community that the individual believer can navi-
gate between the dangers of excessive and careless religiosity.

In the *Dialogue concerning Heresies* More uses a story from ordinary life
to illustrate the importance of the finding the religious mean. Ironically it
is the Messenger who tells the story. He accepts More's claim that one
needs to find a mean in one's religious life and then tells a story that he
thinks, wrongly, illustrates that this is impossible:

> Ye quod he, but wote ye what the wife sayd that complained to her
> gossip of her husdandes forwardnes? She sayde her husbande was
> so wayward that he wold neuer be plesed. For yf hys brede quod she
> be dowe baken, than ys he angry . . . And yf I bake yt all to harde
> cloys yet is he not content neyther by saynt Iame. No quod her gos-
> seppe ye shold bake it in a meane. In a meane quod she? mary I
> can not happen on yt.[103]

The point of this story, which the Messenger misses completely, is that
the mean that the woman is searching for is not an absolute one between

raw and burnt, book 1 and book 2 of *Utopia*. It is rather a commonsensical mean that most bread achieves. The real problem with this story is not the nature of the mean—everyone knows how bread should be baked—the problem is the woman's method, which leads her to lurch from too little to too much.

This passage exemplifies More's use of "merry tales." Throughout his writing More deploys short stories, parables, and proverbs as a deliberate strategy. In place of Pecock's abstract and ultimately tautological notion of reason, and in place of simple assertions of orthodoxy, More uses merry tales to illustrate a communal reason that transcends the limitations of heretical or overscrupulous religious language. In the past historians and critics have rather too quickly linked the merry tales that More tells to oral culture.[104] The work of Adam Fox, among others, has illustrated how problematic it is to separate oral and print culture in this period, perhaps particularly as regards proverbs and parables.[105] Furthermore, More's use of merry tales is unusual. Works like Caxton's version of *Aesop's Fables* (1484) or *A Hundred Merry Tales* (1526) include a range of tales.[106] What separates them from More's merry tales is their lack of an overreaching narrative or even basic ethos. The morals drawn from Aesop's fables in Caxton's work range from the insightful to the banal. They often appear to be almost entirely arbitrary. There is no sense of a coherent philosophy underlying the world depicted in Caxton's *Aesop* or in *A Hundred Merry Tales*. By placing his fables, proverbs, and parables within a narrative, More charges their meaning and at the same time makes them represent an Erasmian proverbial rationality that he associates directly with the church as a space for thought. Merry tales in the world are simply excuses for humor; within the mystical body of the church they become charged with a new, profound meaning.

One of the strangest, but also crucial, passages in the *Dialogue concerning Heresies* is the story of Wilkin and Simkin, which occurs during a lengthy discussion on the limits of knowledge focusing on whether or not one can know Rome exists even if one has never been there. The focus on Rome reflects the extent to which this discussion repeats one that is central to Augustine's *On the Trinity* over the existence of Alexandria.[107] Given this learned reference, the story of Wilkin and Simkin seems at first to be completely out of place. More asks the Messenger:

Yf it so were that Wylken had layd a wager with Symken, that in a certayne way named bytwene them vsuall ynough for men and horse both there had gone of late an horse or two, and that he wolde so clerely proue it that it coulde not be the contrary. If Symken sayd and layd his wager to the contrary, and than they bothe sholde chese vs for Iudges, and we commynge all foure into the way, Wylken wolde shewe vs on the grounde . . . the prente of horse fete and of mennys fete also . . . nowe yf Wylken wold saye that he hadde wonne his wager, for lo here ye se the prente of the horse fete . . . If Symken after all thys wolde saye the wager were hys for it is not proued that any horse hadde gone there, for it myghte be that they were geld-yngys or marys, here were we fallen in a great questyon of the lawe, whyther the gray mare may be a better horse or not, or whyther he haue a wyse face or not that loketh as lyke a foole as an ewe loketh lyke a shepe.[108]

The story of Wilkin and Simkin continues in a similar vein, with the latter insisting that the existence of horse prints in the snow does not prove that a horse has walked down the way. Simkin argues, for example, that "these men whiche wente here had horse shone in theyr handes made fast vpon longe steles, and alway as they wente pricked them downe hard in the grounde."[109] In the end More and the Messenger have to leave Wilkin and Simkin disputing, since there is clearly no way to resolve the wager in either's favor, despite the fact that Wilkin has clearly won.

At one level the point of this story is relatively straightforward, that unless the grounds of a debate are mutually agreed upon in advance, it is extremely difficult to arrive at a result that everyone accepts as legitimate. All the time that Simkin refuses to accept the facts or prints on the ground, and finds ways of explaining them away, the wager will remain open. At the same time More is also making a point about Simkin's lack of good faith, since Simkin is clearly provided with sufficient evidence to accept the presence of men and horses on the path and simply refuses to do so. The far more profound point that More is making is that the kind of legalistic, hair-splitting logic that Simkin uses to defend the undefendable is inappropriate for genuine religious debate, which has to be based on a sense of mutual respect and faithfulness.[110] The example that Simkin provides of human inventiveness and the ability to argue that black is white reflects More's skepticism concerning the value of debating with heretics as opposed to the kind of doubters represented by the Messenger.

In the *Dialogue concerning Heresies* More represents one of the great flaws of heresy as being its desire to live in a world without doubt, its infantile, but also inhuman and antihumanist, rejection of the reality of hesitation and uncertainty in favor of the false illusions of heretical certainty. At times More depicts the targets of his attacks, and in particular Tyndale and Luther, as religious versions of Hythloday, arrogant, foolish, extremist men seeking to place their fantasies above the lived reality of human life. He depicts their desire for certainty, for a fully reformed world consistent with Scripture, as a mirror image of the Utopian world of transparent reason that Hythloday so admired. This is not to suggest that in the *Dialogue concerning Heresies* More adopts a latitudinarian attitude toward doubt. He points out to the Messenger that "in a matter of fayth . . . it is damnable to dwell in doute."[111] More's argument is rather that it is only in the collective reason of the church that one can find an answer to doubt, since relying entirely on Scripture will inevitably produce a sterile situation in which contestants use scriptural citations as counters in a battle of biblical interpretation that cannot be resolved on its own terms.[112]

The need for a point of stability that transcends the individual is a constant theme in the *Dialogue concerning Heresies*. More recounts at length the attempts of the secular lords investigating Hunne's death to discover the source of the rumor that Hunne was murdered.[113] The lords work their way through a number of witnesses, all of whom end up acknowledging that they have no firsthand knowledge of the case, until the investigators reach a witness who refers them to a woman, an "Egypcyan" who, "if a thynge hadde ben stolen," could tell "who hadde it."[114] The Messenger comments at the end of this account that "here was a grete post well thwyted to a puddynge prycke."[115] This section of the *Dialogue concerning Heresies* is not intended to give a serious account of the events surrounding the investigation into Hunne's death, but rather to demonstrate the more general point that large rumors can often result from nothing, that what appear to be great posts are often nothing more than cocktail sticks.[116] More repeats the same point later in the *Dialogue* when he comments, "And a tale that fleeth thorowe many mouthes, catcheth many newe fethers, whyche whan they be pulled away agayne, leve hym as pylled as a cote and somtyme as bare as a byrds ars."[117] More's point in this fictional debate is not to argue that one should aspire toward a model of textual purity in which the only texts accepted as truthful are bare and featherless, but to demonstrate that all texts are feathered, all are passed from mouth to mouth, and it is this that makes them authoritative, since it is precisely the communal nature of the reason embodied in texts that prevents them from being solipsistic. It is only when texts are read within a community that they make sense or have a purpose.[118]

More consistently seeks to demonstrate to the Messenger that the choice is not between accepting the corruptions and failures of the world and embracing an absolute, reformed world of pure scriptural truth, but between the relative certainty of collective human reason—embodied most importantly in the church in relation to religion, but more generally in the textual community that is human society—and the fruitless maze of heretical fantasies. In book 2 the Messenger and More discuss in detail the status of miracles and relics, in particular the problem of counterfeiting. As Peter Marshall suggests, More defends the truth of miracles on the basis of "the common consent of Christ's Church, the testimony of credible men, and a universal belief among all nations."[119] In the course of this discussion More tells the story of the discovery in Barking Abbey of a small wooden cross and some handkerchiefs:

> As my selfe sawe at the abbay of Barkynge besydes London to my remembraunce about .xxx. yeres past in the setting an olde ymage in a newe tabernacle, the backe of the ymage beynge all paynted ouer and of longe tyme layde with beten golde happenyd to crase in one place, and out there fell a praty lyttle dore, at which fell out also many reliques that had lyen vnknowen in that ymage god wote howe longe.[120]

More recounts that while no one was sure how long the relics had been hidden, some people "geesyd that .iiii. or .v. C. yere ago, that ymage was hyden whan the abbey was burned by infydels, and those reliques hyden therin."[121] Having established in some detail the possible authenticity of these relics, More's argument takes a rather surprising turn when he comments:

> as for pygges bones for holy reliques . . . all be it that yf it happened, yet it nothing hurted the soules of them that mysse take it, no more than yf we worshyp an hoste in the masse which percase the neglygence or malyce of some lewde preste hathe left vnconsecrate.[122]

More's acknowledgment in this passage of the possibility of forged relics seems an unnecessary concession, given the detail and care with which he has just discussed the discovery of what clearly seem to have been genuine relics at Barking Abbey. In this exchange, however, More is making two linked points. One is that it is possible, even reasonable, that genuine relics can still be found. Certainly he does not state that the cross and handkerchiefs found at Barking were genuine, but he does create a plausible case for their authenticity. The second point is that even when one is dealing with relics and miracles, the absolute choice put by people like Tyndale between truth and falsehood is inappropriate. During an earlier discussion of miracles in the *Dialogue concerning Heresies*, the Messenger asks More if he is bound to trust a person who has seen a miracle. More's response encapsulates one of the central arguments of the work:

> Whyther ye were bounden quod I or no, we shall se further after. But now why sholde ye not of reason trust them, yf the men be credible, and ernestly report it, and peraduenture on theyr othes depose it, hauyng no cause to fayne it, nor likely to lye and be forsworne for nought?[123]

This is a crucial question for More. Why should the Messenger decide not to trust people who say that they have witnessed miracles? Is this lack of trust reasonable? Can meaning exist in a world without faith?[124]

More makes a very similar point in his "Letter to Martin Dorp," which he wrote in 1515 to defend Erasmus from Dorp's attacks. As well as issuing a number of specific replies to Dorp's criticism of Erasmus's work, More also questions Dorp's basic motives. In particular, he denies that the kind of certainty that Dorp deploys to criticize Erasmus can exist, pointing out that even Augustine considered the book of Revelation impenetrable.[125] More then argues,

> For just as the meaning of many of the things that the prophets foretold about Christ escaped everyone else until all was made plain by Christ's life, passion and resurrection, even so I think that the powers of mortals are not equal to settling the question of whether there may lie still hidden in scripture mysterious truths about either the Last Judgement or other things we cannot even imagine, mysterious truths none has discerned before now or will ever discern before they are unfolded in actual events at a date and a time foreseen only by God in his inscrutable providence.[126]

More concludes this discussion of biblical interpretation by comparing false complexity with practical labor, commenting that while dialectic logic of the kind favored by Dorp is difficult, "so, too, vaulting and tying one's body in knots in the way certain acrobats and mountebanks do are more difficult feats than to walk, and it is easier to chew bread than to grind up potsherds with your teeth, but I think no one would be willing to trade these normal and commonplace functions for such vain displays."[127] The "Letter to Martin Dorp" defends Erasmus's work, and in particular his *Praise of Folly*, not simply from the detailed accusations that Dorp makes against it, but more generally against the kind of absolutist reasoning that Dorp employs. It is not that More did not believe that Scripture was truthful or that he believed that the truths it contained were not absolute. But he did think that as a matter of humility and decorum one should accept one's own, and humanity's general, inability to fully and totally understand God's word.[128]

The *Dialogue concerning Heresies* is a lesson in devotional reading. It concludes with a prayer that God will send heretics the grace to cease and that the author and his fellow Christians "may by the very fayth of Crystes catholyke chyrche so walke with charyte in the way of good warkes in this wretched worlde" that they "maye be parteners of the heuenly blysse, which the blood of goddes owne sonne hath bought [them] vnto."[129] Walking is a constant metaphor in More's work. It reflects his commitment to a practical, affective devotion in which reading is a form of devotional practice; walking the text is a way of following in Christ's footsteps. Book 1 of the *Dialogue concerning Heresies* also ends with an image that collapses reading with tale telling:

> By my trothe quod he I haue another tale to tell you that all thys gere graunted, tournyth vs yet in to as moche uncertayntye as we were in before.
>
> Ye quod I than haue we well walked after the balade, The further I go the more behynde. I pray you what thynge is that? For that longe I to here yet ere we go.
>
> Nay quod he it were better ye dyne fyrste. My lady wyll I were be angry with me, that I kepe you so long therfro.[130]

Walking after the ballad refers to the title, "The Further I Go, the More Behind," but it also suggests a collapse of the learned humanist dialogue of More's work into the commonsense world of ballads. Indeed one senses that all the debate that has filled up book 1 of the *Dialogue concerning Heresies* simply brings it back to the proverbial wisdom expressed in the proverb, "One business begettyth and bringeth forth another," with which More opened the work.

It is this sense of proverbial, practical wisdom that ultimately forms the bedrock of More's opposition not only to heresy but also to forms of absolutist knowledge, religious and secular. As Eamon Duffy has recently argued, "More's handling of criticisms of traditional religion in the *Dialogue* is . . . self-consciously pragmatic and moderating, puncturing rhetorical posturing, challenging sweeping generalizations."[131] In book 1 of the *Dialogue concerning Heresies* the Messenger doubts that God would really help a housewife to find her keys. In the process he articulates an elitist, learned disdain for the reality of lived human life. Implicit in the Messenger's mocking of the idea that God would do something so prosaic is a reforming desire for a greater separation of the spiritual and the profane, and an emphasis on the former over the latter. For the Messenger it is not proper to imagine God in a domestic, practical setting. More's response is humane and deeply revealing: "God hathe I wene so moche wit of hymselfe, that he nedeth not our advyce to enforme hym what

thyng were suffycyent occasyon to worke his wonders for."[132] This acknowledgment of the mysterious workings of God is not for More an
admission of failure. It is rather an acceptance of human limitations that
is at once proportionate and the basis for a good life. More rejects the
attitude of the Messenger toward the possibility of God helping a housewife to find her keys not because he thinks that God does make a habit
of helping people find lost household goods, but because his faith does
not require him to disbelieve it.[133] Indeed More sees the Messenger's dis-
missal of a God who might find a person's lost keys as expressing an arrogant desire to define God's place in the world. It also suggests for More a
dismissive, ultimately un-Christian, attitude to the concerns and needs
of the vast majority of people for whom the idea of a God who inter-
venes in their daily lives makes complete sense.

Telling the Church Tale

Richard Whitford's *The Pype or Tonne of the Lyfe of Perfection* (1532) shares
the polemical agenda of the *Dialogue concerning Heresies* but is ultimately a
very different text. Whitford describes the proper Christian life as like a
pipe or tub, with the rules of good living holding in the truth. Whitford
writes:

> Note well now the example or similitude. For as in the said pipe:
> when the small wickers be broken or loosed: all the residue doth
> follow fail and decay, unto the destruction of the wine. So in like
> manner when the holy ceremonies of religion be neglected, forgot-
> ten, lost, put away, broken, despised, little or nought set by. . . . Reli-
> gion is gone and the life of perfection clean destroyed and lost. The
> decay of religion in this present tyme of our age (pity to say) is evi-
> dent. And surely the great cause and occasion therof is the contempt
> and negligence of the wickers, the small ceremonies.[134]

Although Whitford's main target in this work is monks who fail to keep
their vows, he explicitly extends the scope of his treatise to include all
Christians. The ethos behind this work, which the metaphor of the pipe

or tub perfectly illustrates, is absolutist in its claims to order and containment. The only two options that Whitford entertains are complete wholeness on the one hand and gradual decay and collapse on the other. *The Pype or Tonne of the Lyfe of Perfection* repeats in a slightly different key the pessimistic metaphor at the heart of the prologue to *The Reeve's Tale*. Its bounded, contained absolutism reminds one of the rule-bound world of Utopus and Isope. It is miles away from the acceptance of incompleteness, of human frailty as the basis of Christian life, that flows through the *Dialogue concerning Heresies*.

More's religious thought, and in particular its collapse of walking and reading, leaves open the possibility of religious hesitation, failure, and struggle, albeit in the context of a nonnegotiable acceptance of the church's status as the location of truthful Christian thought. Above all his religious thought reflects a confidence in the ability of stories, fictions, proverbs, and parables to create a space for religious praxis that for him was the church.[135] The *Dialogue concerning Heresies* constructs the true church as a community of tale tellers united in telling a tale that is faith. It is in this process of fabulation that the church exists, and this is why, for More, the tale never should or could end.[136]

Chapter 3

HERESY

Thomas More's career during the 1520s increasingly involved him in the English church's struggle against Luther's teachings and, more generally, the campaign against heresy. In 1521 he helped to edit Henry VIII's *Defence of the Seven Sacraments*, and in 1523 he produced his *Responsio Ad Lutherum*, a detailed assault on Luther's teaching, particularly with regard to the authority of the church. With his appointment as chancellor of the duchy of Lancaster, in 1525, More's role in the campaign against heresy became more active, and he was responsible for a number of raids on German merchants in London as he searched for heretical books. In 1528 Bishop Tunstal, in John Guy's words, "commissioned More to take command of a crash programme of anti-Lutheran propaganda."[1] The first fruits of this campaign were the *Dialogue concerning Heresies* and *The Supplication of Souls*, both first published in 1529.

More always publicly supported the English church's campaign against heresy. His polemical works are replete with comments that express support for heretics being burned alive. More was prepared to mock men like Thomas Bilney—fellow Christians executed by the Tudor authorities for holding beliefs that at the time the established church regarded as heretical. Many, but by no means all, of More's contemporaries shared this attitude. The views of men like John Foxe and William Allen seem a long way from More's celebration of the death of the "devil's stinking martyrs." Foxe and Allen argued that, in a religious context, heresies and treasons should be attacked, not heretics and traitors. For both men the move from heresy to heretic or treason to traitor was so fraught, the boundaries so unclear and porous, as to be dangerous to draw with judicial certainty.[2] Despite his fiery rhetoric, however, More shared Foxe's and Allen's concerns. His antiheretical works are lessons in the dangers of heresy addressed to a number of specific audiences. The most obvious targets for More's polemical works were those who were already attracted to heretical beliefs and practices.

Part of the reason for the violent and often repellent imagery that More uses in his antiheretical writing is to warn potential heretics of the dangers they face. At the same time the extremity of his language and, in particular, the gothic horror of his representations of heresy are designed to protect a relatively large gray zone between orthodoxy and heresy. By making heresy so aberrant, so extreme, More was seeking to defend an area of heterogeneous beliefs and practices that the ultraorthodox regarded with at least suspicion if not downright hostility. More's antiheretical works attempt to protect a space for religious thought and practice between the twin competing absolutes of heresy and ultraorthodoxy. This gives the works their anti- or pre-Reformation feel. More's antiheretical works warn readers not to close down too quickly the space of lay and clerical devotionalism by mistaking popular piety, doubt, or even superstition for heresy. They also contain a series of object lessons in the difficulty of finding or discovering heresy. More's antiheretical writings were clearly designed to support the church's role in pursuing heretics, but they also suggested that real heresy, as opposed to credulity, superstition, anticlericalism, and ignorance, was hard to find, and that the judicial process was at least as likely to produce nonsense and confusion as justice if it ventured too far into the world of popular Christian beliefs and practices.

By none of this do I intend to deny that More supported the persecution of heretics. Nonetheless, as a layman he could not, and did not, take the lead in the examination of suspected heretics. He participated in a number of interrogations, but it was the church's business, not that of the lay authorities, to examine heretics. More was at times responsible for the campaign against heretical books, and he published numerous works attacking what he regarded as heresy, but this hardly makes him the bloodthirsty persecutor that he has been painted as in some recent studies.[3]

More's reputation as an obsessive heresy hunter is partly based on the almost universal view of scholars that his polemical writing reflects some kind of aesthetic and moral fall. In particular, some historians and literary critics have stressed what they see as More's change, and decline, from the witty humanist of *Utopia* to the fanatical reactionary of *The Confutation of Tyndale's Answer*. Alistair Fox's assessment of More's polemical works exemplifies this view: "It is distressing to observe the emotional depths to which More's experience in religious and political controversy sank him. That experience forced changes in his personality that threatened to destroy much of what was most attractive and admirable in him. Equally, it exposed chinks in his intellectual armour that in all the million words of the controversies he refused to acknowledge."[4] Fox views More's controversial works as aberrations. Other scholars, with perhaps Richard Marius in the lead, have instead argued that More the humanist and More the heresy hunter are one and same.[5] For these historians and literary critics the real More is the one revealed in *The Confutation*. The problem with much of this scholarship, however, is that it relies on a naïve, subjective response to More's polemical writings, which are textually complex works. This view also indicates a particular failure within contemporary scholarship: while it praises More the elitist wit, it regards More the committed Christian who wrote to defend his fellow Christians from, as he saw it, the dangers of heresy as an embarrassing problem that needs to be explained away. More's polemical work engages very directly with heresy as a religious, polemical, and ideological concept, and we must understand in this context his often shocking and gleeful support for the execution of men like Bilney. By examining three of More's lesser-known works, *The Supplication of Souls*, *The Confutation*, and *The Apology*, it is possible to understand how More positioned his understanding of heresy within and against a tradition of English antiheretical writing represented in such works as Thomas Hoccleve's *The Remonstrance against Oldcastle*, John Lydgate's *A Defence of Holy Church*, and Nicholas Love's *The Mirror of the Blessed Life of Jesus Christ*. More's antiheretical works are a defense of the place of reason in religion, a rejection of the desire for a purified, godly commonwealth, and a plea for the role of fiction within Christian culture.

Texts like *The Supplication of Souls* (1529) articulate a sense of the religious efficacy of writing in the vernacular that is similar to that expressed in such late fourteenth-century works as *Piers Plowman*. In Passus XVIII of the C Text of *Piers Plowman*, Liberum Arbitrium, "free will," instructs the narrator on charity and church. As part of his teaching, Liberum Arbitrium compares true wisdom with that of "lettered men."

> Me may now likene lettred men to a Loscheborw other worse
> And to a badde peny with a gode printe:
> Of moche mone the metal is nauthe
> And yut is the printe puyr trewe and parfitliche ygraue.[6]

Liberum Arbitrium argues that lettered men who appear to be good Christians but are in practice sinners are like forged pennies. The outer surface words may be good, but their soul or metal is corrupt and sinful. Liberum Arbitrium then relates this image directly to the performance of priests who fail to maintain in themselves the truth of the mark of the cross that is stamped on every Christian at baptism.

> Thus ar ye luyther ylikned to Lossheborwes sterlynges
> That fayre byfore folk prechen and techen
> And worcheth nat as ye fyndeth ywryte and wisseth the peple.[7]

In this passage Langland is repeating a motif that recurs throughout *Piers Plowman*: comparing the truth of Christ's teaching with the false teaching of "lettered" men. The potential scope of this passage is significant. The sinful "lettered" men are like forged coins because the corruption of their souls—the metal upon which Christ writes during baptism— undermines their shiny surface, the value of the image they are marked with. Their corruption is twofold, since not only are they false in themselves but also as coins they circulate within the body of the commonwealth.

The metaphor of the true and false coins relates directly to Langland's poetic endeavor, since he is implying that *Piers Plowman* is a true coin, whose allegorical surface and true meaning are one. Its readerly circulation within the commonwealth provided a potentially universal and communal alternative to the corrupting effects of exchanges based on "Lossheborwes sterlynges." Nicholas Watson comments: "Fundamentally organised around its sense of itself as speaking for, as well as to, Christian society, *Piers Plowman* . . . [argues] that Christ's humanity, the 'lewd' Christians associated with it, and the vernacular poem which represents both come *closer* to the truth than Latin learning."[8] *Piers Plowman*, and other late fourteenth-century works, differ from similar works written during the fifteenth century in their preparedness to deploy images like that of the false and true coins that do not simply advocate the efficacy of vernacular religious writing but also argue that it can be inherently more truthful than the writing of "lettered" men. The image of the false and true coins implicitly celebrates the vernacular, as represented by Langland's own poem, as a vehicle for religious truths. More's use of explicitly fictional writing to defend what he regarded as orthodoxy represents a return to the potential radicalism of works like *Piers Plowman*. *The Supplication of Souls* presents itself to the reader as a good coin, a work that unites good surface teaching in the words of its fictional narrators, souls in purgatory, with a kernel of material Christian truth. It is More's heretics, men like Simon Fish, who take the place of Langland's "lettered" men, producing witty, clever texts whose meaning is "nauthe."

More's Fiction of Heresy

More wrote *The Supplication of Souls* as a direct response to Simon Fish's *Supplication of Beggars* (1529). Fish was a London lawyer who was later accused of heresy and died in 1531. *The Supplication of Beggars* is a vicious attack on the English clergy, and in particular on the doctrine of purgatory. A. G. Dickens points out that the attacks on the clergy contained in Fish's work are cruel, unjust, and exaggerated.[9] *The Supplication of Beggars* has in the past been given a substantial place in accounts of the English Reformation partly as a result of the story that Anne Boleyn presented a copy to Henry VIII. This is, however, highly unlikely. What does make Fish's work significant is that it is a compendium of early

Tudor anticlerical polemics and smears that Fish brought together within a simple but effective literary trope. The timing of the work's publication also helps explain its importance. It happened to be published just when its crude anticlericalism was about to become an aspect of official government policy. More responded to Fish's work by creating a text that claimed to be a supplication written by the souls in purgatory. In the process More pitted souls against beggars in order to defend the idea of purgatory against Fish's attacks.

The Supplication opens with a cry for help from those in purgatory:

> In most pytuouse wyse continually calleth and cryeth voppon your deuout cherite and moste tender pyte, for helpe cumfort and relyefe, your late acquayntaunce, kindred, spouses, companions, play felowes, and frendes, and now your humble and vnacquaynted and halfe forgoten supplyauntys, pore prysoners of god, the sely sowlys of purgatory.[10]

In this opening passage More plunges the reader into his fiction. To read *The Supplication* is to acknowledge this address by the souls in purgatory. Or rather this would be the case were it not for the way in which More subtly points to the fictionality of his work. This is not to suggest that More doubted the reality of purgatory, but rather that he saw its truth as based on an act of faith. *The Supplication* works as a defense of purgatory only if the reader accepts the truthfulness of More's fiction; and to do so one needs to trust in More. *The Supplication* opens by placing a wager on the faithfulness of its readers, their preparedness to hear the text as spoken by 'silly' souls in purgatory while knowing that what they are reading is an imaginary tale, a fable. In *The Supplication* More uses fiction to defend purgatory and in the process distinguishes its fictional truth from Fish's factual lies.

The Supplication mounts a sustained attack upon Fish's polemical strategies. For example, *The Supplication of Beggars* contains a detailed account of the clergy's wealth: Fish states that the Friars alone get each year £43,333 6s. 8d. More mocks this figure ruthlessly by asking the reader, at the end of an incomprehensible discussion of Fish's figures, "Who can now dowte of thys rekenynge when yt cometh so rounde, that of so great a somme he leueth not out the odde noble?"[11] More's comment is intended to be ironic, but it also makes a serious point, since readers have waded through a detailed discussion of Fish's figures before More pulls the rug out from under them. More's polemic in this section aims at two targets: most immediately, the hollowness of the content of Fish's argument; more profoundly, the hollowness of its form. By directly engaging with the detail of the figures in *The Supplication of Beggars*, More's silly souls have produced a text that reflects and repeats the hollowness of the language of heresy. As the numbers pile up, *The Supplication* offers its readers two incompatible options, either that the figures are all totally accurate or that what they are reading is nonsense. More's multiplication of numbers effectively empties them of meaning, since the more numbers there are, the greater the likelihood that the final reckoning will be out by at least the "odde noble." Fish seeks to validate his argument through a display of numerical accuracy, through the "facts"; More mocks Fish's math and at the same time critiques the idea that any number of numbers or facts can provide the certainty Fish desires.

More then suggests that Fish must have heard "these wyse reckenyngis at some congregacyon of beggers."[12] The subtext of this comment is that *The Supplication of Beggars* should really have the title the "Supplication of Heretics." More argues that behind Fish's claim to be concerned with the financial health of the realm is an avaricious desire for personal gain. More's souls tell the reader:

> We dare boldly say whoso gyueth this deuyce as now doth this beggars proctour, we wolde gyue you counsell to loke well what wyll folow. For he shall not fayle as we sayd before yf thys byll of his were sped, to fynde you sone after in a new supplicacyon new balde reasons ynow that shuld please the peoples ears, wherewyth he wold labour to haue lordys landis and all honest mennys goodys to be pulled from them by force and dystrybuted among beggars.[13]

This passage incites a fantasy of social rebellion that is at one level risible, but also refers to the Peasants' Revolt of 1381. More is again playing with his readers' expectations, daring them to believe that such an outcome is possible. If they reject this possibility, then they are committed to reading with a degree of impartial reason that More thinks will render Fish's arguments redundant. On the other hand, if they are prepared to accept the truth of the claims made in *The Supplication of Beggars*, then why not the possibility of a bill to strip lay people of their property?

More backs up the suggestion that Fish's next line of attack will be on property by arguing that "surely as the fyre euer krepeth forward and laboureth to turn all into fyre: so wyll such bold beggars as thys is, neuer cease to solycyte and procure all that they can, the spoyle and robbery of all that ought haue, and to make all beggars as they be them self."[14] *The Supplication* depicts heresy as a protean force burning up the religious and social order. There is, however, something potentially disturbing about this passage given its use of fire as a metaphor for the creeping, remorseless progress of heresy. After all, the narrators of *The Supplication* are speaking from the purifying fire of purgatory. They tell the reader, No matter where we are, "we cary our payne with vs: and lyke as the body that hath an hote feuer as feruently burneth yf he ryde on horsbake as yf he lay lapped in hys bedde: so cary we styll about no lesse hete with vs, then yf we lay bounden here."[15] This pain, the silly souls tell the reader, is greatly augmented by the "evil angels" when they show the souls what happened after their deaths:

What a sorow hath it ben to some of vs when the deuils hath in dispyghtfull mokkage, caste in oure teeth our old loue borne to our money, and then shewed vs our executours as bysyly ryfling and ransakyng our housys, as though they were men of warr that had taken a town by force. . . . Our euyll aungellys haue grynned and lawghed and shewed vs our late wyuys so sone waxen wanton, and forgetyng vs theyre old husbandys that haue loued theym so tenderly and lefte theym so ryche, sytte and lawgh and make mery and more to sumtyme, with theyr new woars, whyle our keepers in dyspyte kepe vs there in payne to stande styll, and loke on.[16]

This is a doubly voyeuristic moment. The silly souls are forced to witness their homes being ransacked and their wives making merry, while the reader is invited to imagine the entire disturbing scene. This passage links the reader's world with that of the silly souls. The fires of purga-

tory are, More suggests, far less painful to the silly souls than is the neglect of their friends and family. James Simpson argues: "The voice of
More's text [*The Supplication*] is communal; its rhetoric deploys imaginative fiction; the dead address themselves to all Christians; the solution it
proposes is one of bottom-up, communal self-help."[17] *The Supplication*
forces the reader, like the silly souls but in reverse, to feel the continuing
pull of the social bond between the living and the dead. The fire of
heresy burns up society in a chaos of spoliation and robbery. The silly
souls, however, remind the reader that even after death familial, social,
and communal ties remain valid; they still have life.[18]

More's *Supplication* demands that its reader engage imaginatively with
the text. At the same time More is clear about the limits of the imagination. For example, the silly souls, after discussing the fate of a soul that
dies in deadly sin, tell the reader of *The Supplication*:

> For as mych as ye can neuer conceyue a very ryght imagynacyon of
> these thyngs whych ye neuer felt, nor yt ys not possyble to fynde
> you eny example in the world very lyke unto the paynys sely sowlys
> fele when they be departed thense: we shall therefore put you in re-
> membraunce of one kynde of payne, whych though yt be nothynge
> lyke for the quantytye of the mater, yet may yt somwhat be resembled
> by reason of the fassyon and maner.[19]

The pain that is like that felt by the souls of those who die in deadly sin
is a seasickness that, More argues, possibly with tongue in cheek, affects
people on the basis of their moral state. Those who are clean from evil
humors do not suffer any sickness, while others, after having purged
themselves through vomiting, no longer feel any displeasure. However,
there are other people

> whose body ys so incurably corrupted, that they shall walter and
> tolter, and wryng theyre handys, and gnash the teeth, and theyr eyen
> water, theyr hed ake, theyr body frete, theyr stomake wamble, and
> all theyr body shyuer for pain, and yet shall neuer vomete at all: or yf
> they vomyte, yet shall they vomyte styll and neuer fynd ease thereof.
> Lo thus fareth yt as a small thyng may be resembled to a great by

the soulys deceaced and departed the world: that such as be clene
and vnspotted can in the fyre feele no dysease at all, and on the tother
syde such as come thense so dedely poysoned with synne, that theyr
spottys bene indelyble and theyre fylthynes vnpurgeable, lye fretynge
and fryenge in the fyre for euer.[20]

Despite More's earlier claim, this passage does invoke very clearly the
pains of those who die in deadly sin, and also positions the reader in the
boat alongside the passengers as they suffer different degrees of sickness.

More implicitly compares the precision of his imagery here during
the course of *The Supplication* with Fish's lack of linguistic care. More
asks his readers:

If this man [Fish] were here matched wyth some suche as he ys hym
selfe, that hathe the eloquence that he hath, that could fynde out
suche comely figures of retoryque as he fyndeth, sette fourthe and
furnyshed wyth suche vehement wordes as he thundreth oute lyke
thunder blastys, that hathe no lesse maters in hys mouth than the
great brode botomlesse ocean see full of euyls, the wekenes and
dulnes of the kynges swerde, the translacyon of the kynges kyng-
dome, the ruyne of the kynges crowne, with greate exclamacyons,
Oh greuouse and paynfull exaccyons, oh case most horrible, oh
greuouse shyp wracke of the comen welth: what myght one that had
suche lyke eloquence saye here to hym?[21]

The obvious answer to the question that opens this section is that what
such a person would say to Fish is what is written in *The Supplication*. This
passage argues that Fish's eloquence is empty, that it comprises nothing
more substantial than bottomless exclamations and windy words. More
explicitly tells his reader that while he will work through all of the points
made in *The Supplication of Beggars*, before doing this he will give an over-
view of Fish's work:

Trewthe yt ys that many thyngs wherewith he florysheth hys mater
to make them seme gay to the reders at a sodayn shew, we leue out
for the while, because we wold ere we come therto, that ye shuld
furst haue the matter self in short set forthe before your eyen. And

than shalle we persue hys prouys, and in such wyse consider euery thynge aparte, that we nothyng dout but who so shall rede hys worshypfull wrytyng after, shall sone parceyue therin, floryshyng wythout frute, suttelte wythout substaunce, rethoryk wythout reason, bolde babelynge wythout learning, and wylynes wythout wyt. And fynally for the foundacyon and ground of all hys prouys: ye shall fynde in hys boke not half so many leuys as lyes, but also as many lyes as lynes.[22]

This is a complex passage. It opens by suggesting that Fish has loaded *The Supplication of Beggars* with rhetorical flourishes that, when read, suddenly or quickly will provide the reader with pleasure. The following lines, however, appear to be an example of precisely the kind of rhetorical language that More accuses Fish of using. The reader is not meant to think seriously about the phrase, "rethoryk wythout reason," so much as to enjoy its structure, the way it exists within a list of equally witty couplings. In *The Supplication* More does not simply rebut Fish's arguments; he also deploys textual play and rhetorical wit in the defense of orthodoxy in a way that seeks to defend the orthodox use of fables. At the same time he is teaching his readers—ironically at times, as in this passage of his own work—to beware of texts that use rhetorical ploys to please the reader. *The Supplication* is a fable that warns against texts that seem gay but are ultimately empty and full of lies, ones that, like Langland's bad pennies, hide sin under an attractive, gaudy surface.

At the end of *The Supplication* More's souls tell the reader:

Yt were impossible to make eny mortall man lyuyng perceyue what maner payn and in what maner wyse we bodylesse soulys do suffer and sustayne; or to make eny man vppon erth perfytely to conceyue in hys ymagynacyon and fantasy, what maner of substaunce we be. . . . And therfore except we shuld of our painfull state tell you nothynge at all . . . we must of necessyte vse you such wordys as your selfe vnderstande, and vse you the symylytudes of such thynges as your self ys in vre with.[23]

More then argues that to reject the reality of purgatory is to take the "story tolde by god for a very fantastyke fable."[24] At the end of *The Supplication*

More's souls announce that their words are a similitude and that purgatory can exist only in a person's imagination or fantasy. This does not render purgatory itself a fiction; rather it insists that the fictional is an essential part of Christian teaching. God's story is a very fantastic fable, More's souls talk in parables, and this is what makes them truthful.[25] In *The Supplication* More creates a situation in which to engage imaginatively with the text is to place oneself within the ship of orthodoxy; to hear More's fictional souls talking and to accept the truth of what they are saying is to take a leap of readerly faith and to believe in the work of fiction.

The Supplication was written with a specific aim: to refute *The Supplication of Beggars*. At the same time More's text, and indeed his whole approach to heresy, needs to be seen within the context of a tradition of fifteenth-century English antiheretical writing. Heresy was not new in early sixteenth-century England, nor was antiheretical writing. More's polemical works draw on the existing tradition of antiheretical polemics but also construct the struggle against heresy in subtly different ways. In particular, writers like John Lydgate and Thomas Hoccleve sought to defend orthodoxy by stressing the need to close down the space for lay religious reflection and by demanding that religious cripples be purged from the realm. More's antiheretical writings are as violently antiheretical as those of any of his fifteenth-century precursors, but they also seek to keep a space open for religious reflection. More's polemical works defend orthodoxy not by assertion or by placing it beyond dispute. Instead he attempts to teach his readers how to read heresy, to recognize its tricks and wiles, and to spot its baneful effects—the subversion and spoliation of all textual, religious, and social boundaries.

Heresy in Fifteenth-Century England

Heresy is written into the Christian church's most basic documents and structures. R. N. Swanson has argued that the development and fixing of orthodoxy during period from 1100 to 1500 created heresy as "a necessary concomitant."[26] Rowan Williams, in his work on Arius, the archetype for all future heretics, points out that the struggle over Arianism "generated the first credal statement to claim universal, unconditional assent."[27] Heresy produces orthodoxy; and in particular it produces definitions of orthodox belief and practice as texts, confessions, and catechisms, which in turn become the source of further heresies and orthodoxies.

When the fifteenth-century English church faced the need to combat Lollardy, it drew upon existing polemical representations of heresy, and in particular the idea of heresy as a disease. The trope of heresy as disease was endlessly productive and could be extended across a range of registers. R. I. Moore has argued that "the comparison of heresy with disease provided not simply a casual or convenient metaphor, but a comprehensive and systematic model."[28] More gives a perfect illustration of the productivity of the trope of heresy as a form of disease in his *A Letter against Frith* (1553):

> For as the canker corrupeth the body ferther and ferther, and turneth the hole partes into the same dedely syckenesse: so do these heretykes crepe forth among good symple souls, and vnder a vayn hope of some hygh secrete learnynge, whych other men abrode eyther wyllyngly dyd kepe from them, or ellys coulde not teche theym, they dayly with such abomynable bokes corrupte and destroye in corners very many before those wrytyngs comme vnto lyght, tyll at the last the smoke of that secrete fyre begynneth to reke oute at some corner, and sometyme the whole fyre so flameth oute at onys, that it burneth vp whole townes, and wasteth whole countrees, ere euer it can be maystred, and yet neuer after so well and clerely quenched, but that it lyeth lurkynge styll in some olde roten tymber under cellers and celynges, and yf it be not wel wayted on and marked, wyll not fayle at lengthe to fall on an open fyre agayne, as it hath fared in late yeres at mo places then one.[29]

Ian Forest has argued that in fifteenth-century England, "The picture of heresy built up from propaganda is not one of an easily distinguished, discrete sect, but rather one of a diffuse crime whose seeds lay dormant in every human being."[30] More's image of heresy as a disease and as fire reflects the perspicacity of Forest's comment. For More heresy was always lurking, hiding in the secret corners of the realm, waiting to spring out.

This could be illustrated, More argued, by studying English history. In particular, in his polemical works More repeatedly refers to the events of Sir John Oldcastle's revolt as a historical lesson of the dangers of heresy. In the *Supplication* he writes:

> In the first yere of the king's mooste noble progenytour Henry the fyfte those heresyes secretely crepyng on styll among the people: a great nomber of theym had first couertely conspyred and after openly gathred and assembled theym selfe, purposyng by open warre and batyle to destroy the king and hys noble and subuerte the realme. Whose traytorouse malyce that good catholyque king preuented, wythstode, overthrew and punyshed: by many of them taken in the feld, and after for theyr traytorous heresyes both hanged and burned.[31]

This passage moves from heresies that creep forth to heretics who conspire together and revolt. More is giving readers a history lesson by showing them a moment when the hidden danger of heresy suddenly emerged and threatened the realm. There is something particularly literary about this structure, since it stages the transformation of the metaphor of heresy as a disease into real, nonmetaphoric heretics. The productivity of the trope of heresy as a disease, both literary and polemical, in More's work reflects the extent to which the current debate over the effect of Archbishop Arundel's *Constitutions* (1407) on religious, and indeed more generally all literary, writing is misplaced.[32]

Arundel intended the *Constitutions*, passed in 1407, to counter the spread of heretical and Lollard ideas. They contain a number of detailed rules and regulations designed to control the circulation of religious discourse, teaching, preaching, and writing. Their potential scope can be seen in their seventh clause, which deals with the publication of books and treatises.

> Item, for that a new way doth more frequently leade astray, then an old way: we wyl and commaund, that no booke or treatise made by Iohn Wycklyffe, or other whō soeuer, about that time or sithēs, or hereafter to be made: be from hencefoorth read in scholes, halles, hospitals, or other places whatsoeuer, within our prouince of Canterbury aforesayd, except the same be fyrst examined by the vniuersity of Oxford or Cambrige, or at the least by .xij. persons, whom

the sayd vniuersities or one of them shal appoynt to be chosen at our discretion, or the laudable discretion of our predecessors: and the same beyng examined as aforesayd, to be expressely approued and allowed by vs or our successours, and in the name and autoritye of the vniuersity, to be deliuered vnto the Stacioners to be copied out, and the same to be sold at a reasonable price, the originall thereof alwayes after, to remayne in some chest of the Vniuersity. But if anye man shall reade anye such kynde of boke in scholes or otherwyse, as aforesaid: he shal be punished as a sower of schisme, and a fauourer of heresy, as the qualitie of the fault shall require.[33]

The initial target of this clause is works written by John Wycliffe; however, it then goes on to extend its scope to all "new" works. This was not, however, simply a question of censorship.[34] As Miri Rubin has recently suggested, the fifteenth-century church took very seriously its pastoral duty to "diminish the occasion for error." In the process, however, it also increasingly limited the subjects it regarded as appropriate for "discussion, preaching and catechism."[35] As part of this agenda, the *Constitutions* sought to contain and control religious writing, while at the same time creating new possibilities in terms of the production of works replete with fantasies of the dangers of heresy, images of total obedience, and descriptions of heretical language. In particular, the sense in which the *Constitutions*, in Steven Justice's words, "regarded all religious discourse as dangerous" gave a new edge to religious works.[36] The need to assert a version of orthodoxy as at once absolute and aware of the dangers of heresy created a set of tropes and metaphors that fed directly into More's polemical works.

Thomas Hoccleve's *The Remonstrance against Oldcastle*, John Lydgate's *A Defence of Holy Church*, and Nicholas Love's *The Mirror of the Blessed Life of Jesus Christ* are exemplary fifteenth-century works of religious orthodoxy. This is not, however, because of the way they represent orthodox positions, but because of the ways in which each advances specific responses to the dangers of heresy while sharing with the others a common, overarching desire to close down or restrict the space of religious debate. Hoccleve's poem, probably written in 1415, encapsulates the orthodox and Lancastrian response to the perceived threat posed by

Lollardy. *The Remonstrance* deploys a class- or estates-based argument to depict heresy as endangering the social order. Hoccleve argues that Lollardy's linguistic proteanness makes it dangerous but also attractive. His solution, aimed directly at the Lollard knight Sir John Oldcastle, but with a much wider scope, is to argue that each estate should stick to its appropriate reading matter, which for Oldcastle, as a knight, means tales of romance and chivalry.

Lydgate probably wrote *A Defence of Holy Church* in the period immediately before Oldcastle's revolt, and it reflects Lydgate's anxiety concerning the attitude of the new king, Henry V, to the church. In this poem Lydgate offers Henry a role in the struggle against heresy that can be seen as a kind of reversal of Hoccleve's criticism of Oldcastle's failure to stay within his proper knightly and chivalric milieu. Andrew Cole comments: "In 'Defence of the Holy Church' . . . [Lydgate] celebrates Prince Henry's orthodoxy as an especially manly form of anti-heresy warfare to protect the church, which is gendered as feminine (as tradition called for) but depicted as something of a romance heroine."[37] *Holy Church* invites Henry to play the role of a romance hero purging his land of spiritual cripples and protecting the church.

The Mirror of the Blessed Life of Jesus Christ is a more substantial work than either *Holy Church* or *The Remonstrance*. Love's work has a claim to be one of the most popular religious works produced during the fifteenth century.[38] Michael G. Sargent comments, "Nicholas Love's *Mirror of the Blessed Life of Jesus Christ* c. 1410 was the most important literary version of the life of Christ in English before modern times."[39] It is based on the Latin, pseudo-Bonaventura *Meditationes vitae Christi*. In *The Mirror*, Love deploys a version of the kind of literary space imagined by Chaucer in, for example, *The Nun's Priest's Tale*. He does so, however, for very different reasons. Chaucer uses the literary in order to create a space for critical political thought. Love aims to offer the laity a fictional text that allows them to engage with Christ's life as a safe alternative to Scripture itself. Indeed, as Michelle Karnes has recently pointed out, in *The Mirror*, Love works against the tradition of meditations on the life of Christ in order to prevent any move beyond the fictional physical world it presents to the reader. Karnes comments, "Love limits the spiritual aims of Gospel meditations by making them resolutely earthbound."[40] Whereas

Piers Plowman consistently offered the reader material or concrete images as the basis for religious reflection, in *The Mirror* Love seeks to close down any move beyond the imagined physical details of Christ's life. *Holy Church*, *The Remonstrance*, and *The Mirror* are exemplary antiheretical works. Although each deploys different strategies and tropes, collectively they aim to curtail the space of religious reflection as the only sure way to defeat heresy and protect orthodoxy.

Hoccleve's *The Remonstrance* accuses Sir John Oldcastle of having made a "fair permutacion" from the "light of trouthe vnto dirk false-nesse."[41] The poem follows Oldcastle's journey as he plunges into the heretical world of Lollardy. Hoccleve argues that Oldcastle's followers are all lower-class ruffians, "heirs of darkness"; that while Oldcastle thinks that he sees clearly, in fact he looks amiss; that Lollards live lives dedicated to bodily lusts; and that heresy has quenched Oldcastle's manhood. Hoccleve's poem does, however, have a positive side, which is to attempt Oldcastle's reform. For example, Hoccleve writes:

> Bewar, Oldcastel, and for Crystes sake
> Clymbe no more in holy writ so hie.
> Rede the storie of Lancelot de Lake
> Or Vegece, *Of the aart of chiualrie*,
> The *Seege of Troie* or *Thebes*. Thee applie
> To thyng that may to th'ordre of knight longe.
> To thy correccioun now haaste and hie,
> For thow haast been out of ioynt al to longe.[42]

The Remonstrance consistently articulates a concern over the regulation and control of knowledge, which this list suggests in how it reflects that what Oldcastle should be reading is works of chivalry and romance, works and genres that belong to the order of knighthood. Andrew Cole has suggested that in *The Remonstrance* Hoccleve "magnifies the issue of lordly identity," which, "when properly recognised and performed," offers Oldcastle a way to escape the clutches of heresy.[43] Hoccleve's model of reading is profoundly conservative. His ideal knight is concerned only with matters of chivalry; he does not seek to climb in holy writ, but instead reads tales of romance and chivalry. Nicholas Watson has argued that fourteenth-century writers like Richard Rolle and William Langland imagined in their work a "vernacular intellectual community"; in Hoccleve's *Remonstrance* the scope of this community has been sharply reduced and refocused.[44] *The Remonstrance* implicitly creates an image of a textual community, or rather communities, locked within islands of class-specific genres and forms. Hoccleve suggests that for Oldcastle to read religious works is to cross a textual boundary that will immediately put into question his social standing. It will also, partly because of the rigorous nature of Lancastrian orthodoxy exemplified by Archbishop Arundel and his clerical supporters, expose Oldcastle to the dangers of heresy, real and potential.

The Remonstrance represents the relationship of the laity — and in particular men like Oldcastle — toward the church as one of complete dependence. There is no room in this relationship, as far as Hoccleve is concerned, for doubt or even reason. The laity must simply obey, unswervingly and uncritically. Hoccleve argues that even if a priest is viciously governed, or his teaching amiss, the laity must obey him and leave his punishment to God:

> Lete holy churche medle of the doctryne
> Of Crystes lawes and of his byleeue
> And lete alle othir folk therto enclyne
> And of our feith noon argumentes meeue
> For if we mighte our feith by reson preeue,
> We sholde no meryt of our feith haue.
> But nowadays a bailiff or reeue
> Or man of craft wole in it dote or raue.[45]

As part of his attack on heresy, Hoccleve insists that faith is beyond reason, and that the one aspect of faith that above all should not be subjected to reason is the requirement to obey the church. Hoccleve's model of proper obedience to the church is almost parodic in its vehemence, and in the process, it acknowledges its own contested status, since demands for complete obedience are in tension with the need constantly to make them. There is also a tension between the valorization of chivalry in *The Remonstrance* as a social identity and the poem's insistence on the paramount need for all members of the commonwealth to accept fully and totally the church's authority. One is left wondering at the end of *The Remonstrance* if anyone, and certainly if any serious Christian, could be sufficiently obedient, and therefore orthodox, to satisfy Hoccleve.

Hoccleve gives the need for absolute obedience to the church a specific social twist when he relates it to status of inheritance:

> If land to thee be falle of heritage
> Which that thy fadir heeld in reste and pees
> With title iust and treewe in al his age,
> And his fadir before him brygelees
> I am ful seur who so wolde it thee reue
> Thow woldest thee deffende and putte in prees.
> They right thow woldst nat, thy thankes, leue.
>
> Right so, where our goode fadres olde
> Possessid were and hadden the seisyne
> Peisible of Crystes feith, it sit vs to enclyne
> Therto, let vs no ferthere ymagyne
> But as that they dide, occupie our right
> And in oure hertes fully determyne
> Our title good, and keepe it with our might.[46]

Paul Strohm has argued that there is something profoundly ironic about Hoccleve's use of inheritance in this passage to set up a standard of obedience to the church that, in terms of the inviolability of inheritance, "the Lancastrian kings will not and cannot meet."[47] Hoccleve's suggestion that obedience to the church is comparable to inheritance also, however, performs a two-way naturalization. The narrator of *The Remonstrance* deploys the acceptance of the legal legitimacy of inheritance as a metaphor for the proper attitude toward the church. Hoccleve uses the term "imagine" simultaneously to acknowledge the possibility of a space outside the logic of his argument and to close it down. Only if it were possible to "further imagine" would *The Remonstrance* need to rule out this possibility. What Hoccleve is explicitly denying here is lay reflection on the church; implicitly the poem acknowledges not only that it is possible to imagine further than the church would allow, but that scope for imagination includes the status of inheritance itself. The implication of Hoccleve's argument is that "excessive" lay imagination in the religious field will lead to social radicalism.

The Remonstrance consistently attacks heresy as irrational, disordered, and disordering. It criticizes Oldcastle's "sly coloured argumentes" and tells him that his "fals conceites renne aboute loos."[48] The problem for Hoccleve is that he wants the reader to use reason to understand the madness of heresy, to imagine its corruption, while at the same he argues that reason has no place in the church and that imagination needs to be under complete control in order to ensure its orthodoxy. *The Remonstrance* ultimately poses a question fraught with danger for Hoccleve and the church—can the imaginary be fully and totally orthodox?

The question at the heart of John Lydgate's *A Defence of Holy Church* (c. 1413) is also a potentially dangerous one—is the king orthodox? *Holy Church* opens by lauding Henry V as a "most worthi prince" and protector of Christ's spouse, the church.[49] The tone of Lydgate's poem, however, changes in stanzas 2 and 3, which focus on the church's perilous state:

> That was oppressid almost in thy rewme
> Even at the poynt of hir destruccioun
> Amyd hit citee of Ierusalem,
> Al bysett with enmyes envyroun:
> Tamade a new transmygracioun
> When she, allas, disconsolat, allone
> Ne kneuh to whome for to make hir moone.

> But on the floodis of fell Babiloun,
> Al solitair and trist in compleynyng,
> Sat with hir children aboute hir euerichoun,
> Almost fordrownyd with teerys in weepyng.[50]

Holy Church moves with incredible speed from an image of Henry as the natural protector of the church to an image of the church weeping and abandoned. The reader is left to ask why, if Henry is so worthy, the church does not know "to whome for to make hir moone?" *Holy Church* uses biblical imagery and history to create a text that simultaneously seeks to instruct Henry on his role as the church's protector and to imagine what would happen if he rejected this role. At the edge of Lydgate's poem lurks the figure of a tyrannical Lollard Henry.

Lydgate asks Henry to consider the example of David:

> And thynke how Dauid ageyn Iebusse
> When that he fouht, in *Regum* as I fynde,
> How he made voide from Syon his Citee
> Unweldly, crokid, bothe lame and blynde:
> By which example always have in mynde
> To void echon, and for to do the same
> Out of thi siht, that in the faith be lame.
>
> For who is blynde or haltith in the faith
> For any doctryne or these sectys newe
> And Cristes techyng therfor aside laith,
> Unto thy corone may he nat be trewe.
> He may dissymule with a feynyd hewe —
> But take good heede, what way that he faire,
> Thy swerde of knyhthoode, that no swich ne spaire,
>
> And Cristes cause always fyrst preferre
> And althirnexte thi knyhtly state preserue,
> And lat this lawe be thi loode-sterre
> Than grace shall thyn honour ay conserue.[51]

In these lines Lydgate reverses the argument of Hoccleve's *Remonstrance* by telling Henry that in the pursuit of a pure church, one from which cripples have been purged, social class should not be a concern. Lydgate places godliness and purity above honor or charity. He tells Henry that it is a king's duty to purify the church by driving out the spiritually blind and halt. In the process *Holy Church* implicitly suggests that in fifteenth-century England the church is dependent to a worrying degree on the secular arm for protection and indeed reform.

One would perhaps expect that, having instructed Henry on his role as monarch, *Holy Church* would end on an optimistic note, with Lydgate assuming Henry will act upon his advice. This is, however, emphatically not the case. Lydgate explicitly warns Henry against taking the church's wealth and tells him:

> Remember also, for swich transgressioun
> What was the fyne of kyng Antiochus
> That proudely tooke by extorsioun
> The sacred iewels from Goddis hooly hous:
> Was he nat slawe, this tiraunt treacherous,
> With smale worms hym fretyng manyfolde
> Whan that he fill down from his chare of golde?
>
> What myht availe his pompe or all his pride,
> Or all the gliteryng of his riche chare
> In which that he so proudely did ride?
> The surquedye also of Baltasar
> Was it nat abatid or that he was war,
> In Babiloun, with a soden fall,
> Whan that the honde wrote upon the wall?[52]

Holy Church maps the transformation of Jerusalem (London) into Babylon and invokes the possible transformation of Henry from worthy prince to treacherous tyrant. The concluding image explicitly warns, indeed threatens, Henry, and its public nature suggests that Lydgate wanted to keep open for his readers the possibility that *Holy Church* was part of a tradition of prophetic warnings to erring kings written on walls.[53]

   In *Holy Church* heresy generates the possibility of godly royal action, purging the realm of spiritual cripples, and simultaneously conjures up a terrifying image of Constantinian Christianity gone wrong — the image of a king acting against the interests of the church. *The Remonstrance* invites the reader to see the irrationality of heresy, to imagine its dangers, and denies reason or imagination any role in the determination of orthodoxy. Nicholas Love's *The Mirror of the Blessed Life of Jesus Christ* (c. 1410) is a more substantial work than either *The Remonstrance* or *Holy Church*. It reflects, however, similar tensions in its engagement with heresy. Love's work is a translation of the *Meditationes vitae Christi*. It recounts the story of Christ's life mapped onto a week, starting with God's decision to send his son to save humanity. The work concludes with a short treatise on the sacrament of the altar.

The Mirror consistently and explicitly rejects Scripture as the source for lay religious instruction in favor of inciting its readers to use their imaginations. In the chapter dealing with Christ's life between his early childhood and the start of his ministry, Love writes: "From the time that our lord Jesus was gone home to Nazareth with his parents, when he was 12 . . . we find naught expressed in scripture authentic, what he did or how he lived and that seemeth full wonderful. What shall we than suppose of him in all this time, whether he was in so much idle: that he did naught or wrought thing that were worthy to be written or spoken of?"[54] Love solves this problem by acknowledging that while the details of Jesus's life cannot be fully affirmed by "holy writ or doctors approved," they can be devoutly imagined.[55] Later Love asks the reader to imagine the domestic life of Jesus and his family: "For as we now imagine they had no great house but a little, in the whiche they had . . . three small chambers, there specially to pray and sleep. And so now we think how our lord Jesus Christ, every night after prayer goes to his bed lowly and meekly."[56] In this passage Love is encouraging his readers to imagine, and identify with, a domestic Jesus. At the same time, however, as part of *The Mirror*'s polemical agenda, Love clearly directs the scope of the reader's imagination. As one reads this passage, imagining the domestic arrangement depicted and Jesus's behavior, one imagines a prototype religious community, a domestic monastery within the house of the holy family.

The idea that the lay reader's imagination can supplement, perhaps even supersede, the scriptural record is fundamental to *The Mirror*. Love's work consistently suggests that its concentration on the physical details of Christ's life is entirely appropriate and commendable for a lay readership. Love introduces his account of the Last Supper by stating that while in other places he has abridged the story, here he will lengthen the process. This is because the Last Supper and the institution of the sacrament of the altar both play central roles in Love's polemical agenda. He asks readers to imagine themselves as spiritual partners in the Last Supper and suggests, "Sit a little longer at this worthy lord's board . . . and take . . . heed inwardly to our ghostly food and comfort."[57] Love links the idea that through devout imagining one can take part in the Last Supper to his argument that reason has no place in true devotion. The account *The Mirror* gives of the Last Supper creates an axiomatic relationship between reason and belief. It equates people who attempt to understand or apply reason to the sacrament with heretics. Love comments that Lollards scorn miracles associated with the sacrament because they "taste not the sweetness of his precious sacrament nor [feel] the gracious working therof."[58] This comment both includes and excludes, suggesting to readers that if their imagination has been devout enough they will have tasted the sweetness of the sacrament, but if not, they are in danger of being labeled a Lollard. For Love the only proper, and perhaps safe, way in which a Christian can participate in the sacrament of the altar is on the basis of an imaginative, affective engagement with its miraculous nature.

Even though *The Mirror* is largely a translation of a continental Franciscan work, Love has shaped its polemical and rhetorical strategies to address the very specific needs of the fifteenth-century English church.[59] Indeed, one can read Love's text as a metaphor for the church's struggle with Lollardy. The vast majority of the work is a moving devotional narrative of Christ's life, while the institutional context and form of the work are motivated by a fear of heresy. H. Leith Spenser has commented on the way that Love's work emphasizes "the more purely narrative aspects of Christ's human existence, rather than the substance of his ministry."[60] Love deploys devout imagination as the narrative motivation for his work, creating a text that formally collapses purposeful reading into its polemical agenda. Richard Beadle argues, "It is clear that Love conceived of devout imagination as essentially a self-validating rhetorical strategy, because if exercised correctly it brought simple souls closer to God, and stimulated the desire for heaven."[61] In Love's work devout imagination irons out the narrative of the New Testament and solves all spiritual problems by suggesting that the reader can address them by engaging imaginatively and devoutly with the narrative of Christ's life. In these terms the operation of devout imagination in *The Mirror* strangely, but interestingly, parallels Pecock's "doom of reason"; both seem able to resolve almost any religious debate or controversy. At the same time, Love's devout imagination seems to require precisely the kind of individuality that writers like Hoccleve associated with heresy. *The Mirror* avoids this danger in a tautological move by equating orthodoxy with successfully learning to use the devout imagination that the work seeks to generate and sustain.

The short treatise on the sacrament of the altar that concludes *The Mirror* opens with a discussion of proper and false dread of God. Love suggests there are two ways people fear God, as servants fear their masters and as children fear their father. He then discusses those people who do not dread God, not surprisingly singling out heretics for particular criticism: "Another manner people that lack the dread of god be heretics, the which in default of buxom dread to god and holy church presumptuously believing upon their own bodily wits, and kindly reason, believe not that holy doctours have taught and holy church determined of this blessed sacrament."[62] To have a proper devout dread of God, to avoid the danger of heresy, means imagining one's relationship with God within a domestic and affective context. Proper dread, proper devout imagination, takes place for Love beyond reason and generates an affective experience of Christ's *life* as a story and not of his *ministry* as a collection of parables, miracles, and sermons.

In these terms *The Mirror* reproduces the rhetorical strategy of anti-Lollard sermons, which, as Katherine C. Little has argued, consistently deploy exemplary narratives in order to "reinforce the authority of the established Church over the laity and not the authority of scripture over the laity."[63] Christ as he appears in *The Mirror* is already a part of the church. Love's work collapses reader and Christ into a narrative that in effect becomes the church—to be outside the narrative, to fail to have a sufficiently devout imagination, is to occupy the position Love creates for Lollards in his work, at the level of form and content. He excludes Lollardy from the textual community of the church at a polemical level and in terms of form, because when he refers to Lollards he does so in such a way as to distinguish these references from the rest of the narrative. In particular, while readers need imaginatively to engage with the narrative, they need not so engage the polemical attacks on the Lollards. Indeed, at one level this is the last thing that Love wants his readers to do.[64] To be part of *The Mirror*'s textual community is to be interpolated into its narrative and in the process to accept Love's clerical authority, sustained and protected by Archbishop Arundel's imprimatur, as the source and basis for the work.

Hoccleve's *The Remonstrance*, Lydgate's *Holy Church*, and Love's *The Mirror* exemplify the productivity of heresy as a literary trope and the ways in which fifteenth-century anti-Lollard writing articulates cultural fears and anxieties that transcend their immediate polemical agendas. In these texts the struggle against heresy escapes its bounds. *The Remonstrance*, *Holy Church*, and *The Mirror* reflect the dangers of writing against heresy. In emphasizing the separation of reason from faith, the need for spiritual cripples to be purged, and the need for the boundaries of religious imagination to be firmly policed, they create an image of an anxious, embattled, aggressive religious orthodoxy. Hoccleve, Lydgate, and Love paint a picture of a true church bound together through bonds of absolute obedience, of a totally devout unity, outside of which lie only doubt, reason, and heresy. This image of the church is miles away from the consensual, copious, communal church that More consistently sought to imagine and defend in his antiheretical works. Hoccleve, Lydgate, Love, and More all agreed that orthodoxy had to be defended from the dangers of heresy, and they used similar antiheretical tropes in their works. More in his antiheretical works, however, as he did in *Utopia*, resists the false choice between two absolutes, heresy and orthodoxy, insisting instead that whereas heresy ultimately destroys the space for religious reflection, orthodoxy has to keep it open: the orthodox position for More is one that has room for doubt, reason, skepticism, and faith.

Battling Heresy in 1533

More resigned the chancellorship on May 16, 1532, the day after the Submission of the Clergy. The following year he published the *Apology*, *The Debellation of Salem and Bizance*, and the second part of *The Confutation of Tyndale's Answer*. More produced all these works in a context very different from that in which he wrote the *Dialogue concerning Heresies* or the *Supplication*. In 1532/33 More was writing from outside Henry's government and court. Despite this changed context, however, More's work of this period remains committed to basic ethos of the *Supplication*, and indeed *Utopia*. The *Confutation* attempted to intervene publicly in the debate over the regime's religious policies and to provide Henry with the good counsel that More clearly felt the king currently lacked.

The Confutation refutes directly and in detail of a number of polemical writings by William Tyndale. More produced it during a period when the future course of Henry's religious policies was unclear. In September 1532 Henry made Anne Boleyn marquis of Pembroke, not marchioness, as she held that title in her own right. Later that autumn Henry and Anne traveled to France to meet Francis I. At this meeting the two kings agreed that, as part of the negotiations for the marriage between Francis's second son and the pope's niece, Catherine de Medici, the pope would be invited to a meeting with Francis that Henry could attend as a prelude to reconciliation between Henry and the pope. It seemed, therefore, in the winter of 1532/33 that Henry might finally achieve a solution to his marital difficulties that had papal approval. Time, however, was not on Henry's side. Anne was pregnant. This became known sometime in late December 1532, and Henry secretly married her on January 25, 1533. From this moment Henry knew he had to take the law into his own hands in order to ensure that the long-awaited heir would be legitimate.

The first part of *The Confutation* was published in 1532, the second in early 1533, during the period when it was unclear how far Henry would need to go to marry Anne. In *The Confutation* More was seeking to guide Henry, and more generally his readers, in a situation that was fluid and, as far as More was concerned, filled with dangers but also possibilities. There was the danger that Henry would listen to those counseling a total split with the papacy, but there was also the equally worrying possibility, from More's perspective, that the regime's religious policies would stabilize around the situation as it existed in 1532/33, with a submissive and defeated clergy confronted by a domineering and vengeful king.[65]

The activity of men like Sir Thomas Elyot reflects the political and religious uncertainty of 1532/33. Elyot spent these years, Greg Walker has suggested, desperately trying to influence royal policy by writing and publishing works like *Pasquil the Plain*, with its barely hidden critique of the political praxis of Henry's government.[66] Also during this period of uncertainty John Heywood produced his *Play of the Weather*, probably writing it during Christmas 1532 and seeing it printed in the spring of 1533.[67] At one level this play is a simple religious parable. It opens with the entrance of Jupiter, who tells the audience:

Before our presens in our hye parliament,
Both goddess and goddeses of all degrees
Hath late assembled by comen assent
For the redress of certayne enormytees.[68]

The enormities that Jupiter's parliament addressed, by the simple Henrician solution of asking Jupiter to take charge, resulted from a dispute between Saturn, Phebus, Eolus, and Phebe over the weather. Having restored order in the heavens, Jupiter descends to earth to resolve similar disputes between his earthly subjects. He listens to a range of people asking for the weather that will suit them best: the Gentleman desires weather that will allow him to hunt, the Wind Miller asks for wind, the Water Miller for rain, the Gentlewoman requests mild weather to protect her complexion, while the Laundress wants sun and wind. The play ends with Jupiter telling all the supplicants, and the audience, that if he were to agree to any of their specific requests, it would lead to disaster, so he will leave the weather as it is:

Wherefore we wyll the hole world attende,
Eche sort, on suche weather as for them doth fall.
Now one, now other, as lyketh us to send.
Who hath yt, ply yt, and suer we shall
So gyde the wether in course to you all,
That eche with other ye shall hole remanye
In pleasure and plentyfull welth, certayne.[69]

The Play of the Weather uses weather as a metaphor for religion. It advances a very specific polemical strategy, since its argument is that Jupiter/ Henry should have control of the weather/religion, and certainly not leave it to parliament or the pope. Heywood, however, is also suggesting that Henry should not do anything with his power over the weather/ religion, since it is impossible to make everyone happy. *The Play of the Weather* is a simple but powerful argument for the religious status quo of 1532/33. *The Confutation* is More's attempt to prevent the emergence of the kind of solution proposed by Heywood. It rejects the idea, implicit in *The Play of the Weather*, that there is nothing really to choose between

heresy and orthodoxy, by stressing the specific dangers of heretical beliefs and practices. It also seeks to advise Henry that it is not too late to
reverse the dangerous, potentially tyrannical, course that More thinks the
king is taking. Finally, *The Confutation* is a reformist text, since, despite the
violence of some of its polemics, it seeks to protect a space for religious reflection free from the emerging confessional norms of sixteenth-
century religion.[70]

In the preface to *The Confutation* More discusses the case of Thomas
Hytton, and in particular how he came to be arrested for heresy:

> Now happed it so that after he [Hytton] had visyted here his holy
> congregacyons, in dyuers corners and luskes lanes, and comforted
> them in the lorde to stande styffe wyth the deuyll in theyr errours
> and heresyes, as he was goynge bakke agayne at graues ende, god
> consyderyng the great labour that he had taken all redy, and de-
> termynyng to brynge his bysynes to his well deserued ende, gaue
> hym sodaynly such a fauour and so great a grace in the vysage, that
> euery man that behelde hym toke hym for a thefe. For where as
> there had ben certayne lynen clothes pylfred away that were hang-
> ynge on an hedge, and syr Thomas Hytton was walkyng not far of
> suspycyously in the medytacyon of hys heresyes: the people dowt-
> ynge that the beggarly knaue had stolen the clowtes, fell in questyon
> wyth hym and serched hym, and so fownde they certayne letters se-
> cretely conuayed in hys cote, wryten from euangelycall brethren here,
> vnto the euangelycall heretykes beyonde the see. And vppon these
> letters founden, he was wyth his letters brought before the moste
> reuerende father in god the archebyshoppe of Canterbury . . . and
> after for hys abominable heresyes delyuered to the secular handes
> and burned.[71]

In this passage More conjures up an ironic, comic, but also threatening
world of heresy in which "holy" congregations of heretics meet in divers
corners and idle lanes. At the center of this world is Hytton, whom More
constructs as an alien, disturbing presence, someone who, while the rest
of the community is going about its normal business, spends time meditating upon his heresies. The contradictory, dual nature of this portrayal

of heresy makes it quite disturbing. More depicts Hytton simultaneously as a real person engaged in purposeful, albeit secret, heretical activity, and as an allegorical figure for heresy lurking in the borders and corners of human society. In this passage heresy is at the edge of the social order and at the same time at its center; a parodic nonsense and a terrifying danger; marked by God as inherently evil and simultaneously capable of hiding itself within normal human society.

More opens the first book of *The Confutation* by comparing a bountiful grain ("corne") harvest with what he claims is the current bumper crop of heretical books:

> Our lorde sende vs nowe some yeres as plentuouse of good corne, as we haue hadde some yeres of late plentuouse of euyll bokes. For they haue grown so faste and sprongen vppe so thykke, full of pestylent errours and pernycious heresyes, that they haue enfected and kylled I fere me mo sely symple soules, then the famyne of the dere yeres haue destroyed bodyes. And surely no lytle cause there is to drede, that the great haboundaunce and plentye of the tone, is no lytle cause and occasyon of the great derth and scarcite of the tother.[72]

As I have already suggested, heresy has long and often been compared to a disease in Western Christianity. More's use of this metaphor is interesting because he develops it so that it becomes in his work a central organizing principle. More concludes the opening passage of *The Confutation* by referring to 2 Kings 4:40, with the phrase "there is death in the pot"—the pot of heresy is filled with death. The phrase "there is death in the pot" collapses the discussion of the lethal effects of heresy into the ordinary and the scriptural. This reference, however, at one level seems out of place, since in the biblical incident God's grace ultimately rendered the deadly substance fit to eat, so that "there was no harm in the pot." In this passage *The Confutation* is using a simple phrase to make the point that while heresy brings death, there is always the possibility of redemption. More's pot is a movable feast, an alchemical vessel transforming death into a life-enhancing biblical saw.

Later in *The Confutation* More uses the phrase "a tale of a tubbe."[73] The editors of the Yale Edition of *The Confutation* gloss this phrase as meaning a cock-and-bull story, and they are clearly correct.[74] Yet with these phrases, "there is death in the pot" and "a tale of a tubbe," More is deliberately constructing a proverbial discourse at key moments within his text to arrest interpretation and to defer readerly consumption of his work. The phrase "a tale of a tubbe" appears commonsensical until the reader pauses to consider its meaning. A tub cannot tell a tale, and even if it could, the tale a tub would tell would be monotonous in the extreme. The obvious metaphorical meaning of this phrase is "a tale generated in a tub"—a tale of a drunk. Another potential meaning, however, is "a tale told by a tub," as it is filled with and emptied of liquid. In these terms More's tub can be related to the stomach, and its tale to belching and farting. "A tale of a tub" therefore includes the idea of drunken non-sense and the meaningless sounds of the body. As such it embodies two key aspects of More's attack on heresy: that heresy is based on an intox-icated, individualizing appropriation of religious authority, and that it is nothing more than guttural, corporeal nonsense.

Of course, writers like William Tyndale made similar arguments in their works. *The Obedience of a Christian Man* depicts papistry as an evil nonsense based on corrupt human fantasies. It is, however, a mistake to ask whether More properly understood Tyndale's position, or indeed Tyndale More's, since to do so is to view their violent debate from a post-Reformation perspective. Richard Rex has recently pointed out that "Thomas More never encountered 'the Reformation'. . . . What More en-countered, as he saw things, were heretics, and if we are to understand More rather than merely pass judgement on him, we must ascertain how he saw things."[75] More did not regard people like Tyndale as members of a specific denomination or valid Christian tradition. For him they were simply heretics. Their arguments might be seductive, even at times correct at the level of fact or detail, but they could never be right or true. This partly explains the circularity of More's and Tyndale's exchanges. More glosses Tyndale in the *Dialogue concerning Heresies*, who replies with his own glosses in his *Answeare unto Sir Thomas More's Dialogue*, which More then re-sponds to with *The Confutation*; the words pile up, but the argument makes very little progress. As Brian Cummings has commented, only More's death, and Tyndale's a year later, "could interrupt the endless glossing."[76]

As an alternative to heresy's tubby tales, *The Confutation* offers its read-ers the certainty of meaning located in the community of the church. More acknowledges that his position cannot be fully supported by Scripture:

As I wote it well that god had good and greate causes why he caused
some thynges to be wryten: so had he causes as good why he lefte
some vnwryten. But neyther can Tyndale tell why he sholde wryte
all, nor I gyve the rekenynge why he lefte some vnwryten.[77]

In this passage More emphasizes the limits of Scripture and criticizes
what he sees as Tyndale's desire to reduce the scope of God's word to
the written text. For More meaning is constrained not in or through
text, even the text of Scripture, but by its place within the community.
This is true not only of religious meaning, which is constrained by the
community of the church, lay and spiritual, but more generally of all
meaning.

   The Confutation consistently returns to the issue of interpretation, and
in particular the relationship between faith, salvation, and the church.
More asserts throughout the work that "there is lyke surety and lyke certayne knowledge of the worde of god vnwryten, as there is of the worde
of god wryten, syth ye knowe neyther the tone not the tother to be the
worde of god, but by the tradycyon of the chyrche."[78] For More it is the
church, temporal and spiritual, that ensures the right interpretation of
Scripture, since without the church—the communal body of Christians
united in a single, faithful story—no one would know what was the
word of God. More clearly regards this argument as unanswerable and
consistently quotes Saint Augustine in support of it.

   This is not to suggest, however, that he is naïve about the difficulties
the church both has and has had in the past in discerning the truth of
Christ's teaching. Indeed at a number of points during *The Confutation*
More acknowledges that the history of the church is littered with moments of dispute and conflict:

God doth reuele hys trouthes not always in one maner, but sometyme he sheweth yt out at onys, as he wyll haue yt knowen and men
bounden forthwith to byleeue yt. . . . Sometyme he sheweth yt
leysourly, suffryng his flokke to comen and dispute theruppon, and
in theyr treatynge of the mater, suffreth them wyth good mynde
and scrypture and naturall wisedome, with inuocacyon of his spiritual helpe, to serche and seke for treuth, and to vary for the whyle in

theyr opynyons, tyll that he rewarde theyr vertuouse dylygence wyth ledyng them secretely in to the consent and concorde and bylyef of the trouth of his holy spirite . . . whyche maketh his flokke of one mynde in hys house, that is to wyt his chyrche.[79]

More's argument here is that while in the past Christians have sometimes differed in their opinions, and have sought the aid of God in various ways during the debates arising from these differences, God has always ultimately, albeit sometimes secretly, restored unity to his house. What is needed, More is arguing, is time and space for concord and consent to emerge. It is almost as though the length of *The Confutation* is itself designed to slow the reader down, to create a pause in the rush for judgment and allow the truth to emerge. In *Burning to Read: English Fundamentalism and Its Reformation Opponents*, James Simpson argues that "More is a textual pragmatist, for whom the sense of texts can be constructed only in the context of non-written, faithful (though credible) *préjugés*. Those pre-textual dispositions have an institutional source, in the Church."[80] More's reference to the history of disputes within the church is an important aspect of his pragmatism. What he violently opposed was what he saw as heresy's rush to judgment, its refusal to defer to the church as an institutional site for the playing out of religious disagreements. In the passage from *The Confutation* quoted above, however, he also implicitly critiqued equally hasty ultraorthodox positions that sought to close down the space of religion before the church, as a mystic and communal corporate body, had a chance to be fully guided by God.

This emphasis on deferment, on protecting the space of reflection, is an important aspect of *The Confutation*'s attempt to offer Henry religious advice. More takes the reader through a detailed discussion of the question of salvation, and in particular the doctrine of justification by faith. He first focuses on the story of David and Bathsheba, asking:

Dyd Dauid in all this whyle amonge all these euyll thoughtes, all these vngracyous wordes, all these abomynable dedes, neuer fall from the loue of the lawe of god, but was all thys whyle a slepe, and neuer consented to synne, nor dyd none of all these thinges wyllyngly? No sayeth Tyndale. I say no more but it is likely yes.[81]

More's lack of certainty in this passage is noteworthy, albeit clearly sarcastic. He is attacking a central paradox of Luther's teaching on salvation, that a believer can be at once righteous and a sinner. Euan Cameron suggests that Luther's teaching "overturned the very basis on which the medieval pastoral cycle of sin, confession, absolution rested. Both the theoretical and the pastoral theology of the late middle ages had assumed that the believer would *alternate* between sin and grace, passing from the former to the latter through the sacraments of penance and communion. By this medieval wisdom, a man was *sometimes* a sinner, *sometimes* righteous — but never both at the same time. For reformers, on the other hand, the oscillating cycle of sin and 'grace' was meaningless."[82] For More the idea that one could be at once a sinner and righteous was ridiculous. David's faith failed him: he was a sinner when he desired and took Bathsheba.

The reference to David may allude to Henry VIII, in which case More's lengthy discussion of David's spiritual state when he was besotted with Bathsheba has political and pastoral implications; Henry, like David, could still redeem himself and his kingship from lechery and tyranny, if he truly repented.[83] The reference to David also implicitly refers the reader, and from More's perspective hopefully Henry, to the Penitential Psalms, which were traditionally associated with the story of David and Bathsheba. Clare L. Costley has recently commented on the persistent use of woodcuts depicting David seeing Bathsheba in the pool to illustrate the Psalms in general during the sixteenth century: "Not only do . . . images of Bathsheba bathing tie the Penitential Psalms to a particular episode in David's life, they also associate sin specifically with sexual transgression."[84] More's reference to David and Bathsheba pointedly attempts to counsel Henry and reminds readers that sexual sin, provoked by voyeurism, led to David's downfall, personal and political. At the same time More perhaps offers David as an example to Henry as a person who in the depth of his sinning found redemption.

Having discussed David's case in detail, More turns to that of Peter and his denial of Christ. More's argues that in this moment of denial Peter's faith failed:

Lette vs deuyde that tyme of that state of hys from hys fyrste denyenge and forswerynge, vnto the very minute of hys dyenge, supposynge to continue styll and dye to in the same state, into fyue

egall parts . . . and then haue we fyue tymes of one fasshyon, to
which fyue tymes Tyndale yf it please hym maye gyue names to, and
call them A, B, C, D, E.

And after that Peters' fayth had fayled in the thre fyrste tymes, that
is to saye those that are named A B C partes of the hole tyme, wherof
A B C D E were all the partes lette vs put, that in the fourth parte
whyche we called D, Peter repented by helpe of goddes grace. . . .
Now I aske Tyndale whether the not faylynge of his fayth now in the
later partes of [Peter's] tyme, that is to wyt in D and E, doth now
make it trewe that hys fayth fayleth hym not before, whyle it fayled
hym in ded in the thre former tymes A B C the thre partes of hys hole
tyme A B C D E.[85]

More is being ironic in this passage by perfectly expressing precisely
the kind of oscillation between righteousness and sin that Protestants
rejected. The passage shows a kind of textual hysteria, since More's use of
the material letters A, B, C, D, and E creates a ludicrous textual image
of the implications of one understanding of the church's penitential
teaching at the beginning of the sixteenth century.[86] Once the soul's state
is reduced to abstract textual units, letters or numbers, then there is
clearly no limit to how often one can imagine it alternating between
the states of righteousness and sin. Why stop at A, B, C, D, and E? Why
not A1, A2, A3, and so on, or even not A1a, A1b? Indeed by the logic
of More's argument the smaller the units used, the more accurate they
should be. By his discussion of Peter's denial of Christ, More aims to
fix, in a very specific graphic form, the falseness of Tyndale's teaching.
It imagines a world in which the believer is caught endlessly oscillating
between A and B, C and D, E and F, and so on. Yet More, quite deliberately, omits faith from this discussion. The material letters, A, B, C, and
so on function in this passage in the same way as the monetary figures
do in More's discussion of Fish's heretical math. In both cases More is
making his argument on two levels. In terms of content he is mocking
the detail of Fish's and Tyndale's work. In terms of form he is attacking
the reductiveness of their language. In the process he is suggesting that to
approach religious questions like salvation or righteousness in a piece-
meal fashion is to produce a nonsensical world. This section of *The
Confutation* illustrates the futility of trying to understand God's promise

of salvation without a prior sense of Christian hope; to do so simply creates a sterile, arid world, a meaningless mass of letters, words, lines, and pages.

The Confutation, in its sheer size and messiness, can be seen as an image of More's church as a place for religious thought. For example, More criticizes Tyndale's claim that More included the papacy in the *Dialogue concerning Heresies* as part of his definition of the true church:

> I purposely forbare to put in the pope as parte of the dyffnycyon of the chyrche, as a thynge that neded not, syth yf he be the necessary hed, he is included in the name of the hole body. And whyther he be or not, yf it be brought in question, were a matter to be treated and disputed besyde.[87]

More here accepts that the position of the pope can be discussed and debated. What cannot, he believes, is the idea of the church as the visible body of all Christians. David Aers has pointed out that for Thomas Aquinas, "people become faithful followers of Christ not as abstract individuals but as members of a specific community where faith, ethics, Christology, and ecclesiology are bound together."[88] In *The Confutation* More seeks to protect this community by violently attacking those he regards as its enemies. He also, however, is reaching out to people like Heywood, and even Henry himself, in order to remind them of the dangers of heresy and the need to distinguish between truth and falsehood. *The Confutation* rejects Heywood's humane but flawed argument that it is better not to take sides and replaces it with an insistence that there is truth and falsehood and that with sufficient care and time they can be discerned. *The Confutation* is a plea, lengthy, in places violent and in others difficult to follow, for the debate to continue. It is a textual representation of the church in the here and now—complex, messy, and compromised, but the only one that actually exists. To keep reading *The Confutation* is to suspend the moment of decision, of confessionalization, and to remain a part of the body of Christian readers that for More was the church.

More published *The Apology* in the spring of 1533, largely as a critique of St. German's *Treatise concerning the Division between Spiritualities and Temporalitie* (1532). St. German was, like Simon Fish, a London lawyer.

But he was a far more dangerous opponent for More to cross swords with, since, unlike Fish, St. German was a religious conservative. His arguments were attractive to those in the Henrician regime seeking to establish royal jurisdiction over the English church. Scholars have typically viewed *The Apology* as More's polemical justification of his actions while he was Lord Chancellor. Its title, and perhaps the coincidence of its being published almost exactly a year after More resigned the chancellorship and a year before he was imprisoned in the Tower, have led scholars to read it as a relatively straightforward defense by More of his actions and those of the church. *The Apology*, however, is a self-consciously literary work. It consistently reflects on the difficulty of defending orthodoxy in a world of polarized religious identities and positions that More thought England was in danger of being divided by. [89]

The Apology opens with a typically witty denial of authorial skill: "So well stand I not (I thanke god) good reader in myne own conceyte, and thereby so myche in myne owne lyghte, but that I can somewhat with egall iudgement and euyn yie, byholde and consider both my selfe and myne owne."[90] The word "conceit" in this opening sentence has a dual meaning, at once "opinion" and also "witty game" or "trick." More's authorial "I" can see itself within its own conceit. The reader is at once plunged back into the world of self-reflecting textual mirrors that More conjured up in the opening of the *Dialogue concerning Heresies*. The first chapter of *The Apology* opens with a self-conscious discussion of its own status as a text. More claims that he has never doubted that readers will find many faults with his work:

> I was neuer so farre ouersene, as eyther to loke or hope that such fautes as in my writyng sholde by myne ouersyght escape me, coulde by the yein of all other men pass forthe vnspyed, but shortely sholde be both by good and well lerned perceyued, and among so many babbe bretherne as I wyst well wold be wroth wyth them, shold be both sought out and syfted to the vttermost flake of branne, and largely theruppon controlled and reproued.[91]

More imagines his own work being examined and reproved by two groups of readers, the bad brethren and the well learned. This passage imagines a form of textual analysis that is totalizing in its completeness, sifting the text down to the last flake of bran. Moreover, in 1533 the people most likely to be subjected to this kind of examination were not necessarily More's opponents. Indeed one of the central arguments of *The Apology* is that heretical works, but more particularly works like St. German's *Division* that hide their heresy under a range of polemical strategies, have not been sufficiently analyzed—they have not been examined to the uttermost flake of bran.

More very quickly, however, qualifies this incitement to examination:

> I nothing douted nor do, but that euery good chrysten reader wyll be so reasonable and indifferent, as to pardon in me the thyng that happeth in all other men, and that no suche man wyll ouer me be so sore an audytour, and ouer my bokes suche a sore controller, as to charge me with any great losse, by gatherynge together of many such thynges as are wyth very fewe men aughte regarded, and to loke for such exacte cyrcumspeccyon and sure syght to be used by me in my wrytynge, as except the prophetis of god, and Cryste and his apostles, hath neuer I wene be founden in any mannes elles byfore, that is to wit to be perfyte in euery poynte clene from all maner of fautes.[92]

The key phrase in this lengthy passage is "good Christian reader." More did not doubt that the bad brethren would be sore auditors of his work, but he was not writing for them. He wrote, rather, for those caught in the middle of the struggle over the future of the English church. More wrote to persuade, and one of his key arguments was that the language and hermeneutics of heresy differed fundamentally from those of its opponents. Heretics played the role of sore auditors of works like More's because for them language was at one level just a game, a hollow performance like Fish's rhetorical broad, bottomless Ohs. Heretical language for More was at once profoundly materialistic and empty: in examining the works of writers like More it oscillated between vague, general accusations and reductive point scoring.

More then discusses in the following chapters the accusation leveled at him by, among others, William Tyndale, that his works are too long and that, from the works he attacked, More picked out at his pleasure pieces particularly well suited to his argument. More comments:

Now on the other syde, as for Tyndale and Barns, I wote nere well whether I may call them longe or short.

For somtyme they be short in dede, bycause they wolde be darke, and haue theyr folyes passe and repasse all vnperceyued.

Some tyme they can vse such a compendyouse kynde of eloquence, that they conuay and couche vp together, with a wonderfull breuyte, four folyes and fiue lyes in lesse then as many lynes.[93]

More's representation of heresy in *The Apology*, and indeed throughout his work, develops and emphasizes aspects of fifteenth-century representations of heresy. Little separates heresy as described by Hoccleve in *The Remonstrance* from heresy as it appears on the pages on *The Apology* in terms of content. The works differ in that More emphasizes the linguistic aspects of heresy. For Hoccleve Oldcastle's loose conceits were a relatively minor part of his heresy; for More Tyndale's compendious empty eloquence is absolutely central. *The Apology* is a book about reading and writing. It is above all concerned with seeking to protect the boundaries of "Christ's Catholic Church" not in confessional terms but linguistic. More saw the church as a space for thought whose boundaries were spiritual, collective, and communal.[94] He perceived heresy as threatening this space by the particular way in which it wrote, spoke, and read.

The Apology is an extended attack on the language of innuendo, exaggeration, and conspiracy theories that More regarded as an important aspect of St. German's *Division* and more generally of all heretical speech. For example, More mocks mercilessly St. German's use of the phrase "some say": "And yet bysyde all the fawtes that he bryngeth in vnder *some saye* and *they say*, some that he selfe sayeth without any *some say*, be such as some say that he can neuer proue, and some they say be playne and open false."[95] More goes on to ask, who says? What is the truth of what they say? How many say it? All the time he is seeking to undermine the way St. German creates a sense of collective anonymous authorship for the complaints against the clergy that fill the *Division*. In these terms one is struck by the perspicacity of More's insistence on authorship, of his rejecting the easy legitimacy of "some say"—is not the Internet the ultimate "some say" world?[96]

In the *Dialogue concerning Heresies*, and in particular during his discussion of the case of Richard Hunne, More repeats in a different key the critique of the world of "some say" that he presented in *The Apology*. More stresses Hunne's heresy and argues that it was this, and the despair that it provoked, that led Hunne to take his own life. More's treatment of the Hunne affair has often provoked critical comment. Richard Marius wrote: "To distort the reported evidence in an effort to protect the Catholic Church would have seemed to a man of More's devout temperament a necessity. His willingness to twist the evidence is a sign of his fear rather than any essential immorality, for he thought that if heresy conquered and the Catholic Church fell, the rational shape possessed by both history and the moment would fall into chaos."[97] Marius is clearly right that there is something excessive about More's discussion of the Hunne case; however, whether or not it amounts to distortion is another matter. In particular, Marius does not really engage with the extent to which status of evidence is at the heart of More's account of Hunne, and in particular the meeting held by Henry VIII at Baynard's Castle to examine the case. More tells the story of the meeting's attempts to find the truth of the rumor that someone knew who had killed Hunne:

> Than was the man asked. Syr knowe you one that can tell who kylled Richard Hunne?
>
> Forsothe quod he and it lyke your lordship I sayd not that I knew one surely that coulde tell who hadde kylled hym, but I sayd in ded that I knowe one which I thought verily could tell who kylled hym.
>
> Well quod the lords at the laste yet with moche worke we come to somewhat. But whereby thynke you that he can tell?
>
> Naye forsothe my lorde quod he it is a woman, I wolde she were here with your lordshyppes nowe.
>
> Well quod my lorde woman or man all is one, she shall be hadde where so euer she be.
>
> By my faythe my lordes quod he and she were with you she wolde tell you wonders. For by god I haue wyst her to tell many maruaylous thynges ere nowe.
>
> Why quod the lordes what haue you herde her tolde?

Forsothe my lordes quod he yf a thynge had ben stolen, she wolde haue tolde who hadde it. And therefore I thynke she coulde as well tell who kylled Hunne as who stale an horse.

Surely sayd the lordes so thynge all we to I trowe. But howe coulde she tell it, by the deuyll?

Naye by my trouthe I trowe quod he, for I coulde neuer se her vse any worse way than lokynge in ones hande.

Therewith the lordes laughed and asked what is she?

Forsothe my lordes quod he an Egypcyan, and she was lodged here at Lambeth, but she is gone ouer see now. Howe be it I trowe she be not in her owne countree yet, for they say it is a grete way hense, and she wente ouer lytell more than a moneth ago.[98]

In this passage More suggests that trying to probe into the roots of the reasons for Hunne's death, for example who killed him, leads into a miasma of rumors, gossip, and popular superstition in which the only certainty is that Hunne was a heretic. More positions the reader of this passage alongside the Lords conducting the interrogation—their attempts to find certainty, to find the truth, are as hopeless as those of the reader. This is clearly an entirely deliberate strategy on More's part. The form of this passage is an essential part of the argument. More is also, however, implicitly distinguishing between the world of popular superstition and the far more specific dangers of heresy. For More the "Egypcyan" and her magic are a joke. It is certainly not something to unduly worry about or seek to destroy.

More ends *The Apology* by refusing to even dignify with an answer the accusation that he brings in "amonge the moste ernest maters, fansyes and sportes, and mery tales."[99] More's insistence on his right to produce texts that are mixed, that ask the reader to deploy a sense of discretion in terms of the different registers and genres that they contain, can be seen as reflecting his commitment to the reformist literature of the fifteenth century, whose fundamental characteristics, Simpson argues, were "an accretive reception of historical artefacts, a complex parcelling out of authority and clearly segmented stylistic and/or structural forms."[100] In these terms More's work is quite reformist in comparison with Love's *Mirror*, which consistently seeks to close down and exclude the use of reason in matters of faith and deploys a range of narrative strategies to smooth away any lack of polemical or formal coherence. In his antiheretical works, More reflects upon the world in which he finds himself—one in which endless texts are being produced, circulated, and read without any control, a world with a readership happy to accept the easy explanations offered by *some say*, regardless of the claims of reason, justice, or truth.

Faith and the Church in *The Confutation*

Enormytes Usyd by the Clergy is a polemical work published in 1532. Jupiter echoes its title in his opening speech in the *Play of the Weather*. *Enormytes* purports to speak for the laity. It accuses the clergy of attacking and persecuting good Catholic laymen, abusing them with terms like "Euangelyke brother" and failing to address such clerical abuses as simony.[101] *Enormytes* tells the clergy that they should "leave their cruel handling of the king's lay subjects for such heresies as be but small heresies in comparison of greater, till they may clear and cleanse themselves from simony that is the greatest and most abominable heresy or else till they can prove by good authority that simony is none heresy."[102] It then argues that because of the prevalence of simony within the church, and the failure of the clergy to take any steps to prevent it, "every bishop and priest heretic may truly be called an arch-heretic in comparison to a lay heretic."[103] *Enormytes* is a prototype confessional text. Its polemical strategy is simply to label its clerical targets heretics, and it advances no real proof that simony is rampant in the English church.

More's antiheretical works are in places violent, and he does indulge in a certain amount of typical polemical mud-slinging, particularly in relation to Luther's marriage. At the same time works like *The Confutation* do try to remain reasonable. This may seem a strange claim to make of More's polemical texts, and in particular *The Confutation*, which, to many critics, represents all that is unreasonable and extreme about the antiheretical writing More produced in the period 1532/33. In particular, the length of *The Confutation* has been seen as indicating More's loss of a sense of proportion, his inability to control his material or his hatred of heresy.

It is possible, however, that the length of *The Confutation* reflects More's awareness that the kind of absolutist claims and demands made by writers like Hoccleve and Lydgate in their antiheretical works would be counterproductive. *The Confutation* is a formal rejection of the argument and style of works like *Enormytes*. It foreshadows an important aspect of the reform agenda pursued by Cardinal Pole during the reign of Mary Tudor, which privileged substantial catechetical and hortatory works over polemical tracts.[104]

In *The Confutation* More tells his readers that "fayth alone may dwell in a man, and dedely synne togyther. But lyuely fayth, that is to wyt fayth not alone, but coupled with hope and cheryte and will of good workes, can not dwell with dedely synne."[105] This passage illustrates another, far more important reason for the length of *The Confutation*. In this work More was writing against what he saw as a sterile, false, and evil religiosity, one that sought to fix and contain the meaning of key Christian terms and words. In particular, More thought that men like Tyndale were committed to a hermeneutics that failed to take any proper note of the linguistic complexity of words, the enabling sensuous, communal, and institutional context of words like "faith" or "church." Faith that is boiled down to the plain, simple, literal word can exist with deadly sin, since it is not really faith at all. Faith that exists within the world, which is linked with hope, charity, and love, cannot.

Chapter 4

DEVOTION

Reading Thomas More's final devotional works, *The Treatise on the Passion*, *A Dialogue of Comfort against Tribulation*, and *De Tristitia Christi*, one senses that More does not feel able to directly face the passion. Instead he walks backwards toward it. This sense of deferral is not simply a product of More's life story. He could have chosen to focus in his final devotional writing upon the passion. Instead the *Treatise* largely deals with the Last Supper, and *De Tristitia* with Christ's agony in the garden at Gethsemane, while the *Dialogue of Comfort* discusses the solace provided by Christian teaching, and explicitly the example of Christ, to those facing worldly troubles and torments. At the same time More's later devotional writings are infused with the reality and experience of the passion. It runs through all of them. In these works More addresses the passion not as an object to be approached or an image to be viewed but instead as an unfolding, ongoing event. The passion in More's late devotional works is all-pervasive. It is an event whose space, form, and time is simultaneously fixed and fluid; it is an endlessly productive text, a path whose end is at once death and life. More's passion is a paradox, but not in a disabling sense. Rather it shares Henri de Lubac's sense of the paradoxical as "the provisional expression of a view which remains incomplete, but whose orientation is ever towards fullness."[1] The passion in *The Treatise*, the *Dialogue of*

Comfort, and *De Tristitia* is a site of possibilities, above all of devotional labour. Participating in the passion in More's later works means working/ reading toward Christ.

In this chapter I focus on two key concepts for understanding More's late devotional works, prayer and the book of Christ. In both cases More seeks to develop a distinctive position that combines late medieval devotionalism with an Augustinian emphasis on the ethics of writing and reading. A key aspect of More's devotional writing is the distinction between the book of Christ as a metaphor and as a metonym. More rejects the metaphoric totalization of either writing or the body. For him the book of Christ is always metonymic.[2] More consistently stresses that all Christians are writers and readers of the book of Christ, not its authors or consumers.[3] Prayer for More is not an individual activity. It is an inherently collective act — a moment of communal solidarity that More feels is being destroyed by the emerging norms of confessional Christianity. Prayer is also, for More, a form of pilgrimage. In More's devotional writing to pray is to travel on the road of Christian renewal that leads to the City of God.

The Treatise opens with an unfinished introduction in which More discusses Hebrews 13: "We haue not here a dwelling citie, but we seeke the citie that is to come."[4] More writes that if Saint Paul is right,

> then semeth me that many men are verye farre ouersene, such men I meane as I am (alacke) my selfe, that so much tyme and studye besette aboute their nyghtes lodgeing here, in passing by the waye, [and] so little remember to labour [and] prouide, that they may haue some house commodious for their ease, [and] well fauoredly trimmed to their pleasure, in [the] whether once go we shal, [and] when we come once there, dwell there we shal, [and] inhabit there for euer.[5]

There is something strangely appropriate in the unfinished nature of these introductory remarks. *The Treatise* focuses on an event, Christ's passion, and yet it opens with a statement of Christian pilgrimage. In his introduction to *The Treatise* More stresses that all Christians are on a journey that will end only in the City of God. *The Treatise*, and More's other late works, are not filled with a sense of enclosure or imprisonment but rather with an expansive sense of Christian devotion and movement, a searching through words and in prayer for the means and strength to live the truth of Christ's message.

This sense of movement distinguishes More's devotional working from important traditions within late medieval and Tudor religious, and in particular penitential, writing. A text like *Everyman* is centrally concerned with the ordering and fixing of sin as a prerequisite for salvation. Chaucer's *Parson's Tale* reflects a similar emphasis. The narrator of this tale consistently warns against the sin of taking "delit in thynkynge" and of being a "talker of ydel wordes of folye or of vileyne."[6] Nicholas Watson has recently argued that *The Parson's Tale* is a lay person's guide to penitence and an "anatomisation, not of holiness, but of everyday sin."[7] Watson then contends that in *The Parson's Tale* Chaucer is writing as a "mediocrist" against "the developing perfectionist definitions of lay devotion."[8] Watson's argument is persuasive, but it does rely on making the relatively restricted scope of *The Parson's Tale* a virtue. It may be more accurate to see the tale as Chaucer's attempt to provide lay people like himself with the tools necessary to survive within the emerging religious ethos of an English church committed to the fight against heresy. In this world, that of Arundel's *Constitutions* and John Lydgate's *Defence of Holy Church*, the Parson's emphasis on cataloguing and containing sin rather than aspiring to holiness was prudent if not inspiring.[9] The last word of *The Parson's Tale* is "synne."[10] It ends where it starts, and in the process brings itself and *The Canterbury Tales* to an abrupt halt.[11] More's last writings, like a number of other late medieval and early Tudor religious works, draw on images of sensuous devotional labor to imagine a collective and communal space of Christian endeavor. *The Treatise*, the *Dialogue of Comfort*, and *De Tristitia* create images of Christian reading as a form of devotional labor, a pilgrimage or search for the truth of Christ's teaching. *The Parson's Tale* offers its readers a guide to defeating or at least ordering sin. Its scope is limited and in some ways impoverished. It suggests that the best, and certainly safest, aspiration a lay Christian should have is to be able to recognize his or her own sinfulness. More's last works are far more ambitious than this. They offer their readers the ideas, images, and tools that More felt were necessary for leading a grace-full Christian life; *The Parson's Tale* ends with "synne"—*The Treatise* with "the spirituall societie of sayntes."[12]

Thomas More and Prayer

Rowan Williams has suggested that prayer is particularly significant in the context of theology because it resists the "urge of religious language to claim a total perspective: by articulating its own incompleteness before God it turns away from any claim of human completeness."[13] For Williams prayer demands an acknowledgment of human failure as the basis for any serious theology. To pray is to accept one's incapacity, one's fears, weaknesses, and failures. In these terms prayer particularly resists forms of totalitarian thought that seek to deny humanity's common, irreducible incompleteness. This unifying aspect of what it means to pray informs Johann Baptist Metz's emphasis on the eschatological and communal nature of prayer. Metz argues that "through prayer we become part of a great historical solidarity. Prayer introduces into the history of mankind a voice that gives expression to our hope and trust."[14] Metz's understanding of prayer relates directly to his sense of Christ as "an emancipative memory, liberating us from all attempts to idolise cosmic and political powers and make them absolute."[15] In prayer, for Metz, the Christian participates in a moment that is oriented simultaneously to the past and the future, that is at once historical and transcendent. More felt that he was caught between a world of endless textuality and one in which the encounter with God was stalled and fixed in such a way as to prevent it from ever actually taking place, a world in which the space for prayer was being drowned in a sea of texts and filled with a cacophony of competing claims to completeness. Like Augustine, More sought in his work to keep open a space for thought as the prerequisite for the emergence of God's truth, at the level of text, believer, and society.

More's *Treatise* was one of the last works he wrote before his martyrdom. It was first published in 1557 as part of William Rastell's edition of More's work. Two manuscript versions of *The Treatise* are extant. It is a complex text, and perhaps for this reason it has suffered disproportionately from the mythology that has grown up around More. *The Treatise* has in the past been seen as the first of More's "Tower works." The use of this label is, however, in many ways unhelpful. It is now generally accepted that *The Treatise* was written, or at least started, in the spring of 1534, before More was incarcerated in Tower on April 17.[16] This dating is important, since it complicates the rather simplistic narrative that has grown up around More's later works, which sees them as becoming progressively more personal and religious as a direct result of the increasingly desperate situation that More found himself in. For example, Peter Ackroyd, in his recent biography, writes that "in 1534 when More saw the rejection of his beliefs, and the destruction of the very order to which he clung, he turned from polemic to meditation and prayer." Ackroyd then suggests that *The Treatise* is a "standard votive work, that combines the exegesis of biblical texts concerning the last days of Jesus with passages of devotion and exhortation."[17] Yet to construct *The Treatise* within this restrictive melancholic context is to ignore the extent to which *The Treatise* is a reforming, humanist work. At its center is not a suffering, tortured, silenced Christ, but instead a Christ who leads and teaches. It is not an enclosed work, looking inwards toward the penitential soul of the narrator, but an expansive work that is learned and witty and whose focus is communal. More's work is a defense of the ideal of the church as a prayerful community united in friendship around the figure of Christ as teacher and leader.

It is also unhelpful to describe *The Treatise* as a "standard votive work." This is partly because it is unclear what "standard" means in this context. Far more problematic, however, is the sense that with *The Treatise* More is returning to the welcoming embrace of a homogeneous medieval tradition of meditations on Christ, and in particular upon the passion. As David Aers has pointed out, the representation of Christ in the fifteenth century was a matter of considerable debate.[18] Not only is *The Treatise* quite different from such works as Love's *Mirror of the Blessed Life of Jesus Christ*; it is also part of a reforming devotional tradition within late medieval English Christianity.

The Treatise is structured around very short harmonies of the gospel story, drawn from John Gerson's *Montessaron*, which are followed by a detailed exposition, each section being completed with a short prayer.[19] This structure is similar to that found in other devotional works of the period and perhaps is most clearly repeated, albeit with important variations, in *The Myrrour or Glasse of Christes Passion* (c. 1533/34; hereafter simply *The Myrrour of Christes Passion*). Each section of *The Treatise* ends with a prayer. Perhaps this is what has led a number of writers, including

Ackroyd, to see *The Treatise* as part of an inward move by More, a withdrawal from the bustle of daily life to the privacy of prayer. To assume, however, that the inclusion of devotional material like prayers in *The Treatise* indicates that in this work More was withdrawing from the world is to ignore the extent to which to pray in pre-Reformation England was a complex act that was not inherently private or personal.[20] More's *Treatise* needs to be seen alongside other early Tudor devotional works aimed at the laity. Texts like William Bonde's *Pilgrimage of Perfeccyon* and *The Myrrour of Christes Passion* provide an essential context for understanding what More was attempting to achieve in *The Treatise* and in particular the way in which he represents prayer in *The Treatise* as a devotional act.

William Bonde's *Pilgrimage of Perfeccyon* was published in 1526 and then republished in 1531. A massive work, it aims to guide its readers, religious and secular, on the road to perfection. Bonde states in the prologue that he started the work as a personal guide but that subsequently it was put into his mind to direct it to "all them that . . . hath a desire to know how to order their life in the pilgrimage of perfection, which is the holy life of religion."[21] There follows a very detailed discussion of what is required to lead a "holy life of religion." Bonde's book is a manual for clerical and lay devotion. It focuses on individual behavior while at the same time expressing real anxieties about what it terms "singularity." Bonde writes, "The enemy uses the singular person as his tables wherein he writes what so ever he will: For the singular person is apt to receive all manner of illusions, both sleeping and waking."[22] It is this skepticism about the value of individual contemplation that makes *The Pilgrimage of Perfeccyon* a very different work from, for example, *The Imitation of Christ*. Bonde's work is not primarily concerned with encouraging either a liturgical or a contemplative approach to religious life; instead it maps out a path between the two. The true Christian as imagined in *The Pilgrimage of Perfeccyon* is in a process of constant devotion, of striving to achieve a holy life. In a very striking image Bonde suggests:

> Our minds or hearts, if they were perfect and clean, should ever be as a ball, which if it be thrown and cast up straight, it falls down again directly, and lightly in the hand of him that cast it up: but if it be cast up crookedly, it swerves and falls on that one side or on the

other, and so misses the hand and falls to the ground. So the mind of every person, should either ascend directly in his service to the contemplation of god . . . or else directly descend to the consideration of the letter of his duty.[23]

Unlike writers of works such as *The Scale of Perfection*, Bonde in this passage creates an image of the ascent toward God as a process of oscillation. The mind or heart is constantly rising and falling, in a metaphor that stresses physical movement; the image of the ball rising and falling evokes the accurate repetition of devotional practice. There is nothing abstract about Bonde's image. It combines material specificity with a pragmatic approach to the devotional practice that reflects the confidence, optimism, and humanity of *The Pilgrimage of Perfeccyon*. It does not ask Christians to throw their ball directly into heaven, nor judge them as failures if it sometimes falls back to the ground; Bonde simply asks that one keep the ball in play.

It is this repetition, and the acceptance of human frailty implicit within it, that informs *The Pilgrimage of Perfeccyon*'s treatment of prayer. At numerous points throughout the work Bonde addresses the question of prayer. He goes out of his way to stress the value of prayer, even when the person praying does not understand the words he or she is saying, and he deploys narrative to sustain the efficiency of such praying. In places this support seems to precisely reflect the "brutal materialism" that Eamon Duffy has suggested was a feature of some fifteenth-century religious practices.[24] For example, in book 3, second day, Bonde discusses the Lord's Prayer. He opens by considering the opening of the prayer. He then discusses the line "Lead us not into temptation" and immediately turns to a short narrative to illustrate his discussion. "So I read in the life of the holy doctor Saint Thomas. . . . He was the son of a noble earl and yet he took this pilgrimage on him, travailing in the religion of Saint Dominic. Whom after great assaults and temptations of the flesh, God delivered by means of his prayer, and sent him a girdle of chastity, by whose virtue he was preserved, and never more troubled."[25] It is possible that Bonde refers to Saint Thomas's girdle of chastity metaphorically, although it does not seem so. Bonde argues that one should pray because, on the basis of this narrative, God will respond with actual practical support in the here and now. Although the story Bonde uses here is not scriptural, the point he is making is. As More suggested to the Messenger in the *Dialogue concerning Heresies*, there is no reason for a Christian not to expect God to intervene in the here and now with practical solutions to pressing problems.

Bonde stresses throughout *The Pilgrimage of Perfeccyon* that the effectiveness of a prayer does not relate to the understanding of the person praying but is rather a property of the words themselves, arguing that when one does not understand a prayer, one should

> do as the enchanter or charmer doth, when he would take a wild venomous serpent. He knows not peradventure, the virtue of the wordes that he speaks, but the serpent knows well the virtue of the same wordes that he speaks, and cannot resist them. And therefore she stoppeth her ears, and would not hear them, yet the enchanter continuing his wordes at the last overcomes her, and brings her to passe as he would. So by holy prayer, we may overcome all passions and temptations, and also our ghostly enemy, that ministered to us the same.[26]

This passage emphasizes the practice of praying, the process, at the expense of the meaning of the words or the intensity of the individual worshiper's religious experience. It articulates very clearly the devotional and practical model of prayer that Bonde advocates throughout *The Pilgrimage of Perfeccyon*. For example, when Bonde discusses the three different degrees of attentiveness that people have when praying—actual, habitual, and virtual—he stresses the virtual over the actual and habitual. Bonde writes that in actual prayer a person's "memory or mind" considers every letter, syllable, word, and sentence of his or her prayer from the beginning to the end. He quickly comments, however, that anyone who could achieve actual prayer would be more like an angel than an earthly creature.[27] At the opposite extreme from this unattainable prayer is habitual prayer, which is simply an outward, empty ritual. The kind of prayer that Bonde argues his readers should aspire to is the mean between these two states of attention, actual and habitual. Following Saint Thomas, Bonde calls this mean virtual.[28]

Bonde explains the nature of virtual attention in prayer through a set of prosaic examples. In particular, he uses the figure of a pilgrim going to Jerusalem whose failure to remember God during the entire course of the journey does not lessen the merit of the act. Bonde then expands further on this argument, commenting, "And as the first intent order to God in all meritorious works, as fasting, watching, alms deeds doing, and pilgrimage, is sufficient, though the mind sometime be otherwise occupied, and not always on his intent, or on God, yet the person does merit . . . so likewise it is in prayer. The virtue of the first intent remains still to the end."[29] The religious practices that Bonde lists in this passage are largely devotional, and his emphasis on a humane, practical spirituality is part of his devotionalism. The *Pilgrimage of Perfeccyon* is a detailed, and in places moving, work of religious instruction. Its intent is to guide clerical and lay readers without imposing aspirations or rules that, in Bonde's words, only angels could keep. *The Pilgrimage of Perfeccyon* stresses the importance of practice, of devotion, while at the same time expressing doubts over the wisdom of pursuing the kind of inner spiritual knowledge advocated in works like *The Imitation of Christ.* James Simpson has pointed out that More's suggestion in his *Confutation of Tyndale's Answer* that good Christians should read such works as *The Scale of Perfection, The Mirror of the Blessed Life of Jesus Christ*, and *The Imitation of Christ* is potentially disingenuous, since the last was not widely read in the late medieval English church and articulated a very different religious agenda from the other works cited by More. Simpson comments, "More's statement that the *Imitatio* was a classic of vernacular spirituality is incorrect: unlike the other two books mentioned by More [*The Scale of Perfection* and *The Mirror of the Blessed Life of Jesus Christ*], the *Imitatio* expresses a chaste, austere, and largely imageless spirituality."[30] *The Pilgrimage of Perfeccyon* can be read as a manifesto of late medieval devotionalism. It provides all the guidance the individual Christian needs to engage in meaningful devotional worship. But the world it evokes is one quite alien to the perfectionist religiosity of *The Imitation of Christ.*

John Fewterer's work, *The Myrrour of Christes Passion* (c. 1533/34), in some ways combines the world of *The Imitation of Christ* with that of *The Pilgrimage of Perfeccyon*.[31] More's *Treatise* shares this synthesizing agenda, and some have speculated that More and Fewterer produced their works as part of a campaign of anti-Protestant publication, although, as Vincent Gillespie has commented, the library at Syon does not appear to have contained a single work by More.[32] Fewterer, like Bonde, was a monk of

Syon Abbey and the last confessor general before the dissolution. J. T. Rhodes has suggested that while "Bonde's *Pilgrimage of Perfeccyon* could be described as a *summa* of late medieval teaching on religious life, *The Myrrour of Christes Passion* (1534) . . . was a *summa* of late medieval devotion to the Passion."[33] *The Myrrour of Christes Passion* is, however, more focused than *The Pilgrimage of Perfeccyon*. It is divided into three parts. The first discusses the spiritual profit of meditating upon the passion; the central part focuses on the events of the passion; and section three addresses the ascension, Pentecost, and the Assumption of the Virgin. Each part is subdivided into sections based upon either specific spiritual graces arising from the study of the passion or events from the gospel. Typically each of these parts contains an extended exposition of the relevant passage, which is followed by a prayer. The first part of *The Myrrour of Christes Passion* also often includes narrative examples of the exposition provided in the text, examples drawn from the life of the thirteenth-century Beguine Saint Mary of Oignies.[34]

The Myrrour of Christes Passion is a guide to Christian meditation that focuses directly on the events of the passion. This focus creates a space that is neither liturgical nor contemplative. In particular, the time of the narrative is collapsed into the process of meditation upon the passion that the work advocates. As Roger Ellis suggests, "The performance of the text . . . enacts [the] very internalisation of the Passion narrative" that Fewterer has urged upon his reader in the work's preface.[35] *The Myrrour of Christes Passion* collapses narrative time into devotional practice. For example, the ninth particle of the first book is entitled "Of the Supper or Maundy of Our Lord."[36] This section opens by briefly recounting the scriptural story of Christ sending Peter and John to prepare a chamber for the Passover. Almost immediately Fewterer gives the story an allegorical gloss: "By Peter is signified good operation or active life. And by John is noted devout contemplation. These two prepare the Pascal lamb, that is, they dispose a man duly and reverently to receive the holy body of our lord, signified by the Pascal lamb. They prepare this spiritual lamb in a great loft or chamber, that is, in the soul of man, elevate and lift up, by fervent devotion and great by forbearance, wide by the bread of charity, and strawed by the diversity of virtues."[37] This passage is typical of *The Myrrour of Christes Passion* in the way it creates an allegorical reading of the gospel story that operates simultaneously on a number of levels. In particular, as one reads this passage one is effectively placed in the "great loft" of devotion alongside Peter and John. Unlike other devotional works, for example Nicholas Love's *The Mirror of the Blessed Life of Jesus Christ*, *The Myrrour of Christes Passion* does not explicitly demand in this passage that readers imagine themselves at the Last Supper; instead they must participate through allegorical identification with the episode's meaning.

The Myrrour of Christes Passion then discusses the relationship between the Old and New Testaments as figured in the Last Supper. The section closes with a prayer that echoes the earlier allegorical exposition of the gospel: "O Lord Jesu Christ, whiche in the eventide made thy last supper with thy disciples in a great and large chamber strawed and made ready for thee, and there fed them with thy most sacred body and blood: make my heart (I beseech thee) a great and large chamber for thee. Enlarge in it true faith, hope, and charity."[38] The repetition of motifs here between exposition and prayer is a constant structural device throughout *The Myrrour of Christes Passion* and gives the work an accumulative momentum as it explains each particle or section of the passion and then bases a prayer on this explanation. In many ways the narrative motivation of *The Myrrour of Christes Passion* is tautological. It is to fashion in the reader a mirror of Christ's passion, in particular through the pattern of gospel, exposition, and prayer; to create a text that weaves together Scripture, teaching, and devotion to create a coherent whole through reading.

Passages detailing events from the life of Saint Mary of Oignies, often relatively long, appear to interrupt the basic narrative coherence of *The Myrrour of Christes Passion*. For example, when discussing the gifts that come to those who meditate upon the passion, the work uses the following to illustrate the gifts of the Spirit.

> Sometime this blessed woman when she was made one spirit with God, and was joined unto him with the glue of fervent love to her great pleasure and sweetness, if she heard of the coming of strangers to speak with her: she would (I say sometime) with great violence withdraw herself from that great pleasure of contemplation, from the sweet embrace of her spouse Christ, lest that she should slander those strangers. I say she would withdraw her mind from that contemplation with so great vehemence of sorrow, that sometime she voided or spitted pure blood, and that in great quantity, to her great

pain and affliction. Willing rather so to punish herself with that great martyrdom, than to trouble . . . the peace and quietness of her sisters and brethren, and especially of pilgrims and strangers.[39]

It is difficult to explain why *The Myrrour of Christes Passion* is peppered with details from the life of Saint Mary, but perhaps the need to explain these passages simply reflects the dominance of post-Reformation assumptions concerning the form and content of religious writing. *The Myrrour of Christes Passion* brings together precisely the different kinds of Christian devotion that More suggested should form the basis of "good Christian reading." It combines an emphasis on the individual prayer with scriptural exposition and exemplary stories drawn from the life of Saint Mary in such a way as to insist on the coherence of all three aspects of Christian life.

It is therefore ironic that within a year of the work's being published, a short text was issued entitled *Deuoute Prayers in Englysshe of Thactes of Our Redemption*, which comprised the prayers from Fewterer's translation without any other supporting material. In the place of the extended discussions of events from the passion that were an integral part of *The Myrrour of Christes Passion, Deuoute Prayers* gives the reader only a bold title and a reference to the relevant New Testament passage. The effect of going from *The Myrrour of Christes Passion* to *Deuoute Prayers* as a reader can be compared to what one would imagine the effect would be of moving from a pre- to a post-Reformation English church. *Deuoute Prayers* reflects an aspect of fifteenth-century English Christianity as represented by *The Myrrour of Christes Passion* stripped of its devotional support. It is perhaps not surprising to find that whereas *The Myrrour of Christes Passion* would be objectionable for a number of reasons to Protestant readers, *Deuoute Prayers*, apart from a few minor references to the specific saints, would not. In the difference between *The Myrrour of Christes Passion* and *Deuoute Prayers* one can see on the page the effects of the Reformation on fifteenth-century religion and in particular on the place of devotional prayer.

More's *Treatise* has an agenda similar to that of *The Myrrour of Christes Passion*. In particular, in his work More attempts to synthesize humanist learning with Christian teaching so as to leave a space for the kind of devotionalism that men like Tyndale ruthlessly mocked. More's work opens with three chapters that address the fall of the archangels, the creation and fall of mankind, the determination of the Trinity, and the restoration of mankind. One senses that More is providing his meditation on the passion with an intellectual context akin to the devotional one provided in *The Myrrour of Christes Passion*. When More turns to the story of the passion, he discusses in detail the moment when Christ asks Peter and John to prepare a room for the Last Supper. At this moment *The Myrrour of Christes Passion* almost immediately turns inward, allegorically relating the room where the Last Supper was to take place directly to the reader's soul. More responds to this story first by discussing the differences of opinion between the Orthodox and Catholic Churches over the timing of Easter. This is a detailed, learned digression, quite unlike the kind of polemics that More wrote against Tyndale and Simon Fish. More then turns to the specifics of the New Testament story. He starts by discussing the fact that Christ did not tell Peter and John the name of the man that they were to go to and ask for a room in which the disciples and Christ could celebrate the Passover:

> Of which thyng dyuers of the olde doctours coniect and tel diuers causes. Some saye [Christ] sente theym to a manne not named, in token that godde wyll come, not only to menne that are in the world famous and of gret name, but also to folke of none estimacyon in the counte of the world and nor of no name. Some other saye (and bothe twayne maye well be trewe) that for as much as oure sauyoure . . . knew the promise of the false traytour Iudas made unto the Iewes vppon the daye before to betraye hym . . . if he shoulde haue named the manne or the place, the traytour mought haue caused hym and hys disciples to bee taken, before his maundy made, and his holy bodye consecrated in the blessed sacrament.[40]

The Treatise treats the New Testament as a meaning-*full* text, a text in which every word has meaning. Thus More makes a typically Augustinian move, since it implies that Scripture is so full of meaning that no human could possibly fully understand it. This passage also, however, refers directly to More's earlier polemic work. In *The Apology* More mocks the use of the phrase "some say" by his opponents, specifically St. German in his *Treatise concerning the Division between Spiritualities and Temporalitie*, to give their attacks on the clergy a spurious legitimacy. In the *Dialogue concerning Heresies* one of the central metaphors for heresy as subversive is the tendency of heretics to have many names and therefore effectively no names.[41]

The whole of *The Treatise* can be read as a provocative revisiting by More of his earlier polemic work. Consistently More reuses tropes and phrases drawn from works very different from *The Treatise*, as if deliberately seeking to purge them of their polemic taint. Why? One explanation would be that More is simply mocking his opponents, but this would not fit with the general tone or ethos of *The Treatise*. I would argue instead that in this work, and in his other late devotional works, More attempts to imagine a use of language that escapes the emerging poetics and polemics of confessionalization. *The Treatise* tries to bring together in a coherent whole for the benefit of the reader a diverse and eclectic collection of materials, so that reading *The Treatise* becomes an act of Christian devotion. In the process More deliberately recycles metaphors and tropes from his polemic work in an act of humanist confidence in the written word. He now deploys for devotional purposes words and phrases, even in the case of the *Dialogue of Comfort against Tribulation* genres, that he earlier associated with the struggle against heresy.

In the *Dialogue concerning Heresies* More stresses the dangers of doubt, arguing that if unchecked it will eat away the very fabric of society by destroying all learning. In *The Treatise* he renders doubt impossible, as he continues his meditation on the preparations for the Last Supper by discussing Christ's instruction to Peter and John to enter Jerusalem and follow a man with a water pot on his head to the house where he works. In this house, Christ assures his disciples, they will be able to celebrate the Passover. More's comment on this story combines a lawyer's appreciation for its improbable aspects with an emphasis on its devotional implications:

> Now who but god coulde surely send menne on suche a maner messages, in which they shoulde be sure to fynde suche thynges as are vnto all creatures vnsure and vncertayne, as thynges accompted to fall vnder chaunce and hap. And therefore whyle they founde euery

thynge come to passe as he hadde before tolde theym, they myght and we maye, surely knowne hym for godde. For whoe coulde tel that the manne with his potte of water walkynge on his errande, and the two apostles goyng forth on theyrs, neyther parte lokynge for other, shoulde so begynne to sette forthe, and in such wyse hold on theyr way, that they shuld at a place whiche neyther of the bothe parties appoynted, so iustely mete together.[42]

One of the things that make this passage striking is that More is depicting here the organization of a clandestine meeting, hidden from the existing religious and political authorities. *The Treatise*, in many ways unavoidably, depicts Christ and his apostles behaving like the heretics that fill More's polemic works. What separates More's work from other meditations on Christ's life is how prepared he is to embrace the subversive aspect of Christ's ministry. For example, Love in *The Mirror of the Blessed Life of Jesus Christ*, when discussing the moment in the gospel where Christ hides from the people he has just fed and who want to make him king, comments, "Take we here good intent how and in what manner Christ fled this worship effectively without feigning."[43] Immediately after this comment, however, Love suggests that Christ was trying to at best mislead the people when he instructed his disciples to board a boat. Love comments that Christ did this "so that if the people would search him among his disciples they should not find him, and so he escaped away from them that sought him to worship."[44] David Aers has discussed the anxieties over interpretation that consistently interrupt Love's work.[45] In this episode Love denies that Christ feigns and then provides a gloss of the gospel passage that could almost have been designed to provoke precisely this reading of Christ's behavior. *The Mirror of the Blessed Life of Jesus Christ* is haunted by a Lollard Christ who is constantly summoned up in order to be denied. *The Treatise* repeats this motif, but with the crucial difference that in More's text Christ as heretic is embraced not denied.

We see how far More is prepared to go beyond the anxious orthodoxy of Love's work when he turns to discuss the presence of Judas at the Last Supper: "Here we se therfore by the euangelystes, not only mencion that [Judas] came with our lord, but also that he sat at the supper with oure lord, so for all the treason that the traytour wrought, yet was the traytoure Christes apostle styll."[46] More then develops this point further by applying it directly to the church: "The vyces of vicious folke in Christes church, can not lette, but that hys catholike church of which they be part, is for all their vnholynes, his holy catholyke churche."[47] Judas is the archetypical despairing heretic. Lee Patterson has pointed out that in medieval exegesis Judas "died suspended between earth and heaven because neither men nor angels would accept him."[48] In *The Treatise* More deploys the figure of Judas as a member of the church to stress its unity and coherence. This is in some ways an outrageous move.

More then makes it even more so when he discusses the two key lessons that one should take from the gospel episode he is discussing. The first is the need to keep the New Law and recognize Christ's role in delivering us from the yoke of the Old. The second is "that Christe had none house of his own, nor none of his apostles neyther."[49] The lesson implies that if we wish to follow Christ, we too should accept that in this world "we be but waye farynge folke."[50] More then, however, acknowledges that while it is easy for a person to say he is a pilgrim, "yet it is harde for many a man to let it fal felyngly, and sincke down depe into his hert."[51] More concludes this section by comparing the reality of pilgrimage to the practice. He suggests that for some people the label "pilgrim" can itself become a snare, a home from which they are reluctant to leave when called by the Lord, "for then fynde they theym selfe much more lothe to parte from this worlde, than pylgrymes to go from their Inne."[52] *The Treatise* represents being or feeling at home as a religious failing; only the itinerant, those on the road, the homeless, are represented in *The Treatise* as truly following Christ's example. More's polemic work consistently equates the trope of homelessness with heresy. In comparison this passage, indeed the whole of *The Treatise*, emphasizes Christ as a social outcast needing to hide from the religious authorities, as if More is daring the reader to see an inevitable conflict between the church and the heterodox, radical preacher depicted in the New Testament.

This section of *The Treatise* ends with a prayer designed to ensure that its lessons sink feelingly into its reader's heart:

Almyghtye Iesu Chryste, whyche wouldest for oure ensample obserue the lawe that thou camest to chaung, and beynge maker of the whole yerth, wouldest haue yet no dwellynge howse therein, gyue vs

thy grace soo to keepe thyne holy lawe, and so to recken oure selfe for
no dwellers but for pylgrymes vppon yerthe, that we maye longe and
make haste, walkynge wyth faythe in the waye of vertuous woorkes,
too come to the gloryouse countrey, wherein thou haste boughte vs
enherytaunce for euer wythe thyne owne precyouse bloude.[53]

In order to understand More's text it is worthwhile to return to the prayer
that concluded the discussion of the same gospel episode in *The Myrrour of
Christes Passion*:

> O Lord Jesu Christ, whiche in the eventide made thy last supper with
> thy disciples in a great and large chamber strawed and made ready
> for thee, and there fed them with thy most sacred body and blood:
> make my heart (I beseech thee) a great and large chamber for thee.
> Enlarge in it true faith, hope, and charity.[54]

The Myrrour of Christes Passion reads as a collection of sermons, each of
which concludes with a prayer that is, like this one, designed to encourage the internalization of the sermon's message. The central metaphoric
conceit of each of the sections of *The Myrrour of Christes Passion* is the use
of allegory to enable the reader to move from exposition to internalization through prayer. The gospel story of finding a room for the Last
Supper becomes a metaphor for the state of the reader's soul. This emphasis on place reflects the enclosing religious ethos of *The Myrrour of
Christes Passion*, its consistent, repetitive staging of moments of expansion
and contraction. More's concluding prayer, in contrast, emphasizes not
place but movement. The Last Supper becomes in *The Treatise* a metaphor
not for closure but for endless wandering. The large "strawed" chamber
of *The Myrrour of Christes Passion* is for More the pilgrim's open road. In *The
Treatise* More consistently asks readers to position themselves, like Peter
and John in this gospel story, as messengers for God on a mission that
escapes human understanding but whose end God already knows.

    The Treatise concludes with a section on the "blessed sacrament."
This gives More's work a recognizable pattern, although also a potentially
misleading one. Nicholas Love's *The Mirror of the Blessed Life of Jesus Christ*
and *The Imitation of Christ* both conclude with discussions of the "blessed
sacrament." These are, however, very different texts. Love's discussion

of the sacrament focuses upon its miraculous nature and includes a number of miracle stories. *The Imitation of Christ* places the sacrament clearly within its contemplative frame of reference, for example, commenting on the need for the believer to approach the sacrament as an "empty vessel."[55] Both texts, however, while approaching the sacrament in very different ways, acknowledge its potentially problematic status.[56] Almost the final words of *The Imitation of Christ* acknowledge, albeit in a displaced way, the problems the church faces in defining the nature of the blessed sacrament: "Go forward . . . with simple, undoubting faith, and come to this Sacrament with humble reverence, confidently committing to almighty God whatever you are not able to understand."[57] Love's work also summons up the specter of doubt, and more specifically heresy, in its discussion of the sacrament. In particular, in an ironic and witty attack on his Lollard enemies Love in one place even suggests that such miracles as the sacrament bleeding or turning into flesh are signs fit only for unbelievers, since true believers require no such signs.[58]

In *The Treatise* More adopts a reforming humanist approach to the sacrament of the altar. Rather than stress its miraculous qualities or its unknowability, he emphasizes its potential as a site or space for meditation and thought. In these terms one could position the approach of *The Treatise* between the worlds of *The Imitation of Christ* and *The Mirror of the Blessed Life of Jesus Christ*. For example, More comments in detail on the problems of nomenclature associated with the sacrament:

> Consider nowe good readers, and remember, that sythe thys excellente high sacrament, vnder a fourme and lykenesse so common and so simple in syghte, couertlye conteyneth in it, a wonderfull secrete treasure, and sygnifieth and betokeneth also manyfold meruelious mysteries, the holye cunninge fathers afore oure dayes, haue hadde much a doe to fynde names ynoughe and conuenient, with wyche they myghte in anye wyse insynuate and shewe, so many suche manner thinges of this blessed sacrament, as are partly conteined therein, and partlye signified thereby.[59]

This passage constructs the multiplicity of the sacrament's names as a source of strength. In the process, however, it performs a profound and risky revision of the norms of early Tudor religious polemics in which all sides ruthlessly used the grammatical metaphor, ultimately derived from Augustine, to tar textual plurality, particularly in relation to names, as a sign of corruption. For example, writers like Tyndale consistently argued that the alleged tendency of their opponents to fill the space of religion with names and labels, especially if they referred to the same thing or concept, clearly signified papist corruption. In this passage More is playing with fire. He is taking what will become a standard Protestant accusation against the Mass, that it has many conflicting names, and turning it on its head. In the process, however, More also rejects the kind of anxiety-ridden approaches to discussing the sacrament exemplified in *The Imitation of Christ* and *The Mirror of the Blessed Life of Jesus Christ*.

The potential provocativeness of More's discussion of the sacrament's many names is reflected throughout the final part of *The Treatise*. For example, More uses a theatrical metaphor to support the idea that the sacrament can at once represent and be Christ, arguing, "If ther were but euen in a playe or an enterlude, the personages of ii or iii knowen princes represented, if one of them now liked for his pleasure to playe his own part himselfe, dyd he not there his owne persone vnder the fourme of a player, represent his owne persone in fourme of his own estate?"[60] At one level this is a daring argument to make. Writers like Tyndale, and indeed earlier critics of the fifteenth-century orthodoxy, consistently argued that the theatricality of church ceremonies indicated their hollowness. There is, however, more to More's use of this theatrical metaphor than a simple desire to mock his enemies. *The Treatise* integrates devotion into its own structure so that its status as a piece of written narrative becomes a complex image of true Christian teaching; it is an interlude that aims to subvert the separation between audience and actors, watching and playing. More's work equates being a pilgrim and being a reader in such a way as to collapse past, present, and future in a moment of readerly labor. More relishes the number of names the sacrament of the altar has in order to construct it as a place for thought, and more accurately for the collective faithful thought of the church.

In these terms More's sacrament takes on the characteristic of proverbs as discussed by Erasmus in his introduction to the 1508 edition of the *Adages*. As was discussed in the chapter 2, in this text Erasmus uses the proverb "Between friends all is common" not only to illustrate the general usefulness of proverbs but also to give proverbial discourse a specifically Christian coloring. Erasmus argues that this proverb is the central tenet of Christ's teaching because of the way it stresses friendship, good company, as a unifying metaphor for a Christian life: "United in friendship with Christ, glued to Him by the same binding force that holds Him fast to the Father, imitating so far as we may that complete communion by which He and the Father are one, we should also be one with Him, and, as Paul says, should become one spirit and one flesh with God, so that by the laws of friendship all that is His is shared with us and all that is ours is shared with Him."[61] Erasmus then expands upon the ideal of Christian friendship centered on Christ by comparing it to the bringing together of many different grains of flour to form the "mystic bread" at the heart of the sacrament of the altar. In the introduction to the 1508 edition of his *Adages*, Erasmus creates an image of Christian friendship united around the image of proverbs as a space for collective communal thought. More's emphasis on the productive exchange engendered by many names that the "old fathers" had for the sacrament of the altar can be read as an adaptation of Erasmus's ideal. At the center of More's and Erasmus's thought is the image of Christ the humanist friend, sharing in the collective, communal, loving exchange of wisdom.

Thomas More and the Book of Christ

Bonde's *Pilgrimage of Perfeccyon* contains a number of striking woodcuts, including a linked pair, the Tree of Virtue and the Tree of Vice. Bonde spends considerable time discussing the meaning of these trees. For example, he informs the reader that

> these three theological virtues, faith, hope and charity, spring out of the root of grace. For as we said before grace is assembled to a tree, of the which tree, faith, hope and charity, be compared to the stock, to the bark, and to the sap. The stock for that it sustains all, is faith. The bark that defends the tree from storms and tempests, is hope. And the sap that gives life to both, is charity. For like as if the stock

or bark receive no moisture from the root they be both dead. So faith and hope when they be not joined to charity, they be likewise dead. Thus these graces and virtues presupposed, we shall climb further in this tree of grace.[62]

Climbing, in this passage, is a metaphor for reading—text and wood-cut. The reader climbs the Tree of Virtue until reaching the body of Christ at the center of the tree. The *Pilgrimage of Perfeccyon*'s image of the Tree of Virtue reflects Bonde's commitment to a devotionalism typical of pre-Reformation Christianity. The metaphor of climbing is far from being simply rhetorical. At one level Bonde expects the reader to imagine reading as a form of physical exercise; as one's eyes scan Bonde's explanatory text, one's fingers climb or trace the woodcut of the Tree of Virtue. Climbing the Tree of Virtue is both a metaphor and metonym for reading.

The Tree of Vice lacks any central image. As a reader one has to constantly rotate the page in order to read the words, since the paired sins or leaves are not symmetrical. Climbing this tree is a pointless exercise. There is no top or bottom. Instead one faces a mass of words, which cannot all be read at once; if one word is the right way up, another will be askew. This is a world of sin imaged as a web of protean textuality. The differences between the Tree of Virtue and the Tree of Vice embody, in pictorial form, Jacques Derrida's discussion of the tension between material and metaphoric writing in *Of Grammatology*. Derrida writes that "in the Middle Ages . . . it is writing understood in the metaphoric sense, that is to say a natural, eternal, and universal writing, the system of signified truth, which is recognised in its dignity. As in the Phaedrus, a certain fallen writing continues to be opposed to it. There remains to be written a history of this metaphor, a metaphor that systemically contrasts divine or natural writing and the human and laborious, finite and artificial inscription."[63] The Tree of Virtue claims a naturalness that is entirely lacking from the Tree of Vice, and it makes this claim partly on the basis of the way it unites the reader's physical experience of the text and its meaning. The Tree of Virtue rewards readerly labor, since the climb, or narrative, ends in the truth, while to expend energy on the Tree of Vice is frustrating and ultimately pointless.

The image of Christ at the center of the Tree of Virtue positions this woodcut within a tradition of images of Christ's body as a text to be read.[64] Bonde's work is an exercise in printed pastoral labor. It incites the reader to climb the Tree of Virtue as a devotional exercise, but it sets out all the footholds in advance; *The Pilgrimage of Perfeccyon* presents the body of Christ as a text, so that it exists between the dangers of excessive lay appropriation and the possibility of voyeurism, of a reading that remains stalled, caught in the surface pleasures of the image, of the corporeal body of Christ. The prologue to *The Myrrour of Christes Passion* echoes this concern over the ways in which lay readers understand passion imagery, telling its readers that "it is not sufficient to a Christian to behold Christ crucified. For so did the Jews and also the gentiles his crucifiers. But it is required of a Christian that he live and work according to the example shown to him in the mount that is Christ crucified."[65] *The Myrrour of Christes Passion* builds on this idea, arguing that God "loves and rejoices in the penance of man for the declaration and example wherof, he would his dear beloved son to be nailed fast unto the cross and spread abroad of the same as a boke open wherein we might read and learn how to do penance. What other thing do signify unto us, his tears or weeping, his sorrow, his wounds, his arms spread abroad, and his most sweet and godly words: but motions and callings unto penance?"[66] *The Myrrour of Christes Passion* is in some ways nothing more than the book of Christ opened and explained to the reader. Its very text is an icon or image of Christ's passion, and this aspect of *The Myrrour of Christ's Passion* reveals the inadequacy of Derrida's insistence upon the tension in the medieval period between divine and human writing. In the devotionalism of Bonde's text and *The Myrrour of Christes Passion* it is precisely the sense of reading as a form of devotional labor, a graphic, material, and corporeal exercise through which the reader can at once understand and participate in Christ's book/body, that undermines a distinction between divine and human, natural and laborious, writing.

Christ's body was everywhere in fifteenth- and early sixteenth-century English religion. It had a central part in the liturgy and was fundamental to the contemplative ideal. Above all, Christ's passion and his body were at the heart of fifteenth-century English devotionalism. In particular, in this period lay people appropriated the body of Christ as an object of devotion in ways that were entirely orthodox and that at the same time potentially subverted existing religious and ecclesiastical hierarchies. To articulate the idea of Christ's body as a text or charter to be read, writers used a number of tropes that existed on the boundary between text and image. *The Pore Caitif*, a late fourteenth-century work whose modern editor, Mary Teresa Brady, describes it as a "manual of religious instruction intended for the use of the laity,"[67] contains an extended Charter of Christ, a medieval religious device in which, as Margaret Aston points out, "the promise of salvation is presented as a charter, in some cases complete with an actual seal and modelled on the structural form of such a document."[68] *The Pore Caitif*'s description of the Charter of Christ opens with the conventional statement that "the parchment of this heavenly charter is neither of sheep neither of calf: but it is the body and the blessed skin of our lord Jesu."[69] The manual then develops this image further:

> and was there never skin of sheep neither of calf, so sore and hard strained on the wooden frame . . . of any parchment maker, as was the blessed body and skin of our lord Jesu Christ for our love strained and drawn upon the gibbet of the cross, heard never man from the beginning of the world till now neither shall hence to doomsday, that ever writer wrote upon sheep's skin . . . with so hard and hideous pens, so bitterly sore and so deep, as wrote the cursed Jews upon the blessed body and sweet skin of our lord Jesu Christ, with hard nails, sharp spear, and sore pricking thorns, instead of pens. . . . There were upon the blessed body of Christ open wounds by number, five thousand four hundred seventy and five, this is the number of letters, with which our charter was written, by which we may claim our heritage . . . for Christ is the coffer, in whom is closed and locked, all the treasure of wit and wisdom of God.[70]

At one level the imagery used in this passage appears entirely conventional; however, as Nicholas Watson has argued, the passage is full of paradoxes. Watson asks, "How . . . can the 'charter' guaranteeing admittance to an all-Christian heaven be described, more than a century before Luther's radical theorizing of law and gospel, as written by Jews?"[71] This passage depicts Christ as a text and at the same time a coffer. These two tropes seem contradictory. *The Pore Caitif*'s deployment of the trope of the Charter of Christ is charged with potentially subversive meanings given the importance of charters, burned and granted, in 1381. Christ's body is the charter that grants freedom to all Christians.[72]

The Pore Caitif then develops the imagery of the Charter of Christ, suggesting that the charter is bound with the laces of the promises of God and sealed with Christ's blood, and that the image on its seal is that of "our lord Jesu hanging for our sin on the cross."[73] This passage employs a recessive logic, in which each detail simply refers to an earlier one, so that the reader's experience is at once complex and simple, complex because the author of this Charter of Christ takes such care to develop in detail the trope of Christ as a text, and simple because ultimately all this imagery and explication returns to the opening statement of Christ's promise of forgiveness. This section of *The Pore Caitif* concludes by explicitly subverting the earlier image of Christ's body as a coffer of wit and wisdom: "Christ hath all his body spread abroad to give him wholly to us, cleaving to him and freely he hath his side opened and his heart made cold for our sake so that without letting we may creep in to Christ's heart. . . . This scripture is our lord Jesu Christ, charter and bull of our heritage of heaven, lock not this charter in thy coffer, but set . . . it in thy heart."[74] *The Pore Caitif* represents Christ's body as at once a book, a charter to be stored and kept safe, and a text to be spread abroad for all. And in this apparent contradiction *The Pore Caitif* creates an image that potentially subverts clerical authority. The metaphor of the Christian creeping into Christ's heart through the wound in his side implies that by doing this one becomes part of the body/Charter of Christ, part of his universal and universalizing promise of salvation. The use of the word "creep" is also significant, since it implies a degree of secrecy or at least tentativeness. One senses that this passage positions the reader as a thief having to steal Christ's salvation. Creeping into the heart of Christ, writing his charter in one's heart, and climbing the Tree of Virtue are images of devotional writing and reading that exist between the liturgical and contemplative. These metaphors reflect the perspicacity of Aston's observation that in the fifteenth century, "there was an equivalence of books and images which is alien to us."[75] *The Pore Caitif* is not simply a book; it is also in its material, textual form an image of the Charter of

Christ; as such, it recognizes itself as an object of devotion, a devotional image, as well as a text to be read.

The early sixteenth-century lyric "Brother, Abide" repeats many of the motifs of *The Pore Caitif*. It is a lament from Christ to "sinfull mane his brother naturall."[76] The poem comprises of a life of Christ leading up to the moment of crucifixion. It stresses Christ's role as a preacher and healer:

> Myn age encresed, and then a-bought I wentt
> Prechinge scripture; and wher-sumeuer I came
> I movyd the people for to be penitent,
> And that I saied, was in my fathers name.
> Some praysed my preching, some said I was to blame,
> Some toke my techyng, sum wold nott of my scole,
> Sum held me wyse, some said I was a fole.[77]

The Christ that is imagined in "Brother, Abide" is recognizably similar to the Christ of More's *Treatise* or indeed of the *York Corpus Christi* plays. He appears to exist at best on the edge of society, "passyng frome place to place / Bare-fotyd, caplese, without syluer or gold."[78] At his death Christ tells the reader:

> My visage changed to pale and blewe as byse,
> My fleshe be-ganne to styff and waxid drye,
> My hart lokyd lyke a plomett of Ise,
> My lyff was spent, myne owre was come to dye.
> Vnto my father I cryd, "heli, heli!"
> And wyth that worde, I layde myne hede a-syde,
> And dolefully gave vp the spret and dyed.[79]

This is a striking image of Christ dying on the cross. In particular, the image of Christ's heart looking like a plummet of ice is horrific, since it suggests, if only for a moment, the terrible possibility that *The Pore Caitif*'s offer of hope that the Christian can always find comfort in Christ's heart might be denied. There is nothing unsophisticated or instrumental about this devotional imagery. It is deliberately and provocatively shocking.

"Brother, Abide" ends with Christ telling the reader to "be-holde this matur welle."[80] This phrase suggests that the reader should at once look upon the picture, the matter, of Christ's death that the poem contains and at the same time internalize, think upon, the message of the poem in its entirety. "Brother, Abide" is an exemplary pre-Reformation devotional text. It aims to encourage and enable the reader to engage emotionally and rationally with Christ's teaching and suffering. It is neither a liturgical nor contemplative work. In particular, its emphasis on the brotherhood between Christ and humanity implies a universalism that Watson has argued was an important feature of fifteenth-century vernacular religious writing.[81] "Brother, Abide" is an entirely orthodox poem. It is not heretical in any sense, nor is it anticlerical. But its incitement to the reader to "be-holde this matur welle" suggests trust in the ability of individual readers, lay or clerical, to participate in the textual community it creates by staging the matter of Christ's address from the cross. It therefore embodies a confidence in relation to lay devotional practice absent from works like *Everyman*. "Brother, Abide" simultaneously presents its readers with an image of Christ on the cross and creates a metonymic relationship between the book of Christ and itself as a graphic text. To hear Christ's words as addressed to us, to read our brother's words, is to accept Christ as our brother. It is to become part of the text of the poem. Reading "Brother, Abide" is a form of devotional labor comparable to praying or going on a pilgrimage.

John Fisher's *A Sermon Preached on a Good Friday* (c. 1520) contains an extended discussion of the book of the crucifix. Fisher was a leading Henrician bishop who had been chaplain to Margaret Beaufort, Henry VII's mother. He was made bishop of Rochester in 1504. As Henry's campaign against the church gathered pace, Fisher took a leading role in opposing it. When Fisher preached and published *A Sermon Preached on a Good Friday*, however, he still had Henry's favor. Richard Rex has suggested that "although . . . this conceit was by no means original, its *bravura* development into an entire sermon certainly was. . . . The whole sermon, in fact, becomes a clever identification of the cross of Christ with scripture, and of the ceremonial part of the Good Friday liturgy (veneration of the cross) with the scriptural readings."[82] In *A Sermon Preached on a Good Friday* Fisher takes an image that played a central role in the kind of devotionalism articulated in works like "Brother, Abide" and develops it within such a form, the sermon, and in such a liturgical context that it becomes the basis for an assertion of clerical control over the meaning of the book of the crucifix. Throughout this piece Fisher aims to simultaneously incite his readers to see Christ's body on the cross as a book to be read and to close down the possibility of variant or individual readings; he asks his readers at once to read and to be read to.

A Sermon Preached on a Good Friday opens with Fisher stating that the book of the crucifix "may suffice for the study of a true Christian man, all the days of his life. In this book he may find all things that be necessary to the health of his soul."[83] He then begins to discuss what is in the book, before suddenly returning to his opening premise: "But you marvel peradventure why I call the crucifix a book? I will now tell you the consideration why? A book hath boards, leaves, lines, writings, letters both small and great. First I say that a book hath two boards: the two boards of this booke is the two parts of the cross, for when the book is opened and spread, the leaves be cowched upon the boards. And so the blessed body of Christ was spread upon the cross."[84] Fisher comments, "This book was written with in and without."[85] The external writing, principally the wounds on Christ's body, are, for Fisher, complemented by internal writing, although Fisher then immediately states that only one word is written within: "Of this word Saint John speaketh . . . the word was in the beginning before all creatures, this word is the second person in the godhead, the son of God which by the holy Ghost was written in the inward side of this parchment. For the Godhead of Christ was covered and hid under the likeness of man. The holy Ghost was the pen of almighty God the father, He set his most mighty word unto the body of Christ, within the womb of the Virgin Mary, and so this book was written within."[86] This is a complex passage, which creates a slightly disturbing analogy between Christ being written in the womb of the Virgin Mary and Christ writing himself on the inward side of Fisher's book of the crucifix. The complexity of this passage reflects the extent to which in this sermon Fisher is seeking to mold the conventional idea of the Book of the Passion to what Brian Cummings has described as the grammar of reformation.[87] Fisher wants to create a written book of the crucifix and at the same time protect the essential meaning of his book from the taint of textuality. In particular, by stressing that it is the Holy Ghost who wields the pen that writes within the book of the crucifix, Fisher moves away from the complexity and productive paradoxes of other medieval depictions of the book of the crucifix, in which Christ's tormentors write on his body.

A Sermon Preached on a Good Friday celebrates and enacts the productivity of the book of the crucifix, while simultaneously seeking constantly to close down the space of interpretation. In a remarkable passage discussing the shame that a Christian should feel when imaging Christ's death, Fisher asks his readers:

> Seest thou not his eyes, how they be filled with blood and bitter tears?
>
> Seest thou not his ears, how they be filled with blasphemous rebukes, and opprobrious words?
>
> His cheek and neck with buffets, his shoulders with the burthen of the cross?
>
> Seest thou not his mouth, how in his dryness they would have filled it with Asell and Gaule?
>
> Seest thou not, how his back is pained against the hard Cross?
>
> Seest thou not his sides, how they were scourged with sharp whips?
>
> Seest thou not his arms, how they were strained by the violence of the ropes?
>
> Seest thou not his hands, how they be nailed just unto the cross? Seest thou not his legs, how they be wearied with labour?
>
> Seest thou not his feet, how painfully they stay and bear up the weight of his whole body?[88]

Eamon Duffy has suggested that this is one of the most eloquent passages in the sermon and that it "invites the sinner to 'read' the message of Christ displayed in the crucifix."[89] Duffy's anxiety over the appropriateness of the word "read" in the context of this section of Fisher's sermon is, however, entirely appropriate, since it is not clear that the reader is being asked to read this passage so much as to see it.

Fisher ends his sermon with a warning:

> Now thou sinful creature, have often before thine eyes this wonder-
> ful book which as I said is written within and with out. In the which
> also thou mayest read three manner of writings, that is to say lamen-
> tation, song, and woe. If thou wilt begin to lament with Jesu, thou
> shalt thereby come to sing with him. And thereby thou shalt be made
> so fully partner of his passion, that the debts of thy sins shall be thor-
> oughly paid, and that thou shalt escape everlasting woe. But if thou
> do refuse this remedy, and follow the desires of this world, and of
> the flesh, be thou assured that then thou shalt pay thine own debts
> amongst the devils in hell, with everlasting woe.[90]

Ultimately for Fisher the book of the crucifix operates as a metaphoric
container for the teaching of God. Fisher's insistence on the book being
written within and without reflects his desire to close down the possibility
of the book having a metonymic relationship to Christ's passion. The
Charter of Christ in *The Pore Caitif* is at once text and image; it contains
Christ's teaching as written on his body by his persecutors and is Christ's
teaching offering forgiveness and freedom for all who can read it. *A Sermon Preached on a Good Friday* deploys imagery similar to that found in *The
Pore Caitif*, but its emphasis is very different. This is partly a product of
the different contexts in which the two works were produced, although
both were ultimately aimed at the same popular religious audience. It
also, however, reflects the extent to which Fisher's clericalism led him
to reduce the universal and potentially subversive scope of the book of
christ's passion; there is no place for creeping in *A Sermon Preached on a
Good Friday*.

We can see a similar process in the late fifteenth-century drama *The
Play of the Sacrament*. In this drama five Jews bribe a Christian merchant
to steal a consecrated Host, which they then torture in a parodic re-
creation of Christ's death. *The Play of the Sacrament* mocks the Jews, and
possibly the Lollards, who may be its real targets, for their failure to understand the nature of the miracle of Mass. Yet the behavior of the Jews in
taking the Host out of a clerical setting and treating it as though it had a
metonymic relationship to the body of Christ reproduces, in parodic

form, the crude materialism that Duffy has suggested was an element of some fifteenth-century devotionalism.[91] *The Play of the Sacrament* ends with the baptism of the Jews by a Bishop:

> **Episcopus:** Now the Holy Gost at thys tyme mot yow blysse
> As ye knele all now in Hys name!
> And with the water of baptyme I shall yow blysse
> To save yow all from the Fendys blame.
> Now, that Fendys powre for to make lame,
> In the name of the Father, the Son, and the Holy Gost,
> To save yow from the Devyllys flame,
> I Crysten yow all, both lest and most.[92]

The Bishop's baptism ushers the Jews into the protected space of the church. In the process the play stages the appropriation of the dangerous liminality of the Host's place in the drama. As the Jews attempt to disprove the miracle of transubstantiation, the play stages ever more literal enactments of the miraculous nature of the Host, until when the Jews throw it into an oven the Host explodes to reveal an image "with woundys bledyng."[93] The image speaks first in Latin and then asks the Jews:

> Why blaspheme yow Me? Why do ye thus?
> Why put yow Me to a newe tormentry,
> And I dyed for yow on the Crosse?[94]

This is the language that one finds in fifteenth-century poetic appeals of Christ to man from the cross. In this play, however, an image makes the appeal, directing it not at ordinary Christians but at Jews. Even so, this moment is deeply disturbing, since it suggests a collapse between image and reality that, in a paradoxical move, relies on sophisticated theatrical business to assert the truth of the doctrine of transubstantiation.[95] *The Play of the Sacrament* stages a moment when sign becomes a reality embodied in a speaking image. In this play icons or images are the laity's books, albeit within a framework that stresses the role of the clergy and church in the process of interpretation. The miracle at the heart of *The Play of the Sacrament* is profoundly devotional. It takes place around a sacred object, outside of the recognized religious boundaries, spatial or temporal. The play ends by imagining an unproblematic act of clerical appropriation and closure, and, in the process, marks the extent to which the central events of the play take place on the boundary of what the fifteenth-century church regarded as acceptable or orthodox religious behavior.

In the *Dialogue concerning Heresies* Thomas More defends visual images with the conventional defense that they should be seen as useful devotional tools for the simple. In the *Dialogue of Comfort* (1534) More explicitly draws on the image of Christ as a book, although in a very different way from Fisher in his *A Sermon Preached on a Good Friday*. The *Dialogue of Comfort* was written at the same time as *The Treatise*. And it has also suffered in the past from being bracketed in the unhelpful category of the "Tower works." The *Dialogue of Comfort* stages a discussion between two Hungarians, Anthony and Vincent, which More depicts as taking place under the shadow of an imminent Turkish invasion. A number of critics have suggested that the Turks symbolize the dangers of Protestantism; however, as Alistair Fox points out, the "allegory of the Turk is polysemous rather than simple."[96] Throughout the dialogue Anthony comforts and reassures his cousin, Vincent, ending by invoking the image of Christ on the cross as an example for those suffering tribulations:

> Yf we could and wold with dew compassion, conceyve in our myndes a right Imagynacion and remembraunce of Christes byttre paynefull passion, of the many sore blody strokes that the cruell tourmentours with roddes and whyppes gaue hym vppon euery part of his holy tender body, the scornefull crowne of sharp thornes beten down vppon his holy hed, so strayght and so diepe, that on euery part his blyssid blode yssued owt and stremyd down, his lovely lymmys drawen and strechid out vppon the crosse to the Intollerable payne of his forebeten and sorebeten vaynes and synewes, new felyng with cruell strechyng and straynyng far passyng any crampe, in euery part of his blyssid body at ones, than the greate long nayles cruelly driven with hamers thorow his holy handes and fete, and in his horrible payne lyft vpp and let hang with the payce of all this body beryng own vppon the paynfull woundid places so grievously percyd with nayles, and in such tourment, without pitie, but not

without many dispightes, suffred to be pynyd and paynid the space of more than three long howres, tyll hym selfe willyngly gave vpp vnto his father his holy soule . . . yf we wold I say remember these things . . . we shuld fynd our selfe not onely content, but also glad and desierouse to suffre deth for his sake.[97]

This passage recognizably draws on the same traditions of passion imagery as Fisher drew on in his sermon, but More's use is very different. This is partly a question of context, although this point can be overemphasized. For More and Fisher what was essential about the image of Christ on the cross was its efficacy as a devotional prompt or aid. More, however, has more confidence in the ability of his readers to understand what they are reading without additional glosses or guides. This passage is, in many ways, provocatively lacking in explanation while being replete with the graphic details of Christ's passion. The space of More's text is filled with the image of Christ on the cross, as though the *Dialogue of Comfort* itself, in formal terms, has become the book of the crucifix.

The *Dialogue of Comfort* stresses the extent to which reading is itself a devotional practice or labor. A. D. Cousins has commented on the two aspects of More's performative spirituality in the *Dialogue of Comfort*: "To Vincent and to the implied reader, Anthony/More's meditation [on the passion] advocates imitation of Christ; already in imitation of Christ, however, Anthony/More plainly teaches divine truths, accommodating them to the same reader."[98] The *Dialogue of Comfort* is an exercise in mapping out and implicitly constructing a space for devotional thinking between the liturgical and the contemplative. Anthony warns Vincent emphatically against having an overscrupulous conscience, which Anthony constructs as a "very timerouse daughter a sely whrechid girle."[99] A person infected by "pevish girl"

fereth that he be neuer full confessed, nor neuer full contrite, and than that his synnes be neuer full forgeven hym, and that he confessith and confessith agayne, and cumbreth hym selfe and his confessour both, and than euery prayour that he sayth though he say it as well as the frayle infyrmyte of the man wil suffre, ye is he not satisfied, but yf he say it agayne and yet after that agayne, and whan he hath said one thyng thrise: as litell is he satisfied at the last as with the first, and than is his hart euermore in hevynes vnquiat and in fere, full of dout and of dulnes without comfort or spirituall consolacion.[100]

This image of a man—and it is important to note the gender slippage from peevish girl to masculine subject—lost in a web of endless confession and empty prayer is a parodic version of the state that works like the *Cloud of Unknowing* construct as an ideal that a Christian should strive toward. This passage may also have had a more immediate and urgent meaning, since at the time More was writing, the whole of the England was being thrown into turmoil because of a scruple of conscience.

The *Dialogue of Comfort* creates images of empty, sterile language that reproduce tropes from medieval contemplative discourse. For example, Vincent tells Anthony about a dinner he once had with a "greate man of the church" who was "gloriouse above all measure."[101] Vincent then tells this uncle that

> so happyd it one day that he had in a greate audience, made an oracion in a certayne maner, wherin he likyd hymselfe so well, that at his diner he sat hym thought on thornes, till he might here how they that satt with hymn at his borde, wold commend it. And whan he had sit musyng a while devising as I thought after, vppon some prety proper way to bryng yt in withall, at the last for lacke of a bettre . . . he brought it evyn blont forth, and askyd vs all that sat at his bordes end . . . how well we likyd his oracion that he had made that daye. But in fayth vncle whan that probleme was ones proponid, till it was full answerid, no man I wene, ete one morsell of mete more, euery man was fallen in so diepe a studye, for the findyng of some exquisite prayse.[102]

In this passage More depicts the corruption of a physical pleasure, good food, by an empty desire. The Great Man's inability to enjoy his own feast is spread over the whole gathering the moment he articulates his desire for praise. It is no coincidence that this story revolves around spoken words. Nor is its conclusion simply a joke, although it clearly is one.

Vincent was initially optimistic that he could win in the battle of flattery that the Great Man's request set in motion, since, as he tells his uncle, he was sitting next to an "vnlernid preest." It becomes apparent, however, that this confidence was misplaced, since when

> this good auncient honourable flaterer . . . saw he could find no wordes of prayse that wold passe all that had bene spoken before all redy, the wily fox wold speke neuer a word, but as he that were ravished vnto havyn ward, with the wonder of the wisedome and eloquence, that my lordes grace had vttrid in that oracion, he fet a long sigh with an oh fro the bottom of his brest, and held vpp both his handes, lyft vpp his hed, and cast vpp his yein into the welkin, and wept.[103]

There is something entirely appropriate about the unlearned priest's response to the Great Man's request for flattery. Both are empty. The unlearned priest satisfies the Great Man's demand for praise not with words, which can be subject to reason and debate, but with a deep sigh, something that in its very nature is irrational or a-rational. The unlearned priest performs, and at the same time corrupts, a moment of contemplative transformation. His sigh is empty, meaningless but potent in the corrupt world created by the Great Man's desire for praise.

In the *Dialogue of Comfort* More uses parables and stories, his infamous "merry tales," to illustrate his argument. For example, he tells the story of the Ass and the Wolf—"Mother Maud's Tale"—who are "confessed" by the Fox. The Ass's confession takes a very long time, since everything he did "was dedly sin to hym."[104] In the end, however, the confession ended and the Fox decided that the chief sin the Ass was guilty of was gluttony, "and thefor he discretely gave hym in penuance, that he shuld neuer for gredines of his mete, do eny other best eny harm or hinderans, and than eate his meate and study for no more."[105] The Ass's overscrupulous conscience, however, led him to eat almost nothing for fear of giving harm to another creature and to practically starve himself to death before his "gostly father [presumably the Fox] came and enformyd hym bettre, and than he cast of that scruple and fell mannerly to his mete, and was a right honest asse many a fayre day after."[106] The Wolf's sin is also gluttony, but the Fox, in an act of solidarity with another predator, imposes a less restrictive penance on the Wolf than on the Ass. He tells the former that in order to curb his gluttony he must eat at one sitting only six pence of food "as nere as your conscience can gesse the price."[107] Not surprisingly, the Wolf finds the penance relatively easy, since when he sees a cow and a calf in the field, he reasons that, "while the cow is in my consciens worth but iiiid, my consciens can not serve me for a sinne of my soule prayse her calfe aboue iid, and so passe they not vid betwene them both. And thefor they twayne may I well eate at this one meale and breke not my penaunce at all. And so thervppon he did without any scruple of conscience."[108] At one level the meaning of this parable is simple; the Ass suffers from a too scrupulous conscience, while the Wolf's is too loose. Certain aspects of this parable, however, reflect More's devotional agenda in the *Dialogue of Comfort*. The parable seems to articulate two possible approaches to religion, both of which depend on contradictory, extreme reactions to its rules and regulations; the Ass takes his penance too seriously, while the Wolf treats his as something to be adapted to allow him to carry on as he was. Neither Ass nor Wolf actually engages with the meaning of his penance, the relationship between his behavior, his sins, and what he needs to do to correct his behavior.

More's "Mother Maud's Tale," however, also clearly has a relationship to the story of the Great Man and the Unlearned Priest. Again what is being staged is a story about eating in which the interpretation of words is crucial. In particular, the parable form of this part of the *Dialogue of Comfort* suggests that it is itself a kind of meal, like that which Conscience offers the narrator in *Piers Plowman*, which is being offered to the reader to be read or consumed. This readerly consumption is, however, not purely metaphoric; it is also metonymic. The material words that make up this section of More's are a textual image of a meaning-producing community that was for More the church, and the parable makes sense only on a communal, ongoing basis. It cannot be owned or understood at the level of the individual, nor can it be reduced to part of the day-to-day worship of the church. Reading Christian parables was for More a, possibly *the*, key way of traveling with and toward Christ.

Fisher's emphasis on the internal writing of his book of the crucifix reflects his desire to at once articulate late-medieval devotional discourse and safely enclose it within a clerical setting. The internal writing of the book of the crucifix stabilizes in advance and forever the possible meanings of the text written on the external body of Christ. More's invocation of the book of the passion in the *Dialogue of Comfort* makes a devotional image of the text itself. Throughout his work More deploys the image of pilgrimage to represent reading. As is typical of devotional imagery, this is entirely conventional and at the same time contains radical possibilities in the way that it collapses distinction—spatial, temporal, and religious. Pilgrimages are located in this world; they take place between the contemplative and liturgical, while being informed by both, and are performative since they implicitly deny any separation between an act and its meaning.

One of the first prayers in More's *Treatise* repeats a motif from Augustine's *Confessions*: "Good lorde gyue vs the grace, not to reade or here this gospel of thy bytter passion with our eyen and our eares in maner of a passetyme, but that it may with compassion so synke in to our heartes, that it maye streche to theuerlastyng profite of our soules."[109] In his *Confessions* Augustine writes, "Preachers of this word pass from this life to another life, but your scripture is 'stretched out' over the peoples to the end of the age."[110] There is a tension in More's prayer between its first part, which focuses on the need for the gospel's message to sink into the reader's heart, and the second part, in which the imagery is much more expansive. Like *The Pore Caitif*, this prayer conceives Christ's message both in terms of images of constriction, coffers, and hearts and in terms of expansion, stretching forth so all can read it and profit their souls. More's prayer constructs the gospel first in metaphoric terms, as sinking into the reader's heart, but then draws on imagery associated with the Book of Christ to imagine it being stretched, like Christ's body, to encompass the reader's soul. In the process More undermines any distinction between internal and external reading/writing. Instead he creates an image of reading as a form of devotional labor in which a focus on one's heart, on interiority, becomes a state that one passes through on the pilgrimage of life, the stretching forth of Christ's body/text, that is, the lived reality of Christian faith.

Reaching toward the unknowable, trying to escape beyond words, is a constant source of potential danger in the *Dialogue of Comfort*. This is, however, not purely a negative position. In all of More's later works words—graphic marks on a page, written textual images—come to represent a collective rationality beyond the limitations of the individual; they act as a kind of material, collective reservoir of knowledge and reason.[111] In *De Tristitia Christi* (The Sadness of Christ, 1534), More pores over the detail of the Christ's moment of agony in the garden of Gethsemane. *De Tristitia Christi* is the only work by More that has survived in manuscript form in his own hand. The manuscript was discovered in 1963 in Spain, although a number of versions of the work were already in circulation. Richard Marius has described *De Tristitia Christi* as "a rationale of faith in the world of agonising doubt that was the Christian Renaissance."[112] More opens *De Tristitia Christi* with a brief but telling discussion of the place names that form part of the apostles' accounts of Christ's last night before the passion:

> And so, since not a single syllable can be thought inconsequential in
> a composition which was dictated by the Holy Spirit as the apostles
> wrote it, and since not a sparrow falls to the earth without God's
> direction, I cannot think either that the evangelists mentioned those
> names accidentally or that the Jews assigned them to the places (whatever
> they themselves intended when they named them) without a
> secret plan (though unknown to the Jews themselves) of the Holy
> Spirit, who concealed in these names a store of sacred mysteries to
> be ferreted out sometime later.[113]

De Tristitia Christi is a principled engagement with the productivity of the biblical text. A minor detail from the Gospels, for example that of a young man clothed in linen who escapes capture by fleeing naked from the crowd that has come to arrest Christ, becomes in More's hands a mine of Christian teaching.

At one level this kind of explication was, and is, the norm of biblical exegesis.[114] What makes More's handling of this story interesting is the way he uses it to generate a hermeneutics for his own text that, while being impeccably orthodox and Augustinian, is also reformist in its implications. More comments that the young man, when he ran away, left his persecutors with the shell while ensuring that the kernel escaped their grasp. More then expands this argument, suggesting, "Now anyone who is willing to devote a little more attention to this deed of the young man can see that it offers us another teaching, even more forceful than the first. For the body is, as it were, the garment of the soul. The soul puts on the body when it comes into the world and takes off the body when it leaves the world at death. Hence, just as the clothes are worth much less than the body, so too the body is far less precious than the soul."[115] More's textual practice in *De Tristitia Christi* is to create more and more opportunities for his reader to set aside the clothes of the text to find the kernel within. More is partly motivated in this by a desire to fully explicate the moment of Christ's agony, but this practice also creates a work that demands a particular kind of devotional reading in which one experiences oneself as an individual participating in a far wider textual community through one's engagement with More's work.[116]

It is instructive to compare More's approach to the story of the young man to that of *The Passion of Christ* (1532), which is a detailed account of Holy Week and Christ's passion.[117] *The Passion of Christ* assumes that the young man stripped of his clothes in the garden of Gethsemane was the disciple John, and it comments: "And in especial it might be conjectured of Saint John the evangelist which was the young man that the Jews bereaved of his mantel by reason whereof he was all naked. Whereof no marvel though he were stricken with a dolorous pang of sorrow and shame, which fled first unto the house where our lady was for succour and garments, but when he was there he could not speak for the great sobbing of his heart."[118] *The Passion of Christ* creates an image of a good Christian as a person stricken dumb by grief, someone committed to an intense emotional engagement with Christ's passion. More, however, uses the story of the young man as, in Frank Kermode's words, a "parable-event" that remains open as a site of interpretation and reflection.[119] *The Passion of Christ* ultimately closes down the space for religious thought through its privileging of an emotional engagement with the story of the passion; *De Tristitia Christi* moves in the opposite direction, seeking to understand the story of Christ in the garden at Gethsemane as a provocation for devotional reading and reasoning. In the process More creates a reformist text that invites readers to see the textual complexity, unevenness, but also the wealth of the Gospels, and to use their intelligence to make those texts meaning-full.

The Space of the Passion

The fifteenth-century lyric "Unkind Man, Take Heed of Me" is a representative devotional text:

> Vnkinde man, take heed of mee!
> Loke, what payne I suffer for the.
> Sinfull man, to the I crie,
> Only for the I die.
> Beholde, the bloode of my handis downe renneth [rinnes]
> Not for my gilte but for youre sinnes,
> Fote and hande with nailes so ben faste,
> That sinoes and vanies alto-berste. [alto-braste]
> The blood of myne hert rote,
> Loke, how hit stremyth downe by my fote.
> Ouer all theeis paines that I suffer so sore,
> With myne herte hit greuith me more,
> That I vnkindnes finde in the
> That for thi loue hongid vpon a tree.[120]

The poem offers not a contemplative experience but rather a devotional one. By the injunction to "Look" it intends to make the reader imagine Christ on the cross, but also demands to be read as a form of looking. However orthodox this text, and however pious the intentions of its author, what it imagines, indeed incites, here is a religious experience that reflects the potential dispersal during the fifteenth century of clerical authority.

The Passion Sunday sermon from John Mirk's *Festial*, a collection of sermons probably written in the late 1380s and intended to be used by parish priests, articulates a very different approach to Christ's passion. The sermon includes an address from Christ on the cross. "I am lift on high for all shall hear me speak. Turn again to me and I will receive you. Lo, mine arms be spread of brode ready for to clyppon you. My head is bowed ready to kiss you. My side is open to show my heart to you, my [hands and] my feet bloody for to show you what I suffered for you."[121] Having discussed this image, the Passion Sunday sermon recounts a miracle story in which a beautiful woman presents a bleeding and scarred child to a magistrate who has been making people swear by "God's passion." The woman asks the magistrate what would be the proper punishment for the person responsible for the child's wounds, and when the magistrate answers death, the woman tells him: "'You and thy men with your horrible oaths have thus dismembered my Son Jesus Christ that I am mother to. And so ye have taught all this land. Wherefore thou shall have now thine awful doom.' Than anone in the sight of all the people the earth opened and the justice fell down to hell."[122] The Passion Sunday sermon deploys Christ speaking from the cross in order to sustain its pastoral message concerning the sin of swearing. The narrative of the sermon progresses from direct Gospel reference to miraculous story, or exempla. In the process the Passion Sunday sermon deploys, albeit in a different key, a strategy similar to that of Nicholas Love in *The Mirror*. This sermon invites listeners to respond emotionally to the image and words of Christ on the cross, but restricts their engagement. The concluding miracle story articulates a hermeneutics that implies an equivalence between Scripture and exempla. In the process, as Katherine C. Little has suggested, the sermon effectively emphasizes the role of the clergy through the performance of bringing together Scripture and exempla in an overarching text at the expense of the individual lay person's direct engagement with Christ.[123]

De Tristitia Christi, while analyzing in detail a very specific scriptural moment, is constantly aware of its own limitation: "Certainly it seems clear to me that no one understands the meaning of all scriptural passages so well that there are not many mysteries hidden there which are not yet understood."[124] One can respond to the mysteries of Christian teaching and Scripture by closing them down in the way that Mirk's Passion Sunday sermon does or, in a different context, *The Play of the Sacrament*. More, however, in his last works presents Christ's passion as a site for ongoing, purposeful devotional labor/reading. He undoubtedly expects readers of *De Tristitia Christi* to emotionally engage with the story, but he also asks them to use their reason and wit. In works like *The Treatise* and the *Dialogue of Comfort* Christ's passion shares the sense of literariness that Chaucer deployed in *The Nun's Priest's Tale* to imagine an open political space under the shadow of 1381; Christ's passion is for More an always open, always giving, always rewarding path to Christian renewal.

CONCLUSION

In the spring of 1534 More was sent to the Tower of London for refusing to take the oath of succession. Although it is tempting to see this as More's first step on the path that led to the execution block and martyrdom, this is misleading. It was entirely reasonable for More to hope that Henry VIII might have another sudden change of mind, "a scruple of conscience," and, like David, see the error of his ways. This did not happen. And by the following year it was clear that Henry was determined either to force More to capitulate or to have him tried for treason. It was during this period that More wrote a number of letters to his daughter Margaret Roper and to Thomas Cromwell. Brad S. Gregory has argued that the writings More wrote between February 1534 and July 1535 are "among the most extensive and elaborate prison writings of anyone executed for religion in the Reformation era."[1] More's letters from prison powerfully influenced later historical accounts of his life. They have often been treated as personal letters that convey More's feelings and thoughts while he was in prison. This use of them started early. For example, this is how Thomas Stapleton viewed them in his influential biography of More produced in 1588. For Stapleton More's prison letters provided an authoritative insight into what More was privately thinking in the months leading up to his trial and execution.[2] Stapleton's use of More's letters is, however,

anachronistic, since it was precisely the religious changes that More strenu-
ously opposed that, as Brian Cummings has argued, fueled the emergence
of a stark dichotomy between the private and public.[3] More wrote as a
humanist, a man for whom letters were rhetorical acts. His Tower letters
display a man using all the linguistic and intellectual tools at his disposal
to explain his beliefs without incriminating himself. At the same time
one senses that More's defense of his position, and in particular his understanding of conscience, within a humanist epistolary discourse pushed
the existing language of religion to its limits.[4]

In his letters to Thomas Cromwell More tried to explain his reasons
for refusing to acknowledge Henry VIII as head of the English church.
His position rested on two key principles: it was not possible for the
church in England to separate itself from the common corps of Christendom, and his conscience prevented him from yielding to Henry in this
matter. The latter principle is the more difficult to understand, largely because More was careful, for obvious reasons, not to state explicitly why his
conscience prevented him from subscribing to the Act of Supremacy.[5]

More spelled out his position with regard to the relationship between the English church and the wider body of Christendom in one of
his early letters to Cromwell: "Sith all Christendom is one corps, I cannot
perceive how any member therof may without the common assent of the
body depart from the common head."[6] More accepted that the nature or
status of the pope's primacy was a matter that could be legitimately debated by the general council of the church:

> For albeit that I have for mine own part such opinion of the pope's
> primacy as I have shewed you [Cromwell], yet never thought I the
> Pope above the general council nor never have in any book of mine
> put forth among the King's subjects in our vulgar tongue, advanced
> greatly the Pope's authority. For albeit that a man may peradventure
> somewhat find therein that after the common manner of all Christian
> realms I speak of him as primate, yet never do I stick with reasoning
> and proving of that point. And in my book [*The Answer to the Poisoned
> Book*] against the Masker, I wrote not I wot well five lines, and yet of
> no more but only Saint Peter himself, from whose person many take
> not the primacy, even those that grant it none of his successors.[7]

Yet More's position on the primacy of the pope does appear to be more papalist in the remarks he is reported to have made at his trial after being sentenced. William Roper in his *Life of Sir Thomas More* quotes More's father-in-law as telling the court: "This indictment is grounded upon an act of Parliament directly repugnant to the laws of God and His Holy Church, the supreme government of which, or of any part whereof, may no temporal prince presume by any law to take upon him, as rightfully belonging to the See of Rome, a spiritual pre-eminence by the mouth of Our Saviour himself, personally present upon the earth, only to Saint Peter and his successors, Bishops of the same See, by special prerogative granted."[8] One needs, however, as John Guy has suggested, to treat Roper's biography of More with caution, since Roper clearly wrote it to address, at least partially, the polemical agenda of the regime of Mary Tudor. In this context papal "supreme governance" of the church was crucial and controversial.[9] What More actually said at his trial is difficult to be sure about.[10] It is, however, clear that his argument rested on the fundamentally different competences and status of secular and spiritual law.

More's position throughout his written work on the papacy is more nuanced and less papalist than is suggested in the speech quoted by Roper. Brian Gogan, in a carefully argued discussion of More's views on the church, suggests that "what a later Catholicism was to make of papal authority in all fields of Christian life, More's 'populist' Catholicism made of the common faith and practice of the believing community, a corporate mind which can never err."[11] As I have suggested, this sense that the church as a space for communal religious belief and practice that in its collectivism and universality cannot err runs through all of More's writings. More understood the church as a mystic corporate body animated by Christ's continuing ministry, and, as George Bernard has argued, it was for this ideal that he gave his life.[12] On the surface, however, More's emphasis on the common corpus of Christendom and his constant references to his conscience as providing the basis for his refusal of the oath of supremacy seem to contradict each other. What was the relationship between More's understanding of the church and the demands of his conscience?

In a letter dated August 1534 Margaret Roper, More's daughter, wrote to Alice Alington, More's step-daughter, passing on a discussion she had with More in the Tower of London.[13] The occasion of this discussion was a letter from Alice to Margaret relating a conversation she had had with the then Lord Chancellor concerning More's fate. The authorship of the *Letter* from Margaret to Alice has from its publication been open to debate. It has been generally assumed that it was written by More, although John Guy has questioned this and has advanced Margaret's claims to be regarded as at least joint-author.[14] Yet not only the authorship of Margaret's *Letter* is unclear. Given the importance of Alice's letter to Margaret, it is at least possible that this letter, too, is less factual and more fictional than is sometimes assumed. Indeed, the basic premises of Alice's letter, that the Lord Chancellor would tell Alice two fables in a response to a request to help More in his predicament, is clearly implausible.

It is, however, less important to decide whether More wrote the *Letter* on his own or in partnership with his daughter than to acknowledge its rhetorical or literary nature. The *Letter* is not a mimetic record of an actual discussion between More and his daughter in the Tower. As Guy has argued, the contents of More's letters from the Tower are "carefully contrived" and "cannot be taken at face value."[15] This is not to suggest that this *Letter* should be regarded as simply a work of fiction, since for More it is precisely its fictionality that makes it truthful. In the world created by Henry's scruple of conscience, which privileged the literal over the figurative and had at its heart a remorseless, absolute demand for obedience, Margaret and More's *Letter* is a religious act of poetic resistance. It mocks the religious ethos of the Henrician Reformation and deploys parables as metaphors for the potential universality of language, specifically writing. To read the *Letter* as revealing, in an immediate or realist fashion, More's inner thoughts and beliefs would be to place it, as Stapleton did in his biography, within the emerging discourse of confessional Christianity that More rejected. Instead it should be seen as deploying the literary in the same way that Chaucer does in *The Nun's Priest's Tale*, to create a space free from the immediate and instrumental religious and political pressures that More faced in 1534.

The *Letter* is a fable, written in response to a fable. It is a joke, but clearly a deadly serious one. It casts Margaret as a tempting Eve to More's resisting Adam: "'I assure you Father, I have received a letter of late from my sister Alington, by which I see well that if ye change not your mind, you are likely to lose all those friends that are able to do you any good.' . . .

With this my father smiled upon me and said: 'What, mistress Eve, . . . hath my daughter Alington played the serpent with you, and with a letter set you at work to come tempt your father again . . . ?'"[16] This passage is typical of the *Letter* in the way it plays with authorial and gender slippage to mock the desire of the reader to create a simple, transparent meaning. If the letter was written by More, he is playing the role of Eve to his own Adam; alternately, if Margaret was the author, then she is at once Eve and the serpent. Passages like this render any attempt to settle the authorship of the *Letter* pointless and reductive, not simply because of the complexity of the different roles being played here, but more importantly because this passage reflects a desire to reject a model of writing that stresses the individual author. The *Letter* was written by Margaret and More, and by More playing Margaret, and by Margaret playing More.

The *Letter* reports More telling Margaret that, while he understands her fears and anxieties, his mind is made up, even if people "say it is no conscience but a foolish scruple."[17] Margaret shows More the letter from Alice as a response to this statement, since one of the parables it contains tells a story of a lion, an ass, and a fox in which the ass is undone by his overscrupulous conscience.[18] This exchange between More and Margaret tempts the reader into a web of parables in which the authorship of the *Letter* is further displaced—who wrote the parable told by the Lord Chancellor, recounted by Alice, read by More, and discussed by Margaret that is the ultimate reason for the *Letter*'s existence? It is easy to forget that the real reason for the *Letter*'s existence was a highly individual, authored scruple of conscience, albeit Henry VIII's and not More's.

In the *Letter* More tells Margaret a story in order to illustrate why he regards as beside the point the fact that other people have found reasons for taking the oath of supremacy. The tale concerns "a poor honest man of the country that was called Company" who found himself in the difficult position of being the only member of a jury not prepared to convict a clearly innocent man.[19] The reason for this reluctance was, as More makes clear, that the accused Londoner was guilty of nothing more than being an escheator (a court officer) who, having arrested a Northern man at Bartholomew Fair, found himself accused by the arrested man's friends and facing a jury composed of Northerners. More's Company was the only non-Northern man on the jury and found that he could not agree with their rush to find the escheator guilty. When he refused to go along with his fellow jurors, they turned on him and asked why: "'What good fellow,' quoth one of the northern men, 'where wonnes thou? Be not we eleven here and you but one la alone, and all we agreed? Whereto shouldst you stick? What is thy name good fellow?' 'Masters,' quoth he, 'my name is called Company.' 'Company,' quoth they, 'now by thy truth good fellow, play then the good companion, come thereon further with us and pass even for good company.'"[20] The phrase "one la alone" indicates the accent of the Northern men, and therefore suggests the extent to which their behavior is partial. More is ironically pointing out that their complaint that Company is standing alone stands alone in its regional specificity. Company explains to the Northern men that he is rejecting their blandishments by asking them whether, if they were sent to heaven for following their consciences while he was condemned for ignoring his, they would then be prepared to keep him company in hell?

Company goes on to tell the Northern men: "Therefore must ye pardon me from passing as you pass, but if I thought in the matter as you do, I dare not in such a matter pass for good company. For the passage of my poor soul passeth all good company."[21] More's Company is a simple soul who refuses to go along with the majority because he fears for his soul. Yet even here More is careful to avoid stating that the Northern men were inherently wrong in their judgment, although he certainly implies this. His central criticism of them is that they have allowed personal, regional considerations to corrupt their duty as jurymen. More's Company stands out against the rest of the jury not simply because he thinks they are wrong to condemn the London escheator, but because they are a false majority, created and designed to enforce a minority view as if it were the norm. The law, which is meant to be universal, is corrupted by the partiality of the Northern men. The implication is that the English are the "Northern men" in the case of Henry's divorce, seeing the situation only from their partial, regional perspective.

The story of "Good Company," however, has a more profound meaning than this one; indeed it would have to, since otherwise it too would be nothing more than another regional tale undermined by its lack of communal or common usage. More uses the term "company" both as the name for one of his protagonists and as the basis for his parable's Christian teaching. Company is good company because he personifies the true meaning of the word. The reader can become part of his company by reading not as a "Northern man" but as one of Christ's friends. More, however, does not present this as the easy or safe option. The other jurors' attempts to get Company to agree with them are more than a little menacing. Placing oneself alongside Company, accompanying him in defending the escheator's right to a fair trial despite the latter's unpopular lowly status, is a metaphor for traveling with Christ against prevailing social norms and cultural demands. Conscience, for More, meant above all making this choice. Indeed, for him to talk about conscience outside Christ's company, outside the church, was simply meaningless.

Having told Margaret the parable of Good Company, More is depicted in the *Letter* as explicitly telling his daughter the reason for his refusal to swear the oath required by the Act of Supremacy. As I already suggested, More ultimately believed that Henry's religious changes represented a fundamental rejection of the integrity of the church. In particular, More tells his daughter that when one part of Christendom regards a law as lawful but another part rejects it, no person, standing on his conscience, is required to accept either position as lawfully made, "other than by the general council or by the general faith grown by the working of God universally through all Christian nations: nor other authority than one of these twain (except special revelation and express commandment of God)."[22] It is difficult to read this list without at least entertaining the possibility that More had his tongue firmly in his cheek. Certainly he consistently maintained a broadly conciliar attitude to the establishment of Christian orthodoxy. The inclusion in this list, however, of the possibility of "special revelation" or "express commandment of God," seems designed to mock the orthodoxy of Henry's religious changes. It is as though More is throwing down the gauntlet and daring his opponents to state that they are working on the basis of God's express commandment, since neither of the alternative options, the general council or the general faith, can be used to legitimate Henry's religious policies.

It seems bizarre that, following such a clear statement of why he regarded the oath demanded by the Act of Supremacy as unlawful, More went on to tell his daughter, "For what causes I refuse the oath, the thing (as I have often told you) I will never show you, neither you nor nobody else, except the King's highness should like to command me."[23] It is, however, crucial to remember that the *Letter* is a work of fiction. It was composed by More and/or Margaret as a public document masquerading as a private letter. Its dialogue is no more real than that which fills such works as *Utopia* or the *Dialogue concerning Heresies*. More's reported refusal to tell Margaret why he will not take the oath is a performance, designed to remind readers of the *Letter* of More's loyalty to Henry. Indeed it is possible to read the entire *Letter* as a final, disguised offer from More to Henry, not simply to explain his position but also to give the king the counsel that More clearly thought he needed and lacked.

Throughout the *Letter* More is depicted as gently mocking Margaret for attempting to persuade him to take the oath. He tells her, "Mary, Marget, . . . for the part that you play, you play it not much amiss."[24] "Part that you play" refers to the ambiguity of the *Letter*'s authorship as well as to the attempts of the Margaret of the *Letter* to tempt her father into taking the oath. In its concluding paragraphs the *Letter* depicts Margaret as giving up on her attempts:

> When he saw me sit with this very sad, as I promise you, sister, my heart was full heavy for the peril of his person, for in faith I fear not his soul, he smiled upon me and said: "How now daughter Marget? What how mother Eve? Where is your mind now? sit not musing with some serpent in your breast, upon some new persuasion, to offer father Adam the apple yet once again?" "In good faith, Father," quoth I, "I can no further go, but am (as I trow Cressida saith in Chaucer) come to Dulcarnon, even at my wit's end."[25]

This passage is another example of the *Letter*'s provocatively playful ethos, which sometimes makes it hard to remember that it was written in the shadow of the executioner's block.

At the end of all of Margaret's attempts to persuade her father to change his mind, the reader is presented with a passage that evokes two famous stories of seduction and changeability. When More calls Margaret Eve and himself Adam, we must remember that Eve ultimately succeeded in tempting Adam. Indeed the *Letter* ends depicting More as acknowledging the possibility that God may intend him to play the role of Saint Peter even if, afterwards, God's goodness would "cast upon [More] his tender piteous eye, as he did upon Saint Peter," and make him "stand up again and confess the truth of [his] conscience afresh."[26] The *Letter* is not an abstract exercise in theological discussion. It is an argument for the importance of fiction, of textual playfulness, in the world created by the Henrician Reformation, which demanded in questions of religious orthodoxy absolute fixity and hermeneutic certainty.[27] The references to Eve and Cressida remind us that despite the refusal of More, old father Adam, to succumb to Eve's/Margaret's temptations, it is impossible to be certain that he would or could sustain his position—if even Saint Peter could doubt, and be forgiven, then why not More? Indeed why not Henry himself?

The reference to "Cressida" in the passage quoted above raises again, and in a particularly dangerous way, the question of the relationship between the *Letter* and Henry's great matter. Geoffrey Chaucer's poem *Troilus and Criseyde* was well known to Tudor readers; More refers to it several times in his work.[28] In 1534, however, referring to Chaucer could also be a political and religious act. Greg Walker has demonstrated the politicized nature of William Thynne and Brian Tuke's 1532 edition of Chaucer's complete works.[29] This edition, however, does potentially make More's reference to *Troilus and Criseyde* difficult to understand fully, since it includes Robert Henryson's *The Testament of Cresseid* as the concluding part of *Troilus and Criseyde*. *The Testament of Cresseid* is far from being a simple continuation of Chaucer's work.[30] Its depiction of Criseyde as a repentant leper provides the moral closure conspicuously lacking from *Troilus and Criseyde*. *The Testament of Cresseid* is a work of certainty, or of a desire for certainty, that in the religious sphere is exemplary of Reformation Christianity; Chaucer's work takes seriously the pagan world of its protagonists, whereas Henryson's poem is, to quote Lee Patterson, "thoroughly and deliberately Christian."[31] Ironically, given the reasons why More found himself in the Tower quoting Chaucer, it is not the world of *The Testament of Cresseid* that informs the *Letter*. Rather, Margaret's claim that she has come to "Dulcarnon" specifically refers to the situation Criseyde faces in the pagan world of Chaucer's Troy.

Troilus and Criseyde is a strange text for the *Letter* to cite. The whole poem is a pagan love story and seems to refer little to the religious issues facing More and his daughter in 1534. Book 3 in particular is the moment when Troilus and Criseyde consummate their relationship. In what ways does courtly love relate to More's imprisonment? A more detailed examination of Chaucer's text, however, reveals that More's citation embodies a profoundly critical stance toward Henry's divorce and the politics it engendered. Criseyde is brought to exclaim that she is at her wits' end by the actions of her uncle, Pandarus, who at the conclusion of numerous tricks and lies has finally maneuvered her into a situation in which she feels forced to become Troilus's lover. Pandarus tells Criseyde that if she does not receive Troilus, she will cause Troilus's heart to break because Troilus thinks that she has been unfaithful. This is, however, a lie. Pandarus's purpose in telling this lie is to engineer a situation in which Troilus and Criseyde are alone together. He tells Criseyde that "harm may ther be non, ne synne" in receiving Troilus, even though all his plotting has been driven by a desire to make Criseyde Troilus's lover. Having been told this by Pandarus, Criseyde comments:

> As wisly God at reste
> My soule brynge, as me is for hym wo!
> And em, iwis, fayn wolde I don the beste,
> If that iche hadde grace to do so;
> But whether that ye dwele or for hym go,
> I am, til God me bettre mynde sende,
> At dulcarnon, right at my wittes ende.[32]

At first sight Margaret's reference to Criseyde, particularly given its proximity to More calling her "mother Eve," could be read as indicating her female changeability. Going back to the original, however, illustrates the complexity of the *Letter*. Criseyde is brought to dulcarnon only by the overwhelming machinations and lies of Pandarus, and even at this stage she is driven by a desire to do the right thing, and to seek God's guidance. Criseyde in the *Letter* represents not female frailty but the limitations of human reason. Indeed Criseyde, although she does not know this, has been brought to her wits' end not by the extremity of her situation but by Pandarus's tricks and stratagems.[33] In her fall she represents those who end up making bad or wrong decisions with good intentions because of the wiles of evil men. Margaret is like Criseyde because she is trying to use reason, her wits, in a thoroughly corrupt situation.

The reference to *Troilus and Criseyde* in the *Letter*, however, also has a wider set of resonances. Chaucer's poem is replete with letters and reports, stories and histories, some honest and truthful, others designed to mislead, seduce, and corrupt. *Troilus and Criseyde*, again like the *Letter*, is concerned with Christian language. Chaucer consistently uses Christ's and the evangelists' favorite words, "grace," "faith," and "love," self-consciously within a pagan world in order to reflect upon different versions of Christianity. The paganism of Troy and the poem's literariness created for Chaucer a space to reflect upon his Christian beliefs. At the center of *Troilus and Criseyde* are two conversions that Dabney Anderson Bankert has persuasively equated with the different conversion narratives of Saint Paul and Saint Augustine.[34] Troilus sees Criseyde and is at once smitten. He falls in love, or at least thinks he does, immediately and violently. Like David when he saw and desired Bathsheba, Troilus allows nothing to stand in the way of his desires. And in this Pandarus aids him, actively colluding in his niece's seduction instead of protecting her. Criseyde falls in love, if she does, slowly and tentatively. She has to be constantly encouraged by Pandarus. *Troilus and Criseyde* is a love story that is also a meditation on the dangers of individualistic revelatory conversion. Certainly Troilus thinks he is in love with Criseyde, that he has suffered a genuine moment of revelation, but at the end of the poem Chaucer creates the sense that Troilus has learned nothing and is trapped in a pagan world where his conversion leads to nowhere.

Troilus and Criseyde was read in Henrician England as an exemplary story of courtly love. In 1534 when the *Letter* was written, however, More would have been very conscious that the boundaries between courtly love, high politics, and religious truth had dangerously blurred. Henry constructed his love for Anne Boleyn in language that Troilus would have instantly recognized. For example, Henry started one of his letters to Anne, probably composed before July 1527, by constructing himself as an anxiety-wracked courtly lover: "My turning over in my thoughts the contents of your last letters, I have put myself into great agony, not knowing how to understand them, whether to my disadvantage, as some passages indicate, or to my advantage, as I interpret other passages."[35] Seth Lerer has pointed out that "[Henry VIII's] letters are shot through with the shards of late medieval Chauceriana: phrases, idioms, allusions, and wordplays that place his letters in a literary trajectory traceable from the late medieval lyrics copied into manuscript anthologies to the Petrarchan sonnets of Sir Thomas Wyatt. If Henry, in some sense, saw himself as Troilus to Anne Boleyn's Criseyde, it was not only as the supplicant letter writer of Chaucer's poem, but as the betrayed epistolarist at the close of Book V."[36] It was not simply in his personal letters that Henry constructed his relationship with Anne in terms of courtly love. Henry's great scruple fed off and fed his revelatory love for Anne. They were parts of one sudden, violent individual conversion moment. The *Letter* is intended not simply to explain More's position as regards the oath of supremacy. It is also a Chaucerian work designed to imagine a literary space for thought as a place of refuge from a world of religious "Troiluses" who, like Henry, never reach dulcarnon, their wits' end, since they are always convinced of their rightness, their revelatory truth.

Troilus and Criseyde ends with Criseyde's betrayal of Troilus and his death. Chaucer, however, stresses the extent to which Criseyde is placed in an impossible position not only by the rulers of Troy when they agree to trade her to the Greeks as part of a prisoner exchange but also by the courtly nature of Troilus's love, which locks him in an infantile state of dependency and passivity.[37] Chaucer reveals Troilus's reliance upon Pandarus to be profoundly corrupt and, at the end of the poem, to be ultimately empty. Troilus responds to Criseyde's betrayal by retreating into self-pitying grievance, complaining to Pandarus that he does not deserve to be betrayed. Given the tricks and lies that he and Pandarus used to seduce Criseyde, this seems at best debatable. Pandarus reacts to the news of Criseyde's betrayal by admitting his inability to provide any help other than to share in Troilus's violent grief:

> If I dide aught that myghte like the,
> It is me lief; and of this tresoun now,
> God woot that it a sorwe is unto me!
> And dredeles, for hertes ese of yow,
> Right fayn I wolde amende it, wist I how.
> And fro this world, almyghty God I preye
> Delivere hire soon! I kan namore seye.[38]

Pandarus has been Troilus's confidant throughout the poem. Whenever the latter had a problem in the past, Pandarus was able through letters and words, texts and stories, to narrate it away. Paul Strohm suggests that

"Pandarus is . . . a master of narratives that are both episodic and highly configured: they possess beginnings, middles, and endings, and feature incidents and observations selected to support predetermined conclusions."[39] At the end of *Troilus and Criseyde* Pandarus finds himself confronted with a world in which he has no power. Indeed it is only within the strange, aberrant world of a besieged city and the intimate space of courtly love that Pandarus has power. In this enclosed, partial, regional space he can make things happen; here his words, narratives, stories, and letters are potent. As Lerer suggests, this is what makes Pandarus a "generative figure" for the "complicated and ultimately self-baffled artfulness of courtly life."[40] Above all Pandarus is the master of the fabricated letter.

The *Letter* is haunted by the possibility that Margaret is playing Pandarus to More's Criseyde, but also by the even more disturbing idea that it is More who is Pandarus. After all, it was More, and not his daughter, who spent years in the service of the king and was one of the most successful members of Henry's court. It was More who congratulated Wolsey on the latter's ability to write a perfect letter in another's hand. To achieve the public success that he did, More mastered the full range of courtly skills. Indeed the *Letter* is a work that at one level Pandarus, or perhaps even Wolsey, would have been proud of. Who is its author? Without knowing the author can one decide what it is saying? What it means? The *Letter* is shot through with profound religious themes and motifs, and yet to interpret it one needs a key that its author(s) has/have denied the reader. This is, however, the case only if one fails to respect the literary, parabolic nature of the *Letter*. It is not a text designed to express a particular individual's thoughts or intentions. The *Letter* is a parable. It mocks emerging forms of confessional writing and reading.[41] It offers its communal, parabolic nature as an antidote to the world that More thought was being created specifically by Henry's religious policies and more generally by the Reformation. In the *Letter* More is implicitly saying to Henry, and Anne, "When the 'Pandaruses' who have allowed you to indulge your desires, who have encouraged you to regard England/Troy as the world, are revealed to be powerless, as having nothing more to say, as being merchants of empty narratives and sterile tales, then there is an escape route that is not Troilus's self-pitying fatalism."

The *Letter* concludes with More speaking: "If anything hap to me that you would be loath, pray to God for me, but trouble not yourself: as

I shall full heartily pray for us all, that we may meet together once in heaven, where we shall make merry for ever, and never have trouble after."[42] This is a strange ending for a letter written by Margaret. There is no coda or comment. The reader is left free to understand More's final words without further authorial or editorial interventions. Conscience for More made sense only within the community of the church. James Simpson points out that for More, "the word 'conscience' has all its etymological force, of a 'knowing together,' a knowing shaped by collective experience."[43] Margaret and More's *Letter* ends with an offer of friendship to all. It implies that anyone can join them in the collective experience offered by the *Letter* and become part of their merry company with Christ.

Thomas More is a complex and controversial figure. He has been regarded as a saint and a persecutor, a leading humanist and a representative of late-medieval culture. In particular, the status of More's religious writings, with their stark and at times violent attacks on what More regarded as heresy, has been hotly debated. It is easy, when working on More's writing, to be seduced by his wit and, in places, charm. It is also easy to be shocked by the violence and, in places, glee with which More celebrated the death of those he considered heretics. This book has attempted to place More within the context of late-medieval and early Tudor culture. It has done so largely without the resort to the confessional labels that have bedeviled the study of More. The danger with this approach is that the More who appears in these pages may seem very much a medieval figure without a place in the emerging conflicts and debates of the Reformation. I am unapologetic about this. The central unifying theme of More's writings, political and religious, is the maintenance of a space for engaged Christian thought. Despite everything, More remained true to the Erasmian ideal of Christian humanist friendship. His final letters, particularly the *Letter*, are epistolary proverbs offering their readers an ocean of learning. More's particular understanding of Christian humanism places him outside the norms of post-Reformation Christianity, Protestant or Roman Catholic. The true inheritors of his legacy are not the religious zealots and confessionalizing leaders of the Reformation but artists like William Shakespeare and Michel Montaigne, who shared More's skepticism toward totalizing confessional discourses, his foolish trust in human reason, and his commitment to the plebeian virtues of faith, hope, and charity.

NOTES

Introduction

1. Thomas More, *The Correspondence of Thomas More*, ed. Elizabeth Frances Rogers (Princeton: Princeton University Press, 1947), 279.

2. Ibid., 280.

3. John Guy, *The Public Career of Sir Thomas More* (New Haven: Yale University Press, 1980), 15.

4. For the way in which More's biography has been mythologized, see John Guy, *Thomas More* (London: Arnold, 2000).

5. William Roper, "Life of Sir Thomas More," in *Two Early Tudor Lives*, ed. Richard S. Sylvester and Davis P. Harding (New Haven: Yale University Press, 1962), 195–254 (198).

6. Ibid.

7. John Guy comments: "In encouraging radically divergent accounts of the same meagre assortment of facts, the Charterhouse debate is typical of the ways in which interpretations of More's life are constructed" (Guy, *Public Career*, 29).

8. Seymour Baker House, "Thomas More," in *New Dictionary of National Biography*, www.oxforddnb.com/view/article/19191, 6.

9. R. W. Chambers, *Thomas More* (London: Jonathan Cape, 1935), 359–60.

10. For the problematic nature of this model of the medieval period, see David Aers, "Rewriting the Middle Ages: Some Suggestions," *Journal of Medieval*

and Renaissance Studies 18 (1988): 221–40, and Lee Patterson, "On the Margin: Postmodernism, Ironic History, and Medieval Studies," *Speculum* 65 (1990): 87–108.

11. Chambers, *Thomas More*, 351.

12. For a discussion of the problematic nature of "conscience" as a category in the fifteenth and sixteenth centuries, see Paul Strohm, "Conscience," in *Cultural Reformations: Medieval and Renaissance in Literary History*, ed. Brian Cummings and James Simpson (Oxford: Oxford University Press, 2010), 206–26.

13. For an excellent recent discussion of More's attitude to conscience and why ultimately he went to his death, see G. W. Bernard, *The King's Reformation: Henry VIII and the Remaking of the English Church* (New Haven: Yale University Press, 2005), esp. 125–51.

14. Richard Marius, *Thomas More* (New York: Knopf, 1984), 426.

15. Ibid., 42.

16. G. R. Elton, "Sir Thomas More and the Opposition to Henry VIII," in *Essential Articles for the Study of Thomas More*, ed. R. S. Sylvester and G. P. Marc'hadour (Hamden: Archon Books, 1977), 79–91.

17. Stephen Greenblatt, *Renaissance Self-Fashioning: More to Shakespeare* (Chicago: University of Chicago Press, 1980), 63.

18. Peter Ackroyd, *The Life of Thomas More* (London: Vintage, 1999), 43.

19. Marius, *Thomas More*, 66.

20. Guy, *Thomas More*, 4; Guy, *Public Career*.

21. Guy, *Thomas More*, 4.

22. For example, Guy points out that a key area of myth building is More's domestic life, the available sources on which, a vignette by Erasmus and Holbein's family portrait, have been blown out of all proportion (ibid., 5).

23. One of the most important developments in the study of medieval and Tudor literature in recent years has been the growing scholarly interest in critiquing dated views of fifteenth-century culture as drab and a new emphasis on its importance. See Maura Nolan, "The New Fifteenth Century: Humanism, Heresy, and Laureation," *Philological Quarterly* 87 (2008): 173–92.

24. Geoffrey Chaucer, *The Pardoner's Tale*, in *The Riverside Chaucer*, ed. Larry D. Benson, new ed. (Oxford: Oxford University Press, 1988), 196–202 (202).

25. William Langland, *Piers Plowman: The C Text*, ed. Derek Pearsall (Exeter: University of Exeter Press, 2008), 252.

26. Nicholas Watson, "The Politics of Middle English Writing," in *The Idea of the Vernacular: Anthology of Middle English Literary Theory, 1280–1520*, ed. Jocelyn Wogan-Browne, Nicholas Watson, Andrew Taylor, and Ruth Evans (Exeter: University of Exeter Press, 1999), 331–65 (339).

27. See Nicholas Watson, "Conceptions of the Word: The Mother Tongue and the Incarnation of God," *New Medieval Literatures* 1 (1997): 85–124, and

"Visions of Inclusion: Universal Salvation and Vernacular Theology in Pre-Reformation England," *Journal of Medieval and Early Modern Studies* 27 (1997): 145–87.

28. Alistair Fox comments: "More's use of proverbs, together with his concern to reinforce the proverbial flavour of his Chaucerian borrowings, suggest his belief in the power of everyday experience, especially as illuminated by poetry, to inculcate wisdom" (Alistair Fox, "Thomas More's *Dialogue* and the *Book of the Tales of Caunterbury*: 'God Mother Wit' and Creative Imitation," in *Familiar Colloquy: Essays Presented to Arthur Edward Barker*, ed. Patricia Bruchmann (Ottawa: Oberon Press, 1978), 15–24 (22).

29. Humanism was not new to England in the sixteenth century. For an important recent study of fifteenth-century English humanist writing, see Daniel Wakelin, *Humanism, Reading, and English Literature, 1430–1530* (Oxford: Oxford University Press, 2007).

30. James McConica, "Thomas as Humanist," in *The Cambridge Companion to Thomas More*, ed. George M. Logan (Cambridge: Cambridge University Press, 2011), 22–45 (23).

31. Brendan Bradshaw, "Transalpine Humanism," in *The Cambridge History of Political Thought, 1450–1700*, ed. J. H. Burns with the assistance of Mark Goldie (Cambridge: Cambridge University Press, 1991), 95–131 (108).

32. Kathy Eden, *Friends Hold All Things in Common: Tradition, Intellectual Property and the Adages of Erasmus* (New Haven: Yale University Press, 2001), 144–45.

33. See Howard B. Norland, "The Role of Drama in More's Literary Career," *Sixteenth Century Journal* 13 (1982): 59–75.

34. Thomas More, "A Mery Gest How a Sergeaunt Wolde Lerne to Be a Frere," in *The Yale Edition of The Complete Works of Saint Thomas More*, vol. 1, ed. Anthony S. G. Edwards, Katherine Gardiner Rodgers, and Clarence H. Miller (New Haven: Yale University Press, 1997), 15–29. All quotes from Thomas More's writing, with the exception of his last letters, are from the authoritative Yale University edition of his complete works.

35. Ibid., 17.

36. Ibid., 28–29.

37. Ibid., 26–27.

38. "Doun ran the blody streem upon his brest; / And in the floor, with nose and mouth tobroke / They walwe as doon two pigges in a poke" (Geoffrey Chaucer, *The Reeve's Tale*, in *Riverside Chaucer*, 77–84 [83]).

39. The Reeve concludes his tale by commenting, "And therefore this proverbe is seyd ful sooth / 'Hyme thar nate wene wel that yvele dooth.' / A gylour shal himself bigyled be." The Reeve appears to assume that his tale illustrates these proverbs, which is clearly not the case (ibid., 84).

40. More, "Mery Gest," 22.

41. See James Simpson, *Reform and Cultural Revolution* (Oxford: Oxford University Press, 2002). On the problematic nature of representations of the medieval as inherently conservative, see Aers, "Rewriting the Middle Ages," and Patterson, "On the Margin."

42. Thomas More, *The Last Things*, in *Complete Works*, 1:125–82 (176).

43. More's tendency to produce "mixed" works and his view of the church overlapped, since both were capacious, embodied, and inclusive. On More's understanding of the church, see James Simpson, "Place," in Cummings and Simpson, *Cultural Reformations*, 95–112.

44. For the importance of language and writing to St. Augustine's thought, see Brian Stock, *Augustine the Reader: Meditation, Self-Knowledge, and the Ethics of Interpretation* (Cambridge, MA: Harvard University Press, 1996).

45. More, *Last Things*, 137.

46. Ibid., 128.

47. Ibid., 129.

48. Ibid.

49. It is interesting to note that penitential manuals, drawing on the language of the Fourth Lateran Council, convoked by Pope Innocent III in 1213, used the idea of the priest as a doctor to stress the clergy's power and authority.

50. More, *Last Things*, 136–37.

51. Ibid., 177–78.

52. Ibid., 180.

53. Ibid., 153.

54. Ibid., 154.

55. Ibid., 155.

56. Ibid., 159–60.

57. Geoffrey Chaucer, *The Parson's Prologue and Tale*, in *Riverside Chaucer*, 287–327 (287).

58. Ibid.

59. Ibid.

60. See Krista Sue-Lo Twu, "Chaucer's Vision of the Tree of Life: Crossing the Road with the Rood in the *Parson's Tale*," *Chaucer Review* 39 (2005): 341–78.

61. For tensions over the status of imagination in the religious sphere in this period, see James Simpson, "The Rule of Medieval Imagination," in *Images, Idolatry, and Iconoclasm in Late Medieval England: Textuality and the Visual Image*, ed. Jeremy Dimmick, James Simpson, and Nicolette Zeeman (Oxford: Oxford University Press, 2002), 4–24.

62. Chaucer, *Parson's Prologue and Tale*, 318.

63. David Aers, *Chaucer, Langland and the Creative Imagination* (London: Routledge, 1980), 109.

64. Katherine C. Little, *Confession and Resistance: Defining the Self in Late Medieval England* (Notre Dame, IN: University of Notre Dame Press, 2006), 99.

65. For a rather different reading of *The Parson's Tale* that stresses its critical engagement with religious orthodoxy, see Karen A. Winstead, "Chaucer's *Parson's Tale* and the Contours of Orthodoxy," *Chaucer Review* 43 (2009): 239–59.

66. Lee Patterson argues that *The Parson's Tale* provides "not a fulfilment to the tales but an alternative, a complete and exclusive understanding of character, action and even language" (Lee Patterson, "'The *Parson's Tale*' and the Quitting of the *Canterbury Tales*," *Traditio* 34 [1978]: 331–80 [379]).

67. More, *Last Things*, 165.

68. Ibid., 165.

69. Ibid., 166.

70. Thomas More, "Letter to a Monk," in *Complete Works*, vol. 15, ed. Daniel Kinney (New Haven: Yale University Press, 1986), 197–311 (279).

71. Hinc pluris multi ceremonias aestimant suas quam cenobij, cenobij quam ordinis, tum quicquid est ordini proprium, quam quae sunt omni religioni communia, sed ea tamen quae sunt religiosorum pluris aliquanto faciunt, quam vilia illa atque humilia quae non sint illis vllo modo priuata, sed cum omni prorsus populo Christiano communia, cuiusmodi sunt virtutes istae plebeae, fides, spes, charitas, dei timor, humilitas, atque id genus aliae (ibid., 280).

72. Watson, "Conceptions of the Word," 107.

73. For the relationship between the two plays, see C. J. Wortham, "*Everyman* and the Reformation," *Parergon* 29 (1981): 23–31.

74. *Everyman*, in *Medieval Drama: An Anthology*, ed. Greg Walker (Oxford: Blackwell, 2000), 280–97 (284–85).

75. Ibid., 294.

76. William Munson, "Knowing and Doing in *Everyman*," *Chaucer Review* 19 (1985): 252–71 (261).

77. Alistair Fox suggests: "Pico's life was clearly a mirror for More in which he saw both sides of himself: worldly ambition resulting from precocity, together with a proclivity towards 'wantoness,' and an otherworldly recoil from it under the pressure of intense spirituality" (Alistair Fox, *Thomas More: History and Providence* [New Haven: Yale University Press, 1982], 31).

78. For a discussion of the identity of Joyeuce Leigh and More's approach to translation, see Anthony S. G. Edwards, introduction to *The Life of Pico*, in *Complete Works*, 1:xxvii–liii.

79. More, *Life of Pico*, 51.

80. Ibid., 52.

81. Gerard B. Wegemer has recently commented: "By eliminating well over one third of the original biography, More changes the focus of the work from emphasis on Pico's extraordinary learning and intellectual gifts used for esoteric studies to an emphasis on issues related to Pico's virtues and responsibilities" (Gerard B. Wegemer, *Young Thomas More and the Arts of Liberty* [Cambridge: Cambridge University Library, 2011], 76).

82. More, *Life of Pico*, 375.

83. Ibid., 106.

84. Ibid., 379.

85. Ibid., 119.

86. On Renaissance Platonism see Paul Oskar Kristeller, *Renaissance Thought and Its Sources* (New York: Columbia University Press, 1979).

87. Eamon Duffy, *The Stripping of the Altars: Traditional Religion in England, 1400–1500* (New Haven: Yale University Press, 1992), 3.

88. For the possible monastic provenance of this play, see Gail McMurray Gibson, *The Theatre of Devotion: East Anglian Drama and Society in the Late Middle Ages* (Chicago: University of Chicago Press, 1989), 128–31.

89. *The N Town Play*, ed. Stephen Spector, Early English Text Society, nos. 11 and 12 (Oxford: Oxford University Press, 1991), 225.

90. Ibid., 227.

91. Ibid.

92. Rowan Williams, *Writing in the Dust: Reflections on 11th September and Its Aftermath* (London: Hodder & Stoughton, 2002), 80–81.

93. Spector, *N Town Play*, 228.

94. Ibid., 227.

95. Peter Meredith comments, "If *Nolo morten peccatoris* clearly deals with both mercy and penitence, it is by no means clear that the story of the woman taken in adultery does. Of mercy there is no doubt" (Peter Meredith, "Nolo Morten and the *Ludus Coventriae* Play of the Woman Taken in Adultery," *Medium Ævum* 38 [1969]: 38–54 [41]).

96. For the importance of this debate as a context for the play *Wisdom*, see Julie Paulson, "A Theater of the Soul's Interior: Contemplative Literature and Penitential Education in the Morality Play *Wisdom*," *Journal of Medieval and Early Modern Studies* 38 (2008): 253–84.

97. Katherine C. Little has argued that a similar clericalist ethos runs through orthodox fifteenth-century sermons. See *Confession and Resistance*.

98. Duffy, *Stripping of the Altars*, 4.

99. See Bob Godfrey, "The Machinery of Spectacle: The Performance Dynamic of the Play of Mary Magdalene," *European Medieval Drama* 2 (1998): 99–116 (100).

100. *The Late Medieval Religious Plays of Bodleian MSSS Digby 133 and E Museo*, ed. Donald C. Baker, John L. Murphy, and Louis B. Hall, EETS 283 (Oxford: Oxford University Press, 1982), 64.

101. Ibid.

102. Ibid., 73.

103. For the importance of wisdom as feminine in the Bible, see Kim Paffenroth, *In Praise of Wisdom: Literary and Theological Reflections on Faith and Reason* (New York: Continuum, 2004).

104. For a discussion of the potentially anticlerical nature of this section of *Piers Plowman*, see Ben Parsons, "Shearing the Shepherds: Violence and Anticlerical Satire in Langland's *Piers Plowman*," *Medium Ævum* 79 (2010): 189–206 (193).

105. Thomas More, *The History of King Richard III and Selections from the English and Latin Poems*, ed. Richard S. Sylvester (New Haven: Yale University Press, 1976), 150.

106. Ibid.

107. Ibid.

108. More, *Last Things*, 128.

109. Ibid.

Chapter 1. Politics

1. On More's early career the most recent authoritative account is in John Guy, *Thomas More* (London: Arnold, 2000).

2. Thomas More, *"The History of King Richard III" and Selections from the English and Latin Poems*, ed. Richard S. Sylvester (New Haven: Yale University Press, 1976), xi. I am using this edition of More's *History of Richard III* and his Latin epigrams because it is more accessible than the Yale *Complete Works* edition, upon which it is based.

3. See Gillian Day, "Sceptical Historiography: Thomas More's History of Richard III," in *The Anatomy of Tudor Literature*, ed. Mike Pincombe (Aldershot: Ashgate, 2001), 24–34; Retha Warnicke, "More's Richard III and the Mystery Plays," *Historical Journal* 35 (1992): 761–78; Arthur N. Kincaid, "The Dramatic Structure of Sir Thomas More's History of Richard III," *Studies in English Literature* 12 (1972): 223–42.

4. On the humanist influences reflected in *Richard III* and in particular More's use of classical models based on the work of Tacitus and Sallust, see

Daniel Kinney, " 'Kings' Tragicomedies: Generic Misrule in More's *Richard III*," *Moreana* 86 (1985): 128–50.

5. Antonia Gransden, *Historical Writing in England II: c. 1307 to the Early Sixteenth Century* (London: Routledge, 1982), 443. See also F. J. Levy, *Tudor Historical Thought* (San Marino, CA: Huntington Library, 1967).

6. For an excellent recent discussion of the classical authors that influenced More's history writing, see George M. Logan, "More on Tyranny: The History of King Richard the Third," in *The Cambridge Companion to Thomas More*, ed. George M. Logan (Cambridge: Cambridge University Press, 2011), 168–90.

7. For a nuanced discussion of the relationship between the various English and Latin versions of *Richard III*, see Alison Hanham, "The Texts of Thomas More's *Richard III*," *Renaissance Studies* 21 (2007): 62–84.

8. James Simpson, *Reform and Cultural Revolution* (Oxford: Oxford University Press, 2002), 219.

9. Herbert McCabe, OP, *The Good Life: Ethics and the Pursuit of Happiness* (London: Continuum, 2005), 6.

10. Walter M. Gordon points out that in *Richard III*, "the very rites and gestures by which the monarch asserts his majesty fall under satirical attack" (Walter M. Gordon, "Maiestas in Thomas More's Political Thought," *Moreana* 34 [1997]: 5–20 [8]).

11. For the importance of the relationship of rhetoric to ethics in relation to humanism, see Peter Mack, "Rhetoric, Ethics and Reading in the Renaissance," *Renaissance Studies* 19 (2005): 1–21.

12. More, "On the Coronation Day of Henry VIII," in *Richard III*, 132.

13. Ibid., 131.

14. Ibid., 132.

15. Alistair Fox, *Thomas More: History and Providence* (New Haven: Yale University Press, 1982), 46.

16. More, *Richard III*, 83.

17. On *Youth* see *Two Tudor Interludes: "Youth" and "Hick Scorner,"* ed. Ian Lancashire (Manchester: Manchester University Press, 1980).

18. Peter C. Herman, *Royal Poetrie: Monarchic Verse and the Political Imagery in Early Modern England* (Ithaca, NY: Cornell University Press, 2010), 30.

19. See John Skelton, *Magnyfycence*, in *Medieval Drama: An Anthology*, ed. Greg Walker (Oxford: Blackwell, 2000), 348–407.

20. For the political sophistication of Henrician history writing that discusses in detail *Richard III*, see Peter C. Herman, "Henrician Historiography and the Voice of the People: The Cases of More and Hall," *Texas Studies in Literature and Language* 39 (1997): 259–83.

21. Lancashire, *Two Tudor Interludes*, 103.

22. Ibid., 105.

23. Ibid., 147–48.

24. Ibid., 149–50.

25. See Lancashire's excellent introductory essay to *Youth* and *Hick Scorner* in *Two Tudor Interludes*, 1–95.

26. Ibid., 54–55.

27. Ibid., 57.

28. More, *Richard III*, 152.

29. Ibid., 153.

30. Ibid., 154.

31. Peter Iver Kaufman has recently suggested that "Thomas More hailed Henry VIII, hoping for advantage for his clients and, likely for himself. He was the crowd and something of a sycophant describing its passions, but he was also the unawed and iconoclastic peasant" (Peter Iver Kaufman, *Augustine and Thomas More* [Notre Dame, IN: University of Notre Dame Press, 2007], 143).

32. For the status of Lady Mede in *Piers Plowman*, see Diane Cady, "Symbolic Economies," in *Middle English*, ed. Paul Strohm (Oxford: Oxford University Press, 2007), 124–41 (136–40).

33. Skelton, *Magnyfycence*, 358.

34. Ibid., 407.

35. Ibid.

36. Ibid., 373–74.

37. Jane Griffiths, *John Skelton and Poetic Authority: Defining the Liberty to Speak* (Oxford: Clarendon, 2006), 138.

38. See T. F. Mayer, "Tournai and Tyranny: Imperial Kingship and Critical Humanism," *Historical Journal* 34 (1991): 257–77. For a critique of several aspects of Mayer's argument, see C. S. L. Davis, "Tournai and the English Crown," *Historical Journal* 41 (1998): 1–26.

39. Greg Walker, "The 'Expulsion of the Minions' of 1519 Reconsidered," *Historical Journal* 32 (1989): 1–16 (14).

40. Mayer, "Tournai and Tyranny," 271.

41. More, *Richard III*, 8.

42. Ibid.

43. Ibid., 9.

44. For the tradition of Aristotelian political theory and advice, see Judith Ferster, *Fictions of Advice: The Literature and Politics of Counsel in Late Medieval England* (Philadelphia: University of Pennsylvania Press, 1996).

45. More, *Richard III*, 9–10.

46. Ibid., 22.

47. Gillian Day comments: "More's Richard is an ambiguous figure who both represents and plays on the inadequacies of human ratiocination. Furthermore, by drawing attention to the constructed nature of his history, More invites the reader to recognise its dual, almost dialectical structure. Form is counterpointed with content in such a way that the discerning reader notes the partiality and potential fallibility of human reasoning" (Day, "Sceptical Historiography," 25).

48. David Lawton, "Dullness and the Fifteenth Century," *English Literary History* 54 (1987): 761–99 (793).

49. Ibid., 788.

50. Patricia DeMarco, "Violence, Law, and Ciceronian Ethics in Chaucer's 'Tale of Melibee,'" *Studies in the Age of Chaucer* 30 (2008): 125–69.

51. David Aers, "Chaucer's *Tale of Melibee*: Whose Virtues?," in *Medieval Literature and Historical Enquiry: Essays in Honour of Derek Pearsall*, ed. David Aers (Cambridge: D. S. Brewer, 2000), 69–82.

52. Steven Justice comments that Walsingham's "narrative happens in a swirl of noise that obscures agency and ignites violence as an impersonal force, a nightmare of clatters and screams that scare dead metaphors back to life" (Steven Justice, *Writing Rebellion in England, 1381* [Berkeley: University of California Press, 1994], 205).

53. Thomas Walsingham, *Historia Anglicana: The Peasants' Revolt, 1381*, ed. and trans. R. B. Dobson, 2nd ed. (London: Macmillan, 1983), 173.

54. Ibid., 167.

55. Ibid., 175.

56. For the relationship between transgressive acts of carnivalesque violence, violent oppression, and political enjoyment, see Slavoj Žižek, *The Plague of Fantasies* (London: Verso, 1997), 57.

57. See David Aers, "Vox Populi and the Literature of 1381," in *The Cambridge History of Medieval English Literature*, ed. David Wallace (Cambridge: Cambridge University Press, 1999), 432–53.

58. Derek Pearsall comments: "*Piers Plowman* is a poem of crisis. It records in minutest detail the conflict which racked medieval society, as the feudal order and the Church of the west moved into their last stages of institutionalised decay, and as the antagonistic forces over which they had presided moved into the open arena" (Derek Pearsall, introduction to William Langland, *Piers Plowman: The C Text*, ed. Derek Pearsall [Exeter: University of Exeter Press, 2008], 6).

59. Langland, *Piers Plowman*, 94.

60. For a discussion of this section of *Piers Plowman* in relation to the grammatical metaphor, see John A. Alford, "The Grammatical Metaphor: A Survey of Its Use in the Middle Ages," *Speculum* 57 (1982): 728–60, esp. 754–59.

61. Langland emphasizes the extent to which defining Mede is, in James Simpson's words, an "intellectual act." See James Simpson, "From Reason to Affective Knowledge: Modes of Thought and Poetic Form in *Piers Plowman*," *Medium Ævum* 55 (1986): 1–23 (13).

62. Mede is in many ways a rather passive figure, lacking positive agency while at the same time inciting all kinds of actions and desires within others. See Elizabeth Fowler, "Civil Death and the Maiden: Agency and the Conditions of Contract in Piers Plowman," *Speculum* 70 (1995): 760–92.

63. See James Simpson, "Spirituality and Economics in Passus 1–7 of the B Text," *Year Book of Langland Studies* 1 (1987): 83–103.

64. Langland, *Piers Plowman*, 91–92.

65. For the relationship between reading and desire in *Piers Plowman*, see James Simpson, "Desire and the Scriptural Truth: Will as Reader in *Piers Plowman*," in *Criticism and Dissent in the Middle Ages*, ed. Rita Copland (Cambridge: Cambridge University Press, 1996), 215–43.

66. David Aers argues: "[Langland's] discourse . . . is fundamentally exploratory, one in which conclusions are risked, tested out, and often shown to be premature, one-sided or mistaken; assumptions made, brought to light and later rejected or developed in fresh perspectives" (David Aers, "Piers Plowman and the Problems in the Perception of Poverty: A Culture in Transition," *Leeds Studies in English* 19 [1983]: 5–25 [5]).

67. Langland, *Piers Plowman*, 92.

68. Ibid., 95–96.

69. Steven Justice comments: "In Fragment VII of the *Canterbury Tales* . . . Chaucer meditates extensively on his authorial identity, and—more importantly—worries the question of reception *as a question of audience*" (Steven Justice, *Writing and Rebellion: England in 1381* [Berkeley: University of California Press, 1994], 218).

70. Helen Cooper, *The Structure of the Canterbury Tales* (London: Duckworth, 1983), 163.

71. Geoffrey Chaucer, *The Shipman's Tale*, in *The Riverside Chaucer*, ed. Larry D. Benson, new ed. (Oxford: Oxford University Press, 1988), 203–8.

72. Emily Steiner, *Documentary Culture and the Making of Medieval England* (Cambridge: Cambridge University Press, 2003).

73. For a reading of an exemplary charter in the *Pore Caitif*, see Nicholas Watson, "Conceptions of the Word: The Mother Tongue and the Incarnation of God," *New Medieval Literatures* 1 (1997): 85–124.

74. Cathy Hume, "Domestic Opportunities: The Social Comedy of the *Shipman's Tale*," *Chaucer Review* 41 (2006): 138–62 (156).

75. Lee Patterson comments: "Just as the economic order represented in the [*Shipman's*] *Tale* lacks an extrinsic norm by which value may be assessed, so does the verbal order from which it is constructed witness to a persistent instability of meaning" (Lee Patterson, *Chaucer and the Subject of History* [London: Routledge, 1991], 358).

76. Anne Middleton, "The Idea of Public Poetry in the Reign of Richard II," *Speculum* 53 (1978): 94–114 (95).

77. For a discussion of Chaucer's engagement with this evolving policy of persecution, see Paul Strohm, "Chaucer's Lollard Joke: History and Textual Unconscious," *Studies in the Age of Chaucer* 17 (1995): 23–42, esp. 28–32.

78. See chap. 3 for a discussion of this work by Love.

79. Geoffrey Chaucer, *Sir Thopas*, in *Riverside Chaucer*, 212–16 (216).

80. Paul Strohm, "Some Generic Distinctions in the *Canterbury Tales*," *Modern Philology* 68 (1971): 321–28 (326).

81. On Chaucer's translation and the incorporation of Melibee into *The Canterbury Tales*, see Dolores Palomo, "What Chaucer Really Did to *Le Livre de Mellibee*," *Philological Quarterly* 53 (1974): 304–20; Diane Bornstein, "Chaucer's *Tale of Melibee* as an Example of the Style Clergial," *Chaucer Review* 12 (1978): 236–54; Lloyd J. Mathews, "The Date of Chaucer's Melibee and the Stages of the Tale's Incorporation in the Canterbury Tales," *Chaucer Review* 20 (1986): 221–34.

82. Geoffrey Chaucer, *The Tale of Melibee*, in *Riverside Chaucer*, 217–39 (217).

83. Paul Strohm, "The Allegory of the *Tale of Melibee*," *Chaucer Review* 2 (1967): 32–42.

84. For a reading that relates Melibee directly to the high political struggles of Richard III's reign, see Ferster, *Fictions of Advice*.

85. Kathleen E. Kennedy, "Maintaining Love through Accord in the *Tale of Melibee*," *Chaucer Review* 39 (2004): 165–76 (165).

86. Chaucer, *Tale of Melibee*, 238.

87. Ibid.

88. Ibid., 239.

89. Ibid.

90. Stephen G. Moore, "Apply Yourself: Learning While Reading the *Tale of Melibee*," *Chaucer Review* 38 (2003): 83–97.

91. David Wallace, *Chaucerian Polity: Absolutist Lineages and Associational Forms in England and Italy* (Stanford: Stanford University Press, 1997), 226.

92. Lee Patterson, "'For the Wyves Love of Bathe': Feminine Rhetoric and Poetic Resolution in the *Roman de la Rose* and the *Canterbury Tales*," *Speculum* 58 (1983): 656–95 (662).

93. Amanda Walling, "'In Hir Telling Difference': Gender, Authority, and Interpretation in the *Tale of Melibee*," *Chaucer Review* 40 (2005): 163–81 (174).

94. Karla Taylor comments, "In the *Melibee* . . . Chaucer aims to create a civil society by means of language—not just to represent one, but genuinely to make one" (Karla Taylor, "Social Aesthetics and the Emergence of Civic Discourse from the *Shipman's Tale* to *Melibee*," *Chaucer Review* 39 [2005]: 298–322 [316]).

95. For the strange absence of the church from a tale that claims to be concerned with penance, see Aers, "Chaucer's *Tale of Melibee*."

96. Geoffrey Chaucer, *The Nun's Priest's Tale*, in *Riverside Chaucer*, 252–61 (252).

97. Ibid., 260.

98. As a fable, *The Nun's Priest's Tale* might be expected to have a clear moral message, but it does not. As Walter Scheps points out, "In the *Nun's Priest's Tale*, the smoothly functioning machinery of the fable is reduced to wreckage" (Walter Scheps, "Chaucer's Anti-Fable: *Reductio Ad Absurdum* in the *Nun's Priest's Tale*," *Leeds Studies in English* 46 [1970]: 1–10 [8]).

99. Helen Barr comments: "[*The Nun's Priest's Tale*] is not just *about* the uprisings in 1381; it participates in the contest for representation which was such a key feature of the revolts. The tale is both a dazzling foray into the arts of fiction-making and an example of the social struggle for empowerment" (Helen Barr, *Socioliterary Practice in Late Medieval England* [Oxford: Oxford University Press, 2001], 126–27).

100. Lee Patterson, "'What Man Artow': Self-Definition in *The Tale of Sir Thopas* and *The Tale of Melibee*," *Studies in the Age of Chaucer* 11 (1989): 117–75 (173).

101. Lynn Staley, "Enclosed Space," in *Cultural Reformations: Medieval and Renaissance in Literary History*, ed. Brian Cummings and James Simpson (Oxford: Oxford University Press, 2010), 113–33 (123).

102. As Derek Pearsall comments, "To recognise that the tale has no point is the start of understanding." However, in comparison to the very pointed texts produced by both sides in 1381, insisting on the integrity of a text that is "pointless" is itself an act of political resistance (Derek Pearsall, "A Reading of the *Nun's Priest's Tale*," in *Geoffrey Chaucer's Canterbury Tales: A Casebook*, ed. Lee Patterson [Oxford: Oxford University Press, 2007], 211–20 [217]).

103. Anne Middleton has argued that the 1388 Act of Vagrancy "emphasizes the control, enforcement, and punishment of mobility as such, in the social as well as the spatial sense, in a manner entirely foreign to any previous

national regulation of labor and wages" (Anne Middleton, "Acts of Vagrancy: The C Version 'Autobiography' and the Statute of 1388," in *Written Work: Langland, Labour, and Authorship*, ed. Steven Justice and Kathryn Kenby-Fulton [Philadelphia: University of Pennsylvania Press, 1997], 208–318 [218]).

104. Daniel Kinney suggests, "More's text may simply point up the folly of trying to sort *texts* as if they had the regular contours of *things*" (Kinney, "'Kings' Tragicomedies," 133).

105. Richard Grafton, *Chronicle* (London, 1543), Hh iiii (1v).

106. More, *Richard III*, 54–55.

107. Ibid., 55.

108. Ibid., 55–56.

109. Patrick Grant comments: "With surprising economy, More manages repeatedly to create, throughout *Richard III*, a sense of how the sheer complexity of circumstances and of our unwitting complicity with past events can be morally compromising, and the single character who understands these facts as fully as More, and who is a master at turning them to sinister advantage, is Richard himself" (Patrick Grant, "Thomas More's *Richard III*: Moral Narration and Humanist Method," *Renaissance and Reformation* 7 [1983]: 157–72 [160]).

110. More, *Richard III*, 57–58.

111. Walter M. Gordon points out that More portrays Shore in such a way that she resists "facile classification." As Chaucer did when he used a beast fable in *The Nun's Priest's Tale* to critique simplistic ways of reading, More used Shore to illustrate the dangers of precisely the kind of moralizing historiography that the story of her life would seem to invite (Walter M. Gordon, "Exemplum Narrative and Thomas More's *History of King Richard III*," *Clio* 9 [1979]: 75–88 [81]).

112. John Bossy, *Christianity in the West, 1400–1700* (Oxford: Oxford University Press, 1985), 153.

113. Elizabeth Story Donno has commented in detail upon what she describes as the "miasma of uncertainty and doubt that pervades" the narrative of *Richard III*. Donno then suggests, "Against such rippling complexity [More's] one-dimensional evil protagonist is allowed to stand out starkly." I would suggest, however, that Richard's undoubted ability to act as a point of clarity reflects the way *Richard III* tempts the reader to gaze exclusively upon Richard and thereby avoid complicity in the political drama that is enfolding (Elizabeth Story Donno, "Thomas More and *Richard III*," *Renaissance Quarterly* 35 [1982]: 401–47 [423]).

114. Hanan Yoran, "Thomas More's *Richard III*: Probing the Limits of Humanism," *Renaissance Studies* 15 (2001): 514–37 (516, 517, 521).

115. Thomas More, "*Historia Richardi Tertii*," in *The Yale Edition of The Complete Works of Saint Thomas More*, vol. 15, ed. and trans. Daniel Kinney (New Haven: Yale University Press, 1986), 318–19.

116. More, *Richard III*, 5.

117. More, "*Historia Richardi Tertii*," 325.

118. More, "Coronation Day," in *Richard III*, 132.

119. Peter C. Herman, "Henrician Historiography and the Voice of the People: The Cases of More and Hall," *Texas Studies in Literature and Language* 39 (1997): 259–83.

120. For the educational agenda of More's work, see Dan Breen, "Thomas More's *History of Richard III*: Genre, Humanism and Moral Education," *Studies in Philology* 107 (2010): 465–92.

121. Edward Hall, *Hall's Chronicle*, quoted in Janette Dillon, *Performance and Spectacle in Hall's Chronicle* (London: The Society for Theatre Research, 2002), 41.

122. Ibid., 42.

123. Jeanne H. McCarthy, "The Emergence of Henrician Drama 'in the Kynges absens,'" *English Literary Renaissance* 39 (2009): 231–66 (253).

124. Maura Nolan, "Beauty," in Strohm, *Middle English*, 207–21 (217).

125. It is for this reason that, in Dan Breen's words, Richard the tyrant is kept at "arm's length." More does not want his readers to become seduced into easy or simple reading; he wants them to remain on their guard. See Breen, "More's *History of Richard III*," 468.

Chapter 2. Reason

1. On the composition of *Utopia*, see J. H. Hexter, "More's *Utopia*: The Biography of an Idea," in *The Yale Edition of The Complete Works of Saint Thomas More*, vol. 4, ed. Edward Surtz and J. H. Hexter (New Haven: Yale University Press, 1965), 15–30.

2. There is no evidence that More read or was even aware of Pecock's work, and given the small number of copies that have survived of works like *The Repressor*, it would be very surprising if More had read any of them. James Simpson has, however, recently commented on the interesting ways in which Pecock's work engages with issues very similar to those on which the confrontation between More and Tyndale was based (James Simpson, *Reform and Cultural Revolution* [Oxford: Oxford University Press, 2002], 471).

3. For a definition of reformist literature, see Simpson, *Reform and Cultural Revolution*, esp. 62–67.

4. J. H. Hexter, "Thomas More: On the Margins of Modernity," *Journal of British Studies* 1 (1961): 20–37.

5. Ibid., 27.

6. Hythloday strongly approves of the politics of Utopia but is totally unaware that Utopus's founding act effectively erased the space of the political. Hanan Yoran quite correctly has recently pointed out that "Utopia is a place without politics." What kind of politics can exist in which all questions about the proper distribution of social and cultural resources have been answered in advance? (Hanan Yoran, "More's *Utopia* and Erasmus's No-place," *English Literary Renaissance* 35 [2005]: 3–30 [18]).

7. The distinction being drawn here is based on John Milbank's work. See "The Double Glory, or Paradox versus Dialectic," in Slavoj Žižek and John Milbank, *The Monstrosity of Christ: Paradox or Dialectic?*, ed. Creston Davis (Cambridge, MA: MIT Press, 2009), 110–233.

8. Stephen Greenblatt, "Utopian Pleasure," in *Cultural Reformations: Medieval and Renaissance in Literary History*, ed. Brian Cummings and James Simpson (Oxford: Oxford University Press, 2010), 305–20 (309).

9. Dominic Baker-Smith comments that the Utopians "distinguish themselves from other nations not on racial grounds but by rational conduct" (Dominic Baker-Smith, "Reading *Utopia*," in *The Cambridge Companion to Thomas More*, ed. George M. Logan [Cambridge: Cambridge University Press, 2011], 141–67 [157]).

10. On the classical and humanist aspects of *Utopia*, see Quentin Skinner, "Sir Thomas More's *Utopia* and the Language of Renaissance Humanism," in *The Languages of Political Theory in Early-Modern Europe*, ed. Anthony Pagden (Cambridge: Cambridge University Press, 1987), 123–57. On the influence of St. Augustine on *Utopia*, see Martin N. Raitiere, "More's *Utopia* and *The City of God*," *Studies in the Renaissance* 20 (1973): 144–68.

11. Daniel Wakelin, *Humanism, Reading, and English Literature, 1430–1530* (Oxford: Oxford University Press, 2007), 182.

12. John Lydgate, *Reson and Sensuallyte*, ed. Ernst Sieper, EETS 84 (1901), 22.

13. Henry Medwall, *Nature*, in *The Plays of Henry Medwall*, ed. Alan H. Nelson (Cambridge: D. S. Brewer, 1980), 91–162 (115).

14. Ibid., 115.

15. Ibid., 161.

16. For northern humanism see Brendan Bradshaw, "Transalpine Humanism," in *The Cambridge History of Political Thought, 1450–1700*, ed. J. H. Burns with the assistance of Mark Goldie (Cambridge: Cambridge University Press, 1991), 95–131.

17. Desiderius Erasmus, *The Adages of Erasmus*, ed. William Baker (Toronto: University of Toronto Press, 2001), 5.

18. Ibid., 13.

19. Ibid., 14.

20. Ibid.

21. Daniel Kinney, "Erasmus' *Adagia*: Midwife to the Rebirth of Learning," *Journal of Medieval and Renaissance Studies* 11 (1981): 169–92 (188).

22. James McConica, "Erasmus and the Grammar of Consent," in *Scrinium Erasmianum*, ed. J. Coppens (Leiden: Brill, 1969), 77–99.

23. The idea of faith as a communicative practice is discussed in detail by Helmut Puekert in his study *Science, Action, and Fundamental Theology*. Puekert argues, "Faith is itself a practice that, as a practice, asserts God for others in communicative action and attempts to confirm this assertion in action. Faith in the resurrection of Jesus is faith as communicative action, factually anticipating salvation for others and thus for one's own existence. As practical solidarity with others, it signifies the assertion of the reality of God for them and for one's own existence" (Helmut Puekert, *Science, Action, and Fundamental Theology: Towards a Theology of Communicative Action*, trans. James Bohman [Cambridge, MA: MIT Press, 1984], 226).

24. For an important comparative discussion of Augustine's and More's political thought, see Peter Iver Kaufman, *Incorrectly Political: Augustine and Thomas More* (Notre Dame, IN: University of Notre Dame Press, 2007).

25. For the importance of Augustine to More's thought, see Åke Bergvall, *Augustinian Perspectives in the Renaissance* (Uppsala: AUU, 2001), 107.

26. Augustine, *On the Trinity*, ed. Gareth B. Mathews, trans. Stephen McKenna (Cambridge: Cambridge University Press, 2002), 224.

27. Ibid., 162.

28. Gerard B. Wegemer has recently pointed out that "one of the most revealing contradictions in Raphael's account [of Utopia] is his boast that fear will disappear once money is eliminated, yet, throughout his story, he points out that Utopia is governed by constant fear, and even terror" (Gerard B. Wegemer, *Young Thomas More and the Arts of Liberty* [Cambridge: Cambridge University Press, 2011], 153).

29. The status of human imagination was a matter of dispute in the fourteenth and fifteenth centuries. While some writers and clergymen regarded it with disdain, others regarded it far more positively. See James Simpson, "The Rule of Medieval Imagination," in *Images, Idolatry, and Iconoclasm in Late Medieval England: Textuality and the Visual Image*, ed. Jeremy Dimmick, James Simpson, and Nicolette Zeeman (Oxford: Oxford University Press, 2002), 4–24.

30. Thomas More, *Utopia*, ed. George M. Logan and Robert M. Adams (Cambridge: Cambridge University Press, 1989), 3. I have chosen to use this edition of More's *Utopia* rather than the version produced as part of the Yale *Complete Works* because it is more accessible.

31. Ibid., 5.

32. Ibid., 6.

33. Ibid., 113.

34. Geoffrey Chaucer, *The Miller's Prologue*, in *The Riverside Chaucer*, ed. Larry D. Benson, new ed. (Oxford: Oxford University Press, 1988), 66–68 (67).

35. One is also reminded of J. R. R. Tolkien's statement in the preface to *The Lord of the Rings* when discussing attempts by readers to impose an allegorical meaning onto his work: "I cordially dislike allegory. . . . I much prefer history, true or feigned." Both Tolkien and More preferred feigned truth to factual lies (J. R. R. Tolkien, foreword, *The Lord of the Rings* [London: George Allen, 1966], 7).

36. For the seminal account of Utopia's relationship to humanist political thought, see Skinner, "Sir Thomas More's *Utopia*."

37. More, *Utopia*, 16.

38. Ibid., 37.

39. Ibid.

40. Daniel Wakelin has recently commented that "Hythloday is an extreme figure, difficult to take seriously; he seems a parody of extreme idealism in scholarship" (Wakelin, *Humanism, Reading*, 196).

41. More, *Utopia*, 13.

42. Ibid.

43. Kaufman, *Incorrectly Political*, 170.

44. More, *Utopia*, 60–61.

45. Lawrence Manley, *Literature and Culture in Early Modern London* (Cambridge: Cambridge University Press, 1993), 30.

46. Although Hythloday seems strangely unaware of Utopia's flaws. Walter Gordon suggests that "Hythloday, in his unqualified and unhesitating acclaim of Utopia, reveals a curious blindness to the dark side of the island. Utopia came into being through warfare, maintains itself by means of a dismal penal code that hardly improves on the unfair laws of England, and extends itself by force wherever it discerns a national failing to use its own resources productively" (Walter Gordon, "The Platonist Dramaturgy of Thomas More's *Dialogues*," *Journal of Medieval and Renaissance Studies* 8 [1978]: 193–215 [204]).

47. Brendan Bradshaw makes the point that "if . . . Utopia represents More's model of true Christianity it must be accepted that he did not consider scripture, the sacraments, the cult of Jesus himself, to be essential features of a truly Christian existence" (Brendan Bradshaw, "More on Utopia," *Historical Journal* 24 [1981]: 1–27 [7]).

48. Richard Marius, *Thomas More* (London: Phoenix Giant, 1999), 167.

49. Arthur F. Kinney, *Rhetoric and Poetic in Thomas More's Utopia* (Malibu, CA: Undena Publications, 1979), 11.

50. Peter Brown suggests that "Pelagius wanted every Christian to be a monk" (Peter Brown, *Augustine of Hippo* [London: Faber, 2000], 348).

51. Martin N. Raitiere comments, in relation to Hythloday's championing of Utopia, that "it is Pelagian presumption to wish to remove the irrational from society" (Raitiere, "*Utopia* and *The City of God*," 163).

52. Gerard Wegemer, "Ciceronian Humanism in More's Utopia," *Moreana* 27 (1990): 5–26 (21).

53. Augustine, *On Christian Teaching*, ed. and trans. R. P. H. Green (Oxford: Oxford University Press, 1997), 5.

54. Brian Stock, *Augustine the Reader: Meditation, Self-Knowledge, and the Ethics of Interpretation* (Cambridge, MA: Harvard University Press, 1996), 190.

55. More, *Utopia*, 109–10.

56. David Norbrook argues, "Utopian laws are based on reason rather than tradition and are drafted so as to be immediately intelligible to all citizens." Utopia's laws are, however, based not on reason but rather on what Utopus thought was rational and set down in laws that are obeyed many years after his death. It is debatable whether the Utopians keep to Utopus's laws because they are reasonable and not simply out of an extreme veneration or a tradition of obedience (David Norbrook, *Poetry and Politics in the English Renaissance* [Oxford: Oxford University Press, 2002], 17).

57. Robert Farrar Capon, *Kingdom, Grace, Judgment: Paradox, Outrage, and Vindication in the Parables of Jesus* (Grand Rapids, MI: Eerdmans, 2002).

58. Lee Patterson, *Chaucer and the Subject of History* (London: Routledge, 1991), 198.

59. Geoffrey Chaucer, *The Knight's Tale*, in *Riverside Chaucer*, 37–66 (65).

60. Ibid., 66.

61. David Aers has argued that the "cursoriness and conventionality" of this concluding comment on Palamon and Emelye's happy marriage "point towards its evasion of the wide range of problems evoked by the poem which is anything but a romance centred on 'Palamon and Emelye'" (David Aers, *Chaucer, Langland and the Creative Imagination* [London: Routledge, 1980], 194).

62. Lee Patterson points out that there is a profound tension between the agenda of Theseus, that of the Knight, and that of the tale itself. See Patterson, *Chaucer and the Subject of History*, 168.

63. Erik Hertog, *Chaucer's Fabliaux as Analogues* (Leuven: Leuven University Press, 1991), 11.

64. Simpson, *Reform and Cultural Revolution*, 313.

65. Maura Nolan, "Beauty," in *Middle English*, ed. Paul Strohm (Oxford: Oxford University Press, 2007), 207–21 (218); Geoffrey Chaucer, *The Miller's Tale*, in *Riverside Chaucer*, 68–77 (69).

66. Geoffrey Chaucer, *The Reeve's Prologue*, in *Riverside Chaucer*, 77–78 (78).

67. V. A. Kolve, *Chaucer and the Imagery of Narrative: The First Five Canterbury Tales* (London: Arnold, 1984), 230.

68. Geoffrey Chaucer, *The Reeve's Tale*, in *Riverside Chaucer*, 78–84 (84).

69. James Simpson, "Faith and Hermeneutics: Pragmatism versus Pragmatism," *Journal of Medieval and Early Modern Studies* 33 (2003): 215–39 (236).

70. For an excellent recent study of Pecock's work, see Kirsty Campbell, *The Call to Read: Reginald Pecock's Books and Textual Communities* (Notre Dame, IN: University of Notre Dame Press, 2010).

71. Norman Doe, "Fifteenth-Century Concepts of Law: Fortescue and Pecock," *History of Political Thought* 10 (1989): 257–80 (271).

72. Reginald Pecock, *The Repressor of Over Much Blaming of the Clergy*, ed. Churchill Babington (London, 1860), 21.

73. Ibid., 18.

74. Ibid., 30.

75. Ibid., 31.

76. Stephen E. Lahey, "Reginald Pecock on the Authority of Reason, Scripture and Tradition," *Journal of Ecclesiastical History* 56 (2005): 235–60 (248).

77. Everett H. Emerson, "Reginald Pecock: Christian Rationalist," *Speculum* 31 (1956): 235–42 (239).

78. Pecock, *Repressor*, 85–86.

79. Ibid., 85.

80. Ibid., 47.

81. Reginald Pecock, *The Folower of the Donet*, ed. Elsie Vaughan Hitchcock, EETS 164 (London, 1924), 14.

82. James Simpson argues that "Pecock is not ordinary or representative, he is extraordinary for his profound, unflinching, and occasionally exasperating commitment to the exercise of human reason, and all that follows from such a commitment" (James Simpson, "Reginald Pecock and John Fortescue," in *A Companion to Middle English Prose*, ed. A. S. G. Edwards [Cambridge: D. S. Brewer, 2004], 271–88 [273]).

83. Joseph F. Patrouch comments, "Pecock insisted on talking things over in the clear light of reason." The problem with this comment is that the more Pecock talks or writes, the less clear reason becomes (Joseph F. Patrouch, *Reginald Pecock* [New York: Twayne, 1970], 38).

84. Simpson, *Reform and Cultural Revolution*, 558–59.

85. For a discussion of the prologue to *The Tale of Beryn*, see Peter Brown, "Journey's End: The Prologue to *The Tale of Beryn*," in *Chaucer and Fifteenth-Century Poetry*, ed. Julia Boffey and Janet Cowen, King's College London Medieval Studies 5 (London: King's College, 1991), 143–74.

86. John M. Bowers, ed., *The Canterbury Interlude and Merchant's Tale of Beryn* (Kalamazoo, MI: Medieval Institute Publications, 1992), 75.

87. Ibid., 77.

88. Richard Firth Green, "Legal Satire in *The Tale of Beryn*," *Studies in the Age of Chaucer* 11 (1989): 43–62.

89. Bowers, *Canterbury Interlude*, 129.

90. Ibid., 128.

91. James H. Landman comments: "The relationship between Isope— an ancient, wise, and remote sovereign—and the law practised in his realm serves as an allegory of the tensions between abstract principles and pragmatic adaptation inherent in medieval legal thought and practice. Isope represents an incorruptible, absolute form of justice" (James H. Landman, "Pleading, Pragmatism, and Permissible Hypocrisy: The 'Colours' of Legal Discourse in Late Medieval England," *New Medieval Literatures* 1 [2001]: 139–70 [162]).

92. In *The Tale of Beryn* Isope is depicted as an aged man living in a heavily fortified castle. The implication is that, having imposed his absolute rule on Falsetown, Isope assumed that the city would run itself, since in a world of truth what need would there be for a ruler? Landman comments, "*The Tale of Beryn* . . . locates a standard of truth in the figure of Falsetown's just lord Isope, but this standard is markedly inaccessible, even irrelevant, for much of the poem" (ibid., 163).

93. John M. Bowers, "*The Tale of Beryn* and *The Siege of Thebes*: Alternative Ideas of *The Canterbury Tales*," in *Writing after Chaucer: Essential Readings in Chaucer and the Fifteenth Century*, ed. Daniel J. Pinti (New York: Garland, 1998), 201–25 (206).

94. I am using "fundamentalism" here in the sense in which James Simpson has developed it in his study *Burning to Read: English Fundamentalism and Its Reformation Opponents* (Cambridge, MA: Harvard University Press, 2007).

95. It is debatable to what extent More fully or properly understood Luther's ideas, or indeed those of other people like Tyndale, whom he attacked as heretics. In practice, the fact that More regarded Luther's, and Tyndale's, ideas as heretical means that their actual coherence or even validity was not fundamentally important to More.

96. In a recent article, "Charity of Fire? The Argument of Thomas More's 1529 *Dyaloge*," Craig W. D'Alton has suggested that More's text marked a watershed in the English campaign against heresy, inaugurating a more aggressive public policy in place of the relative passivity of the years of Wolsey's ascendancy. D'Alton comments that from the opening discussion of the proverb "One busynes begettyth and bryngeth forth another," More's reader is propelled "not into a world of reasoned philosophical debate, but into the world of

the proverb and the anecdote" (Craig W. D'Alton, "Charity of Fire? The Argument of Thomas More's 1529 *Dyaloge*," *Sixteenth Century Journal* 33 [2002]: 51–70 [54]).

97. Richard Hunne was a Londoner whose suspicious death in the Tower of London in 1514 sparked the first real confrontation between royal power and the church of Henry VIII's reign. Thomas Bilney was martyred in Norwich in 1531 for preaching against a range of devotional practices, including pilgrimages.

98. Thomas More, *Dialogue concerning Heresies*, in *Complete Works*, vol. 6, ed. Thomas M. C. Lawler, Germain Marc'hadour, and Richard C. Marius (New Haven: Yale University Press, 1981), 254.

99. Ibid., 301.

100. Simpson, *Burning to Read*, 271.

101. More, *Dialogue concerning Heresies*, 258.

102. Ibid., 255.

103. Ibid., 258.

104. Peter Ackroyd, *The Life of Thomas More* (London: Vintage, 1998), 275.

105. Adam Fox, *Oral and Literate Culture in England, 1500–1700* (Oxford: Clarendon, 2000).

106. R. T. Lenaghan, ed., *Caxton's Aesop* (Cambridge, MA: Harvard University Press, 1967).

107. Augustine, *On the Trinity*, 15–16.

108. More, *Dialogue concerning Heresies*, 274.

109. Ibid., 275.

110. Simpson, *Burning to Read*, 251.

111. More, *Dialogue concerning Heresies*, 159.

112. Ibid., 160.

113. For a more detailed discussion of this episode, see chap. 3 below.

114. More, *Dialogue concerning Heresies*, 321.

115. Ibid.

116. Later in the discussion of Hunne's case More tells the more serious story of his own examination of an Essex carpenter for robbery, an examination in which the carpenter confessed to attending heretical midnight lectures also attended by Hunne (ibid., 328).

117. Ibid., 324–25.

118. Joan Curbet comments: "The main aim of the *Dialogue* . . . is to question the notion of free interpretation of scripture; but this cannot be done without actively exemplifying the impossibility of reaching truth from the isolation of individualism. It is especially necessary, therefore, to deconstruct the illusions of intellectual autonomy, which the dialogue identifies as the main

form of pride; dialectical exchange destabilises the belief in direct, unmediated communion with God and works towards the establishment of a firm common theological knowledge" (Joan Curbet, "Lutheranism and the Limits of Humanist Dialogue: Erasmus, Alfonso de Valdés and Thomas More, 1524–1529," *Literature & Theology* 17 [2003]: 265–80 [274]).

119. Peter Marshall, *Religious Identities in Henry VIII's England* (Aldershot: Ashgate, 2006), 130.

120. More, *Dialogue concerning Heresies*, 222.

121. Ibid.

122. Ibid., 223.

123. Ibid., 71.

124. On the importance of faith to all forms of interpretation, see Simpson, "Faith and Hermeneutics."

125. Thomas More, "Letter to Dorp," *Complete Works*, vol. 15, ed. Daniel Kinney (New Haven: Yale University Press, 1986), 58–59.

126. Ibid., 60–61.

127. Ibid., 60–61 and 62–63.

128. Constance M. Furey comments, "At the heart of his critique in his *Letter to Dorp*, More claims that Dorp violated communal ethics by launching an intemperate attack against Erasmus" (Constance M. Furey, "Invective and Discernment in Martin Luther, D. Erasmus and Thomas More," *Harvard Theological Review* 98 [2005]: 469–88 [483]).

129. More, *Dialogue concerning Heresies*, 435.

130. Ibid., 185.

131. Eamon Duffy, "'The Comen Knowen Multytude of Crysten Men': *A Dialogue concerning Heresies* and the Defence of Christendom," in Logan, *Cambridge Companion to Thomas More*, 191–215 (200).

132. More, *Dialogue concerning Heresies*, 81.

133. Alastair Minnis suggests that in the *Dialogue concerning Heresies*, "the sympathy and fellow-feeling [More] brings to the practices of vernacular religion are quite remarkable" (Alastair Minnis, *Translations of Authority in Medieval English Literature: Valuing the Vernacular* [Cambridge: Cambridge University Press, 2009], 141).

134. Richard Whitford, *The Pype or Tonne of the Lyfe of Perfection*, ed. James Hogg, Salzburg Studies in English Literature 89 (1532; Salzburg: Institut für Anglistik und Amerikanistik, 1979), A.ii (v)–A.iii.

135. R. R. McCutcheon comments that "dialogue is integral to More's conception of Christianity" (R. R. McCutcheon, "Heresy and Dialogue: The Humanist Approaches of Erasmus and More," *Viator* 29 [1993]: 357–84 [377]).

136. Eilén Ní Chuilleanáin points out that "for More no opinion exists in the abstract; it needs to be held by some person embedded in his own society, culture, tradition" (Eilén Ní Chuilleanáin, "The Debate between Thomas More and William Tyndale, 1528–33: Ideas on Literature and Religion," *Journal of Ecclesiastical History* 39 [1988]: 382–411 [400]).

Chapter 3. Heresy

1. John Guy, *Thomas More* (London: Arnold, 2000), 119.

2. See Thomas Betteridge, *Tudor Histories of the English Reformations* (Aldershot: Ashgate, 1991), chap. 4.

3. Guy, *Thomas More*, 120.

4. Alistair Fox, *Thomas More: History and Providence* (New Haven: Yale University Press, 1982), 205.

5. Richard Marius, *Thomas More* (London: Phoenix Giant, 1999), 339.

6. William Langland, *Piers Plowman: The C Text*, ed. Derek Pearsall (Exeter: University of Exeter Press, 2008), 285.

7. Ibid., 286.

8. Nicholas Watson, "Conceptions of the Word: The Mother Tongue and the Incarnation of God," *New Medieval Literatures* 1 (1997): 85–124 (118).

9. A. G. Dickens, *The English Reformation*, 2nd ed. (London: Batsford, 1989), 122.

10. Thomas More, *The Supplication of Souls*, in *The Yale Edition of the Complete Works of Saint Thomas More*, vol. 7, ed. Frank Manley, Germain Marc'hadour, Richard Marius, and Clarence Miller (New Haven: Yale University Press, 1990), 107–228 (111).

11. Ibid., 124.

12. Ibid., 126.

13. Ibid., 148–49.

14. Ibid., 149.

15. Ibid., 221.

16. Ibid., 221–22.

17. James Simpson, "Diachronic History and the Shortcomings of Medieval Studies," in *Reading the Medieval in Early Modern England*, ed. Gordon McMullan and David Matthews (Cambridge: Cambridge University Press, 2007), 17–30 (24).

18. Eamon Duffy comments that the "souls in Purgatory were part of the church of the redeemed, and prayer for the dead was one of the principal

expressions of the ties that bound the community together" (Eamon Duffy, *The Stripping of the Altars: Traditional Religion in England, 1400–1580* [New Haven: Yale University Press, 1992], 348–49).

19. More, *The Supplication of Souls*, 188–89.

20. Ibid., 189.

21. Ibid., 136.

22. Ibid., 118.

23. Ibid., 226.

24. Ibid., 227.

25. Germain Marc'hadour, "Introduction to Supplication of Souls," in *Complete Works*, 7:lxv–cxvii (xci).

26. R. N. Swanson comments: "Because Western Christianity developed, indeed was transformed between 1100 and 1500, heresy was almost a necessary concomitant. Necessary, because the development reflected a succession of choices in terms of doctrine and acceptability, often with little real precision in formulation or interpretation" (R. N. Swanson, "Literacy, Heresy, History and Orthodoxy: Perspectives and Permutations for the Later Middle Ages," in *Heresy and Literacy, 1000–1530*, ed. Peter Biller and Anne Hudson [Cambridge: Cambridge University Press, 1994], 279–93 [280]).

27. Rowan Williams, *Arius: Heresy and Tradition* (London: SCM Press, 2001), 1.

28. R. I. Moore, "Heresy as Disease," in *The Concept of Heresy in the Middle Ages*, ed. W. Lourdaux and D. Verhelist (Leuven: Leuven University Press, 1976), 1–11 (9).

29. Thomas More, "A Letter against Frith," in *Complete Works*, 7:233–34.

30. Ian Forrest, *The Detection of Heresy in Late Medieval England* (Oxford: Clarendon, 2005), 168.

31. More, *Supplication of Souls*, 143.

32. For the argument that Archbishop Arundel's *Constitutions* had a "narrowing" effect on fifteenth-century English literary and religious writing, see Nicholas Watson, "Censorship and Cultural Change in Late Medieval England, the Oxford Translation Debate and Arundel's Constitutions," *Speculum* 70 (1995): 822–64. For a trenchant rejection of Watson's argument, see Eamon Duffy, "Religious Belief," in *A Social History of England, 1200–1500*, ed. Rosemary Horrox and W. Mark Ormrod (Cambridge: Cambridge University Press, 2006), 293–339 (330–31).

33. John Foxe, *Acts and Monuments* (London: John Day, 1570), 627.

34. For the problematic nature of censorship in a preprint culture, see Kathryn Kerby-Fulton, *Books under Suspicion: Censorship and Tolerance of Revelatory*

Writing in Late Medieval England (Notre Dame, IN: University of Notre Dame Press, 2006).

35. Miri Rubin, "Identities," in Horrox and Ormrod, *Social History of England*, 383–412 (410).

36. Steven Justice, "Lollardy," in *The Cambridge History of Medieval English Literature*, ed. David Wallace (Cambridge: Cambridge University Press, 2002), 662–89 (676).

37. Andrew Cole, *Literature and Heresy in the Age of Chaucer* (Cambridge: Cambridge University Press, 2008), 131.

38. Kantik Ghosh, "Nicholas Love," in *A Companion to Middle English Prose*, ed. A. S. G. Edwards (Cambridge: D. S. Brewer, 2004), 127–50.

39. Michael G. Sargent, introduction to Nicholas Love, *The Mirror of the Blessed Life of Jesus Christ: A Reading Text* (Exeter: University of Exeter Press, 2004), ix–xlvii, (ix).

40. Michelle Karnes, "Nicholas Love and Medieval Meditations on Christ," *Speculum* 82 (2007): 380–408 (399).

41. Thomas Hoccleve, *Selections from Hoccleve*, ed. M. C. Seymour (Oxford: Clarendon, 1981), 61.

42. Ibid., 66.

43. Cole, *Literature and Heresy*, 112.

44. Nicholas Watson, "Middle English Mystics," in Wallace, *Cambridge History of Medieval English Literature*, 539–65 (551).

45. Hoccleve, *Selections*, 64.

46. Ibid., 65.

47. Paul Strohm, *England's Empty Throne: Usurpation and the Language of Legitimation, 1399–1427* (New Haven: Yale University Press, 1998), 146.

48. Hoccleve, *Selections*, 68, 69.

49. John Lydgate, *A Defence of Holy Church*, in *John Lydgate: Poems*, ed. John Norton-Smith (Oxford: Clarendon, 1966), 30–34 (30).

50. Ibid., 30.

51. Ibid., 32–33.

52. Ibid., 34.

53. Michael P. Kuczynski, *Prophetic Song: The Psalms as Moral Discourse in Late Medieval England* (Philadelphia: University of Pennsylvania Press, 1995), 156–64.

54. Love, *Mirror of the Blessed Life*, 61.

55. Ibid., 61.

56. Ibid., 64.

57. Ibid., 150.

58. Ibid., 152.

59. Elizabeth Salter, *Nicholas Love's "Myrrour of the Blessed Lyf of Jesu Christ"* (Salzburg: Analecta Cartusiana, 1974).

60. H. Leith Spencer, *English Preaching in the Late Middle Ages* (Oxford: Clarendon, 1993), 187.

61. Richard Beadle, "'Devoute ymaginacion' and the Dramatic Sense in Love's *Mirror* and the N-Town Plays," in *Nicholas Love at Waseda*, ed. Shiochi Oguro, Richard Beadle, and Michael G. Sargent (Cambridge: D. S. Brewer, 1997), 1–18 (11).

62. Love, *Mirror of the Blessed Life*, 225.

63. Katherine C. Little, "Catechesis and Castigation: Sin in the Wycliffite Sermon Cycle," *Traditio* 54 (1999): 213–44 (224).

64. Kantik Ghosh comments, "The *Mirror* counters Lollardy not only through its very form—a series of emotive 'imaginations' on the life of Christ as different as possible from the kind of scriptural argumentation evidenced in the Wycliffite sermons—but also through explicit doctrinal arguments as well as implicit hermeneutic strategies" (Kantik Ghosh, *The Wycliffite Heresy: Authority and the Interpretation of Texts* [Cambridge: Cambridge University Press, 2002], 19).

65. The most recent authoritative account of the Henrician Reformation is G. W. Bernard's magisterial study, *The King's Reformation: Henry VIII and the Remaking of the English Church*. Bernard argues in this work that Henry was in charge of religious policy during the period 1527–36, and indeed for the rest of his reign. Bernard argues that as "early as 1527 Henry threatened to go it alone; from 1533 that is what he did" (G. W. Bernard, *The King's Reformation: Henry VIII and the Remaking of the English Church* [New Haven: Yale University Press, 2005], 68).

66. Greg Walker, *Writing under Tyranny: English Literature and the Henrician Reformation* (Oxford: Oxford University Press, 2005), 214.

67. For a detailed discussion of *The Play of the Weather*, see Greg Walker, *The Politics of Performance in Early Renaissance Drama* (Cambridge: Cambridge University Press, 1998), esp. chap. 3.

68. John Heywood, *The Play of the Weather*, in *Medieval Drama: An Anthology*, ed. Greg Walker (Oxford: Blackwell, 2000), 456–78 (457).

69. Ibid., 478.

70. In hindsight it is clear that Heywood's Henrician solution to the religious issues facing England in 1532/33 could not produce stability. Alec Ryrie, however, has pointed out that this was not obviously the case at the time and that Henry VIII's religious settlement "did not die with him. It was killed by Edward's Reformation and Mary's Restoration, and it did not die quickly or easily" (Alex Ryrie, "Paths Not Taken in the British Reformation," *Historical Journal* 52 [2009]: 1–22 [19]).

71. Thomas More, *The Confutation of Tyndale's Answer*, in *Complete Works*, vol. 8, ed. Louis A. Schuster, Richard C. Marius, James P. Lusardi, and Richard J. Schoeck (New Haven: Yale University Press, 1973), 14.

72. Ibid., 3.

73. Ibid., 71.

74. More, *Complete Works*, 8:1491.

75. Richard Rex, "Thomas More and the Heretics: Statesman or Fanatic?," in *The Cambridge Companion to Thomas More*, ed. George M. Logan (Cambridge: Cambridge University Press, 2011), 93–115 (97).

76. Brian Cummings, *The Literary Culture of the Reformation: Grammar and Grace* (Oxford: Oxford University Press, 2002), 196.

77. More, *Confutation of Tyndale's Answer*, 157.

78. Ibid., 226.

79. Ibid., 248.

80. James Simpson, *Burning to Read: English Fundamentalism and Its Reformation Opponents* (Cambridge, MA: Harvard University Press, 2007), 253.

81. More, *Confutation of Tyndale's Answer*, 537.

82. Euan Cameron, *The European Reformation* (Oxford: Clarendon, 1991), 123.

83. Lynn Staley has recently suggested that the Psalms, and in particular the Penitential Psalms, were used by writers during the fourteenth, fifteenth, and sixteenth centuries to reflect upon the "nature of secular sovereignty" (Lynn Staley, "The Penitential Psalms: Conversion and the Limits of Lordship," *Journal of Medieval and Early Modern Studies* 37 [2007]: 221–70 [253]).

84. Clare L. Costley, "David, Bathsheba, and the Penitential Psalms," *Renaissance Quarterly* 57 (2004): 1235–77 (1247).

85. More, *Confutation of Tyndale's Answer*, 557–58.

86. In this passage More is clearly criticizing what he sees as Tyndale's reductive understanding of purgatory and, in particular, of indulgences. For the importance of indulgences to pre-Reformation Catholicism, see Robert W. Saffern, *The Penitents' Treasury: Indulgences in Latin Christendom, 1173–1373* (Scranton, PA: University of Scranton Press, 2007), and R. N. Swanson, *Indulgences in Late Medieval England* (Cambridge: Cambridge University Press, 2007).

87. More, *Confutation of Tyndale's Answer*, 577.

88. David Aers, "Faith, Ethics, and Community: Reflections on Reading Late Medieval English Writing," *Journal of Medieval and Early Modern Studies* 28 (1998): 341–69 (345).

89. On the poetics of More's polemical writing, see William J. Rogers, "Thomas More's Polemical Poetics," *English Literary Renaissance* 38 (2008): 387–407.

90. Thomas More, *The Apology*, in *Complete Works*, vol. 9, ed. J. B. Trapp (New Haven: Yale University Press, 1979), 3.

91. Ibid.

92. Ibid., 4.

93. Ibid., 8–9.

94. See Brian Gogan, *The Common Corps of Christendom: Ecclesiological Themes in the Writings of Thomas More* (Leiden: Brill, 1982).

95. More, *Apology*, 60.

96. Timothy Bewes argues that the Internet has become, despite the fantasies of it being a realm of pure, unmediated, authentic freedom, a space in which banal conspiracy theories and paranoid delusions are as valid as reasoned truth (Timothy Bewes, *Cynicism and Postmodernity* [London: Verso, 1997], 65).

97. Marius, *Thomas More*, 141.

98. Thomas More, *A Dialogue concerning Heresies*, in *Complete Works*, vol. 6, ed. Thomas M. C. Lander, Germain Marc'hadour, and Richard C. Marius (New Haven: Yale University Press, 1981), 321.

99. More, *Apology*, 170.

100. James Simpson, *Reform and Cultural Revolution* (Oxford: Oxford University Press, 2002), 62.

101. *Enormytes Usyd by the clergy* (London, 1532), A.ii (2).

102. Ibid., C. I (v)–C. II.

103. Ibid., C.ii (2).

104. See Eamon Duffy's important discussion of this aspect of Mary Tudor's religious policies in *Fires of Faith: Catholic England under Mary* (New Haven: Yale University Press, 2009), esp. chap. 3.

105. More, *Confutation of Tyndale's Answer*, 424.

Chapter 4. Devotion

1. Henri de Lubac, *Paradoxes of Faith* (San Francisco: Ignatius Press, 1987), 9.

2. I distinguish here between metaphor and metonym on the basis of the theoretical work of Ernesto Laclau, who uses the terms to refer to different models of democracy. Laclau argues that while models of democracy that stress homogeneity are predominantly metaphoric, and run from Robespierre to Pol Pot, those that respect difference are predominantly metonymic and as such always keep traces of their contingency and incompleteness visible. Ernesto Laclau, *The Politics of Rhetoric* (Colchester: University of Essex, 1998), 25–26.

3. For the importance of writing and reading to Augustine's religious thought, see Brian Stock, *Augustine the Reader: Meditation, Self-Knowledge, and the Ethics of Interpretation* (Cambridge, MA: Harvard University Press, 1996).

4. Thomas More, *Treatise on the Passion*, in *The Yale Edition of The Complete Works of Saint Thomas More*, vol.13, ed. Garry E. Haupt (New Haven: Yale University Press, 1976), 3.

5. Ibid.

6. Geoffrey Chaucer, *The Parson's Tale*, in *The Riverside Chaucer*, ed. Larry D. Benson, new ed. (Oxford: Oxford University Press, 1988), 288–327 (the tale), 289 and 299 (the quotations).

7. Nicholas Watson, "Chaucer's Public Christianity," *Religion & Literature* 37 (2005): 99–114 (103).

8. Ibid., 104.

9. Lee Patterson has commented on the way in which *The Parson's Tale* discusses different sins: "The effect of this procedure is to contain each specific act within a controlling theoretical perspective. The arrangement stems not from a bureaucratic impulse towards neatness but from a vision that sees all experience as reflecting a universal and rationally apprehensible order and coherence." *The Parson's Tale* contains and orders sin. In the process it offers a guide to the lay reader while reflecting upon the ordering and closing down of the space for lay devotional thought and practice that was an aspect of the English church's response to heresy (Lee Patterson, "The *Parson's Tale* and the Quitting of the *Canterbury Tales*," *Traditio* 34 (1978): 331–80 (343).

10. Chaucer, *Parson's Tale*, 327.

11. As Katherine Little comments: "The Parson invokes a particular ideal, but it is one that seems unable to extend reform beyond itself. Even his isolation from the other pilgrims reveals a certain hopelessness about the possibility of his reforming influence" (Katherine C. Little, *Confession and Resistance: Defining the Self in Late Medieval England* [Notre Dame, IN: University of Notre Dame Press, 2006], 90).

12. More, *Treatise on the Passion*, 177.

13. Rowan Williams, *On Christian Theology* (Oxford: Blackwell, 2000), 13.

14. Johann Baptist Metz, *Love's Strategy: The Political Theology of Johann Baptist Metz*, ed. John K. Downey (Harrisburg, PA: Trinity Press International, 1999), 158.

15. Johann Baptist Metz, *Faith in History and Society: Toward a Practical Fundamental Theology*, trans. David Smith (London: Burns and Oates, 1980), 91.

16. Louis L. Martz, "Thomas More: The Tower Works," in *St. Thomas More: Action and Contemplation*, ed. Richard S. Sylvester (New Haven: Yale University Press, 1972), 57–84.

17. Peter Ackroyd, *The Life of Thomas More* (London: Vintage, 1999), 248.

18. David Aers, "The Humanity of Christ: Reflections on Orthodox Late Medieval Representations," in David Aers and Lynn Staley, *The Powers of the Holy: Religion, Politics, and Gender in Late Medieval English Culture* (University Park: Pennsylvania State University Press, 1996), 15–42.

19. For details of the sources of *The Treatise on the Passion*, see Garry E. Haupt, introduction to vol. 13 of *Complete Works*, xv–clxxxiv.

20. See Eamon Duffy, *Marking the Hours: English People and Their Prayers, 1240–1570* (New Haven: Yale University Press, 2006), 63–64.

21. William Bonde, *The Pilgrimage of Perfeccyon* (London, 1526), a (v).

22. Ibid., f.iiii. (1v).

23. Ibid., E.iiii.

24. Eamon Duffy, *The Stripping of the Altars: Traditional Religion in England, 1400–1580* (New Haven: Yale University Press, 1992), 296.

25. Bonde, *Pilgrimage of Perfeccyon*, r.iiii. (v).

26. Ibid., v.iiii (1v).

27. Ibid., D.iiii.

28. A similar discussion takes place in the early Tudor work *The Pomander of Prayer*. In this text the three types of prayer discussed are vocal, mental and mixed vocal, and mental. *The Pomander of Prayer* (London, 1528), B.ii (1)–B.ii (1v).

29. Bonde, *Pilgrimage of Perfeccyon*, E.

30. James Simpson, *Reform and Cultural Revolution* (Oxford: Oxford University Press, 2002), 453.

31. Alexandra da Costa has recently established that Fewterer's text, with the exception of the prefatory letter, is "a very close translation of Ulrich Pinder's *Speculum passionis domini nostri*" (Alexandra da Costa, "John Fewterer's *Myrrour or Glasse of Christes Passion* and Ulrich Pinder's *Speculum Passionis Domini Nostri*," *Notes and Queries* 56 [2009]: 27–29).

32. Vincent Gillespie, 'Introduction', *Corpus of British Medieval Library Catalogues 9: Syon Abbey* (London: The British Library, 2001), xxix–lxv, lx.

33. J. T. Rhodes, "Syon Abbey and Its Religious Publications in the Sixteenth Century," *Journal of Ecclesiastical History* 44 (1993): 11–25 (22).

34. Roger Ellis, "Further Thoughts on the Spirituality of Syon Abbey," in *Mysticism and Spirituality in Medieval England*, ed. William F. Pollard and Robert Boening (Cambridge: D. S. Brewer, 1997), 219–43.

35. Ibid., 236.

36. James Fewterer, *The Myrrour or Glasse of Christes Passion* (London, 1534), I.iii (3).

37. Ibid., H.iii.

38. Ibid., K.i.

39. Ibid., H.iii (3).

40. Thomas More, *Treatise on the Passion*, 93.

41. Thomas More, *Dialogue concerning Heresies*, in *Complete Works*, vol. 6, ed. Thomas M. C. Lawler, Germain Marc'hadour, and Richard C. Marius (New Haven: Yale University Press, 1981), 268. Thomas More, *The Apology*, in *Complete Works*, vol. 9, ed. J. B. Trapp (New Haven: Yale University Press, 1979), 60.

42. More, *Treatise on the Passion*, 95.

43. Nicholas Love, *The Mirror of the Blessed Life of Jesus Christ: A Reading Text*, ed. Michael G. Sargent (Exeter: University of Exeter Press, 2004), 103.

44. Ibid.

45. David Aers, *Sanctifying Signs: Making Christian Tradition in Late Medieval England* (Notre Dame, IN: University of Notre Dame Press, 2004), 27.

46. More, *Treatise on the Passion*, 96.

47. Ibid., 97.

48. Lee Patterson, "Chaucer's Pardoner on the Couch: Psyche and Clio in Medieval Literary Studies," *Speculum* 76 (2001): 638–80 (673).

49. More, *Treatise on the Passion*, 99.

50. Ibid.

51. Ibid.

52. Ibid., 100.

53. Ibid.

54. Fewterer, *Myrrour or Glasse of Christes Passion*, K.i.

55. Thomas À Kempis, *The Imitation of Christ*, trans. Leo Sherley-Price (London: Penguin Books, 1952), 212.

56. See Gary Macy, "The Dogma of Transubstantiation in the Middle Ages," *Journal of Ecclesiastical History* 45 (1994): 11–41, and James F. McCue, "The Doctrine of Transubstantiation from Berengar through Trent: The Point at Issue," *Harvard Theological Review* 61 (1968), 385–430.

57. Kempis, *Imitation of Christ*, 217.

58. Love, *Mirror of the Blessed Life*, 232.

59. More, *Treatise on the Passion*, 140.

60. Ibid., 157.

61. Desiderius Erasmus, *The Adages of Erasmus*, ed. William Baker (Toronto: University of Toronto Press, 2001), 13–14.

62. Bonde, *Pilgrimage of Perfeccyon*, h.

63. Jacques Derrida, *Of Grammatology*, trans. Gayatri Chakravorty Spivak (Baltimore: Johns Hopkins University Press, 1976), 15.

64. Vincent Gillespie, "Strange Image of Death: The Passion in Later Medieval English Devotional and Mystical Writing," *Analecta Cartusiana* 117 (1987): 111–59.

65. Fewterer, *Myrrour or Glasse of Christes Passion*, +iii (v).

66. Ibid., +iii (1).

67. *The Pore Caitif*, ed. Mary Teresa Brady, PhD diss., Fordham University, New York, 1954, ix.

68. Margaret Aston, *Lollards and Reformers: Images and Literacy in Late Medieval Religion* (London: Continuum, 1984), 104.

69. *Pore Caitif*, 128.

70. Ibid., 128–29.

71. Nicholas Watson, "Conceptions of the Word: The Mother Tongue and the Incarnation of God," *New Medieval Literatures* 1 (1997): 85–124 (107).

72. Sarah Beckwith has argued that in late medieval England Christ's body, while ostensibly being the very symbol of unity, in practice functioned as arena for intense struggles between identity and society, agency and structure (Sarah Beckwith, *Christ's Body: Identity, Culture and Society in Late Medieval Writings* [London: Routledge, 1993], 41).

73. *Pore Caitif*, 130.

74. Ibid., 131.

75. Aston, *Lollards and Reformers*, 118.

76. "Brother, Abide," in *Religious Lyrics of the Fifteenth Century*, ed. Carleton Brown (Oxford: Clarendon, 1939), 169–75 (169).

77. Ibid., 170.

78. Ibid.

79. Ibid., 174.

80. Ibid., 175.

81. Nicholas Watson, "Visions of Inclusion: Universal Salvation and Vernacular Theology in Pre-Reformation England," *Journal of Medieval and Early Modern Studies* 27 (1997): 145–87 (169).

82. Richard Rex, *The Theology of John Fisher* (Cambridge: Cambridge University Press, 1991), 46.

83. John Fisher, *English Works of John Fisher, Bishop of Rochester: Sermons and Other Writings, 1520–1535*, ed. Cecilia A. Hatt (Oxford: Oxford University Press, 2002), 301.

84. Ibid., 303.

85. Ibid.

86. Ibid., 303–4.

87. Brian Cummings, *The Literary Culture of the Reformation: Grammar and Grace* (Oxford: Oxford University Press, 2002).

88. Fisher, *English Works*, 307.

89. Eamon Duffy, "The Spirituality of John Fisher," in *Humanism, Reform and Reformation: The Career of Bishop John Fisher*, ed. Brendan Bradshaw (Cambridge: Cambridge University Press, 1989), 213.

90. Fisher, *English Works*, 323.

91. Duffy, *Stripping of the Altars*, 256.

92. *The Play of the Sacrament*, in *Medieval Drama: An Anthology*, ed. Greg Walker (Oxford: Blackwell, 2000), 212–33 (232).

93. Ibid., 228.

94. Ibid.

95. Jannette Dillon, "What Sacrament?," *European Medieval Drama* 3 (1999): 187–200.

96. Alistair Fox, *Thomas More: History and Providence* (New Haven: Yale University Press, 1982), 224.

97. Thomas More, *A Dialogue of Comfort against Tribulation*, in *Complete Works*, vol. 12, ed. Louis L. Martz and Frank Manley (New Haven: Yale University Press, 1976), 313.

98. A. D. Cousins, "Role-Play and Self-Portrayal in Thomas More's A Dialogue of Comfort against Tribulation," *Christianity and Literature* 52 (2003): 457–70 (462).

99. More, *Dialogue of Comfort*, 112.

100. Ibid., 113.

101. Ibid., 213.

102. Ibid.

103. Ibid., 215–16.

104. Ibid., 115. This parable, in a slightly different form, is central to the letter from Margaret Roper to Alice Alington that I discuss in detail in the book's conclusion.

105. Ibid.

106. Ibid., 117.

107. Ibid.

108. Ibid., 119.

109. Ibid., 52.

110. Augustine, *Confessions*, trans. Henry Chadwick (Oxford: Oxford University Press, 1992), 283.

111. This is obviously an aspect of More's profound Augustinianism.

112. Richard Marius, *Thomas More* (New York: Knopf, 1984), 483.

113. Thomas More, *De Tristitia Christi*, in *Complete Works*, vol. 14, ed. and trans. Clarence H. Miller (New Haven: Yale University Press, 1976), 15.

114. It is important to note that, as Garry E. Haupt points out in his introduction to vol. 13 of *Complete Works*, while exegesis was itself recognized as an entirely proper form of devotional exercise in this period, More makes a number of choices in *De Tristitia Christi* that are far from conventional. See Garry E. Haupt, introduction to *De Tristitia Christi*, in *Complete Works*, 14:xvii–clxxxiv.

115. More, *De Tristitia Christi*, 605.

116. Louis L. Martz comments: "The *De Tristitia* is a document of the most profound humanism, using the letter to hold body and spirit together, using the word to maintain in the mind a vision of Christian unity that spanned all history, all nations, all creatures, all being." Louis L. Martz, *Thomas More: The Search for the Inner Man* (New Haven: Yale University Press, 1990), 86.

117. *The Passion of Christ* (London: Wynkyn de Worde, 1532). The text claims in its prefatory material to be a translation by Andrew Chertsey from an existing French work.

118. Ibid., F.iii–F.iii (v).

119. Frank Kermode, *The Genesis of Secrecy: On the Interpretation of Narrative* (Cambridge, MA: Harvard University Press, 1979), 24.

120. "Unkind Man, Take Heed of Me," in Brown, *Religious Lyrics*, 158.

121. John Mirk, *Festial*, ed. Susan Powell (Oxford: Oxford University Press, 2009), Early English Text Society, Volume 334, 99.

122. Ibid., 100.

123. Katherine C. Little, "Catechesis and Castigation: Sin in the Wycliffite Sermon Cycle," *Traditio* 54 (1999): 213–44 (224–25).

124. More, *De Tristitia Christi*, 441.

Conclusion

1. Brad S. Gregory, "Tyndale and More, in Life and in Death," *Reformation* 8 (2003): 173–97 (192).

2. See Thomas Stapleton, *The Life and Illustrious Martyrdom of Sir Thomas More*, ed. E. E. Reynolds (London: Burns and Oates, 1966).

3. Brian Cummings, "Swearing in Public: More and Shakespeare," *English Literary Renaissance* 27 (1997): 197–232 (202–3).

4. Brian Cummings, "Conscience and the Law in Thomas More," *Renaissance Studies* 23 (2009): 463–85 (482).

5. John Guy has commented, "The trouble with any discussion of More's stand against Henry VIII is that we always seem to be standing in a hall of mirrors" (John Guy, *Thomas More* [London: Arnold, 2000], 205).

6. Thomas More, *The Last Letters of Thomas More*, ed. Alvaro de Silva (Grand Rapids, MI: Eerdmans, 2000), 54.

7. Ibid., 54–55.

8. William Roper, "The Life of Sir Thomas More," in *Two Early Tudor Lives*, ed. Richard S. Sylvester and Davis P. Harding (New Haven: Yale University Press, 1962), 195–254 (248).

9. Guy singles out this passage from Roper's work as one that is particularly problematic (Guy, *Thomas More*, 7).

10. The most recent authoritative analysis of More's trial is J. Duncan M. Derrett, "The Trial of Sir Thomas More," in *Essential Articles for the Study of Thomas More*, ed. R. S. Sylvester and G. P. Marc'hadour (Hamsden: Archon Books, 1977), 55–78.

11. Brian Gogan, *The Common Corps of Christendom: Ecclesiological Themes in the Writings of Sir Thomas More* (Leiden: Brill, 1982), 170.

12. G. W. Bernard, *The King's Reformation: Henry VIII and the Remaking of the English Church* (New Haven: Yale University Press, 2005), 148–50.

13. Margaret's letter to Alice will henceforth be referred to in the text as the *Letter*.

14. John Guy, *A Daughter's Love: Thomas and Margaret More* (London: Fourth Estate, 2008), 239–42.

15. Guy, *Thomas More*, 175.

16. More, *Last Letters*, 73.

17. Ibid., 74.

18. More also gives a version of this parable in the *Dialogue of Comfort*, discussed in chap. 4.

19. More, *Last Letters*, 79.

20. Ibid., 80–81.

21. Ibid., 81.

22. Ibid., 83.

23. Ibid., 84.

24. Ibid., 82.

25. Ibid., 86.

26. Ibid., 88.

27. For the extreme anxieties of the Henrician authorities over the possibility of equivocation and a gap existing between public statements of obedience and private thoughts, see Peter Marshall's outstanding essay, "Papist as Heretic: The Burning of John Forest, 1538," *Historical Journal* 41 (1998): 351–74.

28. See Francis X. Ryan, "Sir Thomas More's Use of Chaucer," *Studies in English Literature* 35 (1995): 1–17.

29. Walker argues: "For Thynne and Tuke . . . the Chaucer canon represents a profusion of diverse materials, a 'compendiousness in narratioun' of 'doctrynes and sciences' that in itself spoke against the narrowness and exclusivity of the highly vocal evangelical polemicists" (Greg Walker, *Writing under Tyranny: English Literature and the Henrician Reformation* [Oxford: Oxford University Press, 2005], 97).

30. See George Edmondson, "Henryson's Doubt: Neighbours and Negation in *The Testament of Cresseid*," *Exemplaria* 20 (2008): 165–96.

31. Lee Patterson, "Christian and Pagan in *The Testament of Cresseid*," *Philological Quarterly* 52 (1973): 696–714 (697).

32. Geoffrey Chaucer, *Troilus and Criseyde*, in *The Riverside Chaucer*, ed. Larry D. Benson, new ed. (Oxford: Oxford University Press, 1988), 471–585 (526).

33. Tison Pugh comments, "No tactic of cruelty, even threatening a woman marginalized from Trojan community, lies outside of [Pandarus's] 'playful' arsenal" (Tison Pugh, "Christian Revelation and the Cruel Game of Courtly Love in *Troilus and Criseyde*," *Chaucer Review* 39 [2005]: 379–401 [386]).

34. Bankert suggests: "Whereas Paul's interpretation of his one moment of grace is provided by Christ . . . Augustine explicates his own. In like manner Troilus' experience is consistently interpreted by Pandarus, but Criseyde must, like Augustine, read herself, her environment and the people and events that influence her; or perhaps, more accurately, this interpretative task is split between Criseyde and the narrator" (Dabney Anderson Bankert, "Secularizing the Word: Conversion and Gender in Chaucer's *Troilus and Criseyde*," *Chaucer Review* 37 [2003]: 196–218 [203]).

35. Jasper Ridley, ed., *The Love Letters of Henry VIII* (London: Cassell, 1988), 41.

36. Seth Lerer, *Courtly Letters in the Age of Henry VIII: Literary Culture and the Arts of Deceit* (Cambridge: Cambridge University Press, 1997), 89.

37. Mary Behrman, "Heroic Criseyde," *Chaucer Review* 38 (2004): 314–36 (330).

38. Chaucer, *Troilus and Criseyde*, 583.

39. Paul Strohm, *Social Chaucer* (Cambridge, MA: Harvard University Press, 1989), 121.

40. Lerer, *Courtly Letters*, 6.

41. See James Simpson, *Burning to Read: English Fundamentalism and Its Reformation Opponents* (Cambridge, MA: Harvard University Press, 2007).

42. More, *Last Letters*, 89.

43. James Simpson, "Rhetoric, Conscience, and the Playful Positions of Sir Thomas More," in *The Oxford Handbook of Tudor Literature, 1485–1603*, ed. Mike Pincombe and Cathy Shrank (Oxford: Oxford University Press, 2009), 121–36 (135).

INDEX

THOMAS BETTERIDGE

is professor of theater at Brunel University.

He is the author of a number of books,

including *Literature and Politics in the English Reformation*,

and co-editor of *The Oxford Handbook of Tudor Drama*.